T0320328

The End of Individualism and the Economy

Individualism has been one of the driving forces in the rise of modern capitalism, and methodological individualism has been dominant in social science for many years. In this paradigm the economy is seen as a machine to routinize production and improve efficiency, and the discipline of economics has come to focus on control and automation. Recent innovations in natural and social sciences, however, indicate a shift in thinking away from individualism and towards interconnectedness.

The End of Individualism and the Economy: Emerging Paradigms of Connection and Community traces the origins of "the individual" in history, philosophy, economics, and social science. Drawing from linguistic philosophy, there is increasing attention to language as a social substrate for all institutions, including money and the market. One irony is that the "individual" is a key term, related to distinct institutions and associated expertise; that is, "the individual" is social. The book explores the influence of individualism in the subversion of class consciousness, the view of impersonality as a virtue, and the rise of financialization. The founding assumption of economics, the rational autonomous individual with exogenous tastes, undercuts social solidarity and blocks awareness of interconnections and interdependencies. The text looks forward and embraces the new paradigms and alternative forms of governance, economics, and science which can be developed based on collectives and communities, with new values, frameworks, and world views.

This work is suitable for academics, students, scholars, and researchers with an interest in economic and social collectives and methodological individualism, as well as those studying the connections between economics and other disciplines in the social and natural sciences.

Ann E. Davis is Associate Professor of Economics at Marist College, USA, and author of *Money as a Social Institution: The Institutional Development of Capitalism* (Routledge, 2017).

Routledge Frontiers of Political Economy

For more information about this series, please visit: www.routledge.com/books/series/SE0345

The End of Individualism and the Economy

Emerging Paradigms of Connection and Community

Ann E. Davis

Routledge
Taylor & Francis Group

LONDON AND NEW YORK

First published 2020 by Routledge

2 Park Square, Milton Park, Abingdon, Oxon OX14 4RN

605 Third Avenue, New York, NY 10017

Routledge is an imprint of the Taylor & Francis Group, an informa business

First issued in paperback 2021

Publisher's Note

The publisher has gone to great lengths to ensure the quality of this reprint but points out that some imperfections in the original copies may be apparent.

British Library Cataloguing-in-Publication Data
A catalogue record for this book is available from the British Library

Library of Congress Cataloging-in-Publication Data
Names: Davis, Ann E., 1947– author.
Title: The end of individualism and the economy : emerging paradigms of connection and community / Ann E. Davis.
Description: Milton Park, Abingdon, Oxon ; New York, NY : Routledge, 2020. | Series: Routledge frontiers of political economy ; 270 | Includes bibliographical references and index.
Identifiers: LCCN 2019049993 (print) | LCCN 2019049994 (ebook) | ISBN 9781138321267 (hardback) | ISBN 9780429452703 (ebook)
Subjects: LCSH: Individualism—Economic aspects. | Capitalism.
Classification: LCC HM1276 .D385 2020 (print) | LCC HM1276 (ebook) | DDC 330.15/3—dc23
LC record available at https://lccn.loc.gov/2019049993
LC ebook record available at https://lccn.loc.gov/2019049994

ISBN: 978-1-138-32126-7 (hbk)
ISBN: 978-1-03-217468-6 (pbk)
DOI: 10.4324/9780429452703

Typeset in Bembo
by Apex CoVantage, LLC

To Bob, the Tireless Interlocutor

Contents

Preface

In a period when the journal *American Historical Review* (2012) has a second forum on "turns," changing methods of writing history, within the memory of contemporaries, there is a certain self-awareness, if not insecurity, regarding the choice of particular approaches. There are new reflections beyond critique, with an emerging literature addressing the possibility of "post critique" (Felski 2015; Anker and Felski 2017).

For this book, the method is historical institutionalism, focusing on a key term, like "the individual," along with the associated institutions and expertise. This tripartite interrelated complex varies historically and can be documented with archival research to examine its evolution. The key term is often associated with an overarching narrative which provides meaning for a given historical context and then structures institutional operations. In this sense, the method is both linguistic and material since the meanings organize activities of production and consumption.

This work draws upon key sources and influences as follows:

Historically specific institutions: Polanyi and Marx, MacPherson and Pateman regarding fictional commodities; individualism as discipline; Mazower; free trade as utopian global governance; Hegel, Fukuyama, and Habermas regarding the liberal state; Thelen, Streeck, Hodgson, Blyth, and Pistor regarding historical institutions;

Expertise: Michel Foucault, Lorraine Daston, Peter Galison, Caroline Merchant, Evelyn Fox Keller, Sarah Hrdy, Donna Haraway, Bruno Latour, Thomas Kuhn, and Naomi Oreskes regarding historicization of knowledge;

Language: Searle, Austin, Wittgenstein, Taylor, Koselleck, Joan Scott, and Harrison White on terms, concepts, and categories; Cambridge School (Pocock; Skinner) on history of concepts; Moyn and Sartori on intellectual history; "historic epistemology" (Daston, Poovey, Wahrman; Somers).

More specifically, building on the work of Hegel and Marx, Honneth, Honig, and Lukacs, throughout this book the concept of reification will be an especially important aspect of language. That is, the use of a term to refer to a human institution, with the implicit metaphor of an object, tends to reinforce the stability and resilience of that human institution. For example, the term "property" is often taken to mean land instead of the complex set of human legal and economic institutions. In addition, the term "economy" is often taken to mean a self-regulating machine, with predictable and repeated processes, instead of contingent institutional forms. The term "money" is taken to refer to gold, an inert element, instead of a symbol of value in a complex interdependent "hybrid" social and natural system.

Reification may be particularly important in a capitalist society, where humans are treated as commodities, and commodities are assumed to have "value." This "value" is taken to be an aspect of the commodities themselves, compared with other commodities, instead of in reference to humans and their needs and preferences. Humans are regularly considered workers, available for employment, compared with others in the labor market. That is, there is a regular reversal of subject and object, between living agent and concrete matter, assumed to be the normal operation of modern market economies. This normalization of subject/object reversal makes critique more difficult and tends to naturalize what are actually historically specific institutions. Modern social science is characterized by the pursuit of "objectivity," presumably value-free. Reification is also a form of cultural transmission, enabling us to see ourselves more easily as objects, as if from a "view from nowhere" (Nagel 1986), as abstract "individuals" competing with others.

Rather than self-evident and autonomous, the modern "individual" is more dependent than during earlier periods of history. A single, lone person could not exist without the infrastructure of roads, water, and communication systems, or the division of labor in the market, technology and science, or money. The awareness of this vulnerability is avoided by the objectification and naturalization of "the economy" and the removal of the awareness of alternatives (a form of power, according to Searle 2010).

The economy, seen as a machine, is a way of monetizing human life, which is gated and channeled to power financial flows with human energy. Market "incentives" make life contingent, such as the requirement to work to live. Humans have become the motive power behind the economic machine, like the horse driving the grinding stone inside the mill, which is later substituted by hydro and then electric power. As a machine, the economy is beyond conscious choice, in spite of the long legacy of "democracy" and "collective intentionality" in Western civilization. Economics constrains the political, while Hayek argues that the market cannot be known, or consciously designed (Mirowski 2013; Davies 2017). The market as a steering mechanism allows politicians to disavow responsibility for its outcomes and impact on humans and the environment.

Rather than a convenience (Searle 2010) for managing time (Goetzmann 2016), the exploration here is that money is a form of taking time and dominating human lifetimes. One is required to "make money" in order to live, and one's life is devoted to that necessity. There is no "voluntary" choice regarding work or participating in the market (Friedman 1962 vs. MacPherson 1973 debate).

This exploration of the role of reification is consistent with the methodology of historical institutionalism discussed in earlier work (Davis 2015a, 2017c). The organization of this book also interrogates key concepts, meanings and history of each term, as well as institutional manifestations and related expertise.

We will seek to use increasingly the first-person plural voice, as this author addresses you, the reader, in engaging with the literature on modernity. Whenever we speak of what markets do, we have relinquished human agency to a social construct and deny responsibility for its outcomes. The "individual" is seen from outside, within the operations of this system, disempowered to affect its operation or to undertake critique. Agency is recovered only by collective deliberation and examination of the institutions which guide our lives, a political and moral assignment.

We will explore major themes and classic works. From Adam Smith, we will discuss the goal of the "wealth of nations." From Marx, we will explore the nature of the commodity. The commodity has both use value (or utility) and exchange value (or price), which Marx sees as potentially contradictory (Marx 1967, Vol. I, Chapter 3 Section 2.a., 114). The typical division of a bourgeois society, the public/private divide (Habermas 1989), can be seen as an institutional expression of these dual aspects of the commodity for human use, on the one hand, represented in the public sphere, and for private profit represented in the private sphere on the other. The potential resolution, or potential gridlock, between these two dimensions of the commodity is expressed in a "double movement," according to Polanyi (1944), and manifested in political extremes in the current period, like populism on the one hand and neoliberalism on the other.

Having written recent books on "property" and "money," and now "the individual," I hope to now be able to understand the role of these key concepts of Western modernity, apparently universal and eternal, while they are actually relative and historically specific. The supposed objective scientific status of these concepts masks a domination of nature and anthropocentrism which risks relationships with humans and other living species on the earth. It is time to relativize or to "provincialize" Western science and philosophy for the purposes of gaining a perspective on ecological limits and providing alternative world views.

There is a distinct irony: "individualism" is part of a modern world view which affects how the economy operates. It is performative, disciplinary, and normative, not neutral, objective, or universal. In that sense, "individualism" cannot fully account for itself.

The book will proceed as follows:

Chapter 1 will review the literature on "individualism" from multiple points of view and disciplines.

Chapter 2 will examine the notion of "property" and its relation to "the individual" while exploring the concept of reification.

Chapter 3 will examine the divisions in modern society, like the public/private divide and the connection to the "individual" and to "property."

Chapter 4 will examine the evolution of the liberal state and its relationship to the key terms, "individual" and "property."

Chapter 5 will explore the metaphor of the economy as a machine and determine whether this implies a form of autophagy with respect to humans and the environment.

Chapter 6 will examine the methodology of modern natural and social science to explore whether "objectivity" is part of the strategy of reification.

Chapter 7 will explore the characteristic "unique individuals" of the modern liberal state, like corporations and families, to explain the disappearance of the "social."

Chapter 8 reviews the property paradigm and the ways in which it structures one's self-concept, human institutions, and relationships.

Chapter 9 examines the contradictions of the form of the liberal state based on the individual and property, along with the social divisions.

Chapter 10 explores the political and social backlash associated with the operations of these contradictory institutions.

Chapter 11 explores alternative world views and institutions.

Chapter 12 concludes with a review of methodology and a critical overview of the concepts of the individual and property.

We begin by taking Margaret Thatcher seriously in her declaration that "there is no such thing as society," and use the concept of reification to explain how "society" disappears, along with the implications of this absence.

This work is a synthesis of other sources for the purposes of reviewing these major concepts of the "individual" and "property." The purpose is to interrogate these conventional terms and to realize the implications of accepting them without question.

Partial bibliography

Anker, Elizabeth S. and Rita Felski (eds.). *Critique and Postcritique.* Durham, NC: Duke University Press, 2017.

Davies, William. *The Limits of Neoliberalism: Authority, Sovereignty, and the Logic of Competition.* London: Sage, 2017.

Davis, Ann E. *The Evolution of the Property Relation: Understanding Paradigms, Debates, Prospects.* New York: Palgrave MacMillan, 2015a.

Davis, Ann E. "The Process of Provisioning: The Halter for the Workhorse," *Journal of Economic Issues,* Vol. XLIX, No. 2, June 2015b, 449–457.

Davis, Ann E. "Paradoxical Positions: The Methodological Contributions of Feminist Scholarship," *Cambridge Journal of Economics,* Vol. 41, No. 1, 2017a, 181–201.

Davis, Ann E. "The Practical Utopia of Ecological Community," in Richard Westra, Robert Albritton, and Seongjin Jeong (eds.), *Varieties of Alternative Economic Systems: Practical Utopias for an Age of Global Crisis and Austerity.* New York: Routledge, 2017b, 52–70.

Davis, Ann E. *Money as a Social Institution: The Institutional Development of Capitalism*. New York: Routledge, 2017c.

Davis, Ann E. "Fetishism and Financialization," *Review of Radical Political Economics*, Vol. 49, No. 4, December, 2017d, 551–558.

Felski, Rita. *The Limits of Critique*. Chicago: University of Chicago Press, 2015.

Friedman, Milton. *Capitalism and Freedom*. Chicago: University of Chicago Press, 1962.

Goetzmann, William N. *Money Changes Everything: How Finance Made Civilization Possible*. Princeton, NJ: Princeton University Press, 2016.

Habermas, Jurgen. *The Structural Transformation of the Public Sphere: An Inquiry into a Category of Bourgeois Society*. Cambridge, MA: MIT Press, 1989.

MacPherson, C. B. *The Political Theory of Possessive Individualism: Hobbes to Locke*. Oxford: Clarendon Press, 1962.

MacPherson, C. B. *Democratic Theory: Essays in Retrieval*. Oxford: Clarendon Press, 1973.

Marx, Karl. *Capital*. New York: International Publishers, 1967.

Mirowski, Philip. *Never Let a Serious Crisis Go to Waste: How Neoliberalism Survived the Financial Meltdown*. New York: Verso, 2013.

Nagel, Thomas. *The View from Nowhere*. New York: Oxford University Press, 1986.

Polanyi, Karl. *The Great Transformation*. Boston: Beacon Press, 1944.

Searle, John R. *Making the Social World: The Structure of Human Civilization*. New York: Oxford University Press, 2010.

Acknowledgements

I would like to thank many colleagues for vital and provocative discussions related to the topic of "the individual" and to the importance of methodology and world views, including Bas van Bavel, Jim Challey, Asimina Christoforou, Mark Cladis, Thorvald Gran, Janet Gray, Armin Haas, Dirk Hartog, Edith Kuiper, Bob McAulay, Jeff McAulay, Perry Mehrling, Kirsten Munro, John Najemy, Julie Nelson, John Padgett, Paddy Quick, and Randy Wray. All remaining errors and omissions are entirely my own.

Chapter 5 is a revised version of a conference presentation. I acknowledge extremely helpful comments from participants in the Allied Social Science Association meetings, sponsored by the Association for Social Economics panel on "The Market as Metaphor," January 4, 2019, Atlanta, GA.

Acknowledgements

1 The individual as a key term

"Modern Times"

In an interview in 1987, Margaret Thatcher famously said, "There's no such thing as society. There are only individuals" (www.margaretthatcher.org/document/106689).

Thatcher was also famously part of a "battle of ideas" to challenge the reining orthodoxy in Britain of Fabian socialism and Keynesian economics and is the only British prime minister in the twentieth century "whose name has become synonymous with a political philosophy" (Yergin and Stanislaw 1998, 101, 105). Her fame and influence, helping to establish "neoliberalism" in the 1980s (Harvey 2005), attest to the power of discourse in influencing forms of self-consciousness and political world views. That is, the very "individuals" of whom she speaks are influenced by social forces and political tides which she herself exemplifies.

The notoriety of her statement is partly due to her bold claim, like a grand truth proclamation, "There is no such thing as . . ." but also because her statement goes to the core of the divide between political perspectives, between right and left, and partly because "society" is truly strange; it is not a tangible "thing." There is no object to which to point, to verify the existence of this "reifying abstraction" (Poovey 2002). Thatcher's stark statement draws upon the work of Friedrich von Hayek, who held similar beliefs. But even his view of "individualism" gives more credence to society.

> The first thing that should be said is that [true individualism] is primarily a *theory* of society, an attempt to understand the forces which determine the social life of man . . . the silliest of the common misunderstanding [is] the belief that individualism postulates . . . the existence of isolated or self-contained individuals, instead of starting from men whose whole nature and character is determined by their existence in society.
>
> (italics in original; Hayek 1948, 6)

The special relevance to this book is that Hayek believed in money as an object rather than a social symbol. Hayek's view of money supports the proposition of the non-existence of society, especially since there is an inherent social dimension to money which he denies (Davis 2017; Yuran 2014, 125–139). There is also a "disciplinary" aspect to Thatcher's statement. As she continues,

> And no government can do anything except through people, and people must look to themselves first. It's our duty to look after ourselves and then, also, to look after our neighbours. People have got their entitlements too much in mind, without the obligations. There is no such thing as entitlement, unless someone has first met an obligation.
>
> (quoted in Brittan 1992, 7)

That is, Thatcher is implying that "individuals" have responsibility for themselves rather than a reliance on government assistance.

Now, more than 30 years after her statement, Thatcher's ideas are still influential, even if under some challenges. As with the Charlie Chaplin movie *Modern Times*, there is much disruption of late to everyday existence and conventional wisdom. The January 1, 2019, (179:1, 52–55) issue of *Fortune* magazine had a cover story on the disappearance of the middle class; the population is not reproducing itself, and life expectancy is declining for white males (Case and Deaton 2017). The US government shutdown of December 22, 2018, to January 25, 2019, was the longest on record, and the liberal democratic form of government is no longer the global ideal (Bell 2019; Barber, Foy, and Barker 2019). The attempt to extract Britain from the European Union is in chaos. In the neoliberal European Union, it is possible that Merkel's attempts to save the euro is repeating the history of the interwar attempt to save the gold standard (Polanyi 1944), with the same disastrous effects.

Since the mid-twentieth century, there has been a critical perspective on "modernity," with a continuing stream of "turns" in social science methodology. At such a time, it is propitious to examine fundamental assumptions, such as "the individual." The related perplexity of money and society will be discussed more fully later in this book.

This chapter will conduct a selected review of the literature on the definition and history of this key term, "the individual." We will interrogate this sense of the ubiquitous unitary individual with an examination of the variety of meanings and methods of differentiating the individual. We will conclude the chapter with a summary of the methodology of historical institutionalism which will guide us in this interrogation, to be further developed in Chapters 2 and 3.

Introduction to "the individual"

The "individual" seems self-evident to the modern observer.

One's body seems to be a coherent whole, with an integrated system of organs, covered and protected by skin, operated by cognition, capabilities, and memories located in the brain. The boundaries between self and other seem clearly demarcated, with the nutrition consumed by one no longer available to the other. Personalities are unique, as are facial formations, irises, DNA, and fingerprints.

On the one hand, some view individualism as one of the highest achievements of Western Civilization (Berlin 1969; Habermas 1989; Davis 2011; Fukuyama 2018) and Enlightenment rationality (Israel 2004), while others view individualism as a disciplinary technique (Polanyi 1944; Poovey 1998, 2008), a technology of power of "liberal governmentality" (Foucault 1991). Arguably Marx viewed the "individual" as a bourgeois category, with de jure rights different from de facto powers (Cohen 1978).

There are even diametrically opposed conceptions of individual "consciousness," such as the biophysical explanations of Gazzaniga (2018) compared with the social class dimension in Lukacs (1971).

Contrasting perspectives

One example of contrasting perspectives is in the opening paragraph of a recent highly regarded book on economics methodology, specifying the normative significance of the individual (Davis 2011, 16–19, 215–235).

> Economics has long been seen as the social science that makes the individual central. . . . It is surely one of the great normative assumptions of contemporary human society – one not held in much of the past – that the human individual counts or should count, that the individual is important, and that individuals have an inherent moral value, despite all the evidence of human practices to the contrary.
>
> (Davis 2011, 1)

While noting the inadequacies of the isolated, asocial, self-interested concept of the individual as **Homo Economicus** (Davis 2011, 6–10), Davis proceeds to propose a reconceptualization of the individual as embedded in social systems (Davis 2011, 13–16, 191–214; Huddy 2013). Bowles goes further and proposes an alternative characterization of human nature as *homo socialis*, who is motivated by social norms and ethical values (Bowles 2016, 41–56). Other possibilities include "expressive" individuals from the Romantic era (Cortois and Laermans 2018, 69–72). Marglin (2008) distinguishes between biological individualism and political or economic individualism, among others ways of conceptualizing a given human person.

Some historians see the "individual" as an expression of the gift of Western civilization to the world, drawing from roots in Christianity (Siedentop 2014). Others see the notion of human rights as ancient, as early as Roman law, but varying as to whether rights are individual or collective and whether inalienable or transmissible to the state or the sovereign (Edelstein 2019).

Some philosophers of modernity see a teleology towards ever greater freedom for individuals, as the course of human history, what some sociologists have called the "revolutionary idiom" (Somers and Gibson 1994, 45–50). Taylor bemoans the loss of a moral framework by which to establish the "good," the goals for which life becomes worthwhile. He attributes this loss to the modern secular instrumental world view (Taylor 1989, 4–5, 49, 514). Taylor's view of the modern self is defined relative to a "moral" standard which is not equally accessible to all human persons (Lemert 1994, 116–121). Yet he attributes a "long march" towards human rights to a Grotian-Lockean strand of moral economy, with values of equality, self-government, and mutual benefit gradually permeating the "modern social imaginary" (Taylor 2002, 98, 111).

By contrast, other renowned commentators see the social as a moral dimension, not just the individual. For example, Rorty sees a welcome corrective to American individualism in the tradition of American socialism in the first half of the twentieth century in association with the Progressive movement (Rorty 1998, 47–50). Rorty quotes Herbert Croly in saying that "the traditional American confidence in individual freedom has resulted in a morally and socially undesirable distribution of wealth . . . [so that] the whole associated life of that community rests on an equivocal foundation" (Rorty 1998, 47).

Even though the discrete human body has a sense of the eternal, formed in the image of the Creator, it has been shaped by the long-term forces of evolution and has not necessarily been recognized as an "autonomous individual" in all periods of history. Some commentators on the individual place even the formulation of the issue as related to the emergence of modernity, or the "modern self" (Giddens 1991; Beck 2002), associated with increasing reflexivity as well as anxiety and risk. The well-known contrast of ideal types between *gemeinschaft* and *gesellschaft* (Weber 1978; Calhoun 2012, 95–102; Appadurai 2016a, 74) compares the presumed cohesion of traditional society with the processes of individuation and mobility of modern industrial society. Drawing on Luhmann, White builds on a unitary person with multiple identities, seeking control in complex social settings from which meaning emerges (White 2008).

The concept of the individual is related to Western philosophy, drawing upon the ancient Hebrews and ancient Greeks, as well as Locke and the natural law theorists (Calhoun 2007, 124–127; Pierson 2013a, 2016). Rather than focus strictly on the boundaries between individuals, there is also an issue of the boundaries within individuals, such as Smith's "impartial spectator" and Locke's "inner legislator" as well as the management of passions and the threat of the subconscious (Mehta 1992, 74–75). There is a list of specific types of modern individuals whose emergence can be noted but not always explained, such as Charles Cooley's "looking-glass self" (Konings 2015, 58, 81) or Riesman's "inner-directed" vs. "other-directed" self (Konings 2015, 69, 93–100; Riesman 1954, 100–114). For George Herbert Mead, the self is that human capacity to be an object to itself (Lemert 1994, 120). For William James, "each of us" possesses a Self which is "what a man calls *me*," with the obvious cultural assumptions of gender and class (Lemert 1994, 100). For Seigel, there is a "multi-dimensional self" (Sennett 2012, 126–127). Based on Kant's distinction between the "subjective" and the "objective," there developed a "scientific" self and an "artistic" self, the former reducing the influence of the individual's own perspective and the latter explicitly expressing it (Daston and Galison 2010, 198–251).

Others see the focus on individualism as undermining human community by changing values and behavior. Without strong sanctions or absolute moral principles, any "free," self-interested individual may be tempted to become a "free rider."

> Individualism is one way of being in the world rather than the only way . . . an important piece of the ideology of modernity . . . It is rather a characterization of people that makes us believe that a certain set of institutions – markets and private property – are the most sensible way of organizing production and exchange.
>
> (Marglin 2008, 58)

The possible implication of hierarchy and domination is considered part of Western dualism.

> Chief among these troubling dualisms are self/other, mind/body, culture/ nature, male/female, civilized/primitive, reality/appearance, whole/part, agent/resource, maker/made, active/passive, right/wrong, truth/illusion, total/partial, God/man. The self is the One who is not dominated, who knows that by the service of the other, the other is the one who holds the future, who knows that by the experience of domination, which gives the lie to the autonomy of the self. To be One is to be autonomous, to be powerful, to be God; but to be One is to be an illusion, and so to be involved in a dialectic of apocalypse with the other.
>
> (Haraway 2016, 59–60)

The individual and the social

"The individual" seems to exist by itself, with no need for another, completely autonomous and self-sufficient. This concept is descriptive but also normative. Any self-respecting individual *would be* autonomous and self-sufficient. Dependency is a sign of failure, inadequacy. The myths of heroic individuals, such as Robinson Crusoe, derive from the time of the origin of the market, which presumes such an individual agent (Poovey 1998; Grapard and Hewitson 2011; Brantlinger 1990). Ownership of property provides a source of this independence, since property is often assumed to be land, which can provide subsistence with appropriate effort, which is then assumed to be forthcoming from any worthy individual.

The notion of "the individual" seems to be particularly important in the modern West (Appadurai 2016a, 102, 147). Western political theory conceives of "the individual" as universal, bounded within a discrete bodily envelope, with self-consciousness and memory.

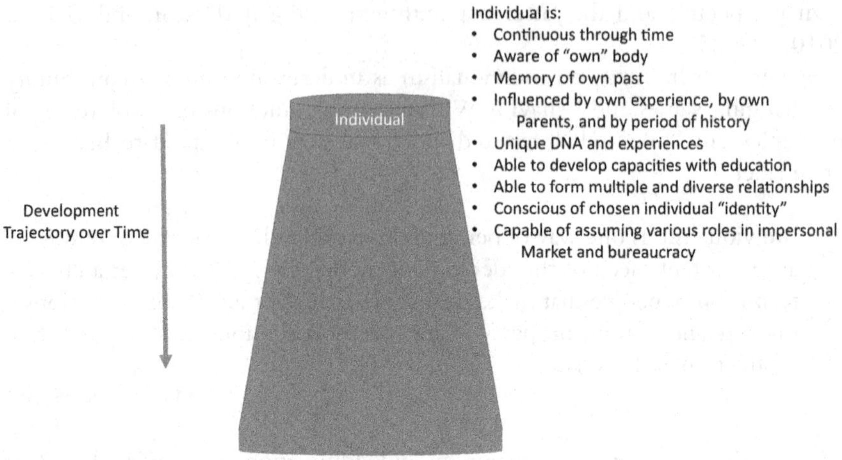

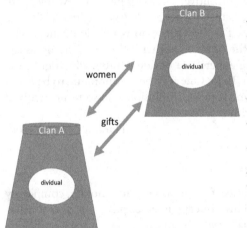

Individual is:
- Continuous through time
- Aware of "own" body
- Memory of own past
- Influenced by own experience, by own
  Parents, and by period of history
- Unique DNA and experiences
- Able to develop capacities with education
- Able to form multiple and diverse relationships
- Conscious of chosen individual "identity"
- Capable of assuming various roles in impersonal
  Market and bureaucracy

Development
Trajectory over Time

Individual

Figure 1.1 The Western Self

Clan B

dividual

women

gifts

Clan A

dividual

The "Dividual" is:
- Part of a distinct clan
- Part of unique relationships with kin,
  spouse, and gender collective
- Responsible for particular roles and
  ritual performances
- "Gender" influenced by specific role
  And relation for each act
- Exchange of symbolic body parts
  in ritual acts
- Exchange of women and gifts among
  clans
- Capable of "agency" and "performance"
- No sense of fixed individual "identity"

Figure 1.2 Melanesian "Dividual"

The contributions of prominent anthropologists contrast this model with the "dividual," who is part of a social whole, whose characteristics are known and revealed in relationships, whose bodily parts can be shared and symbolically redistributed. The unity of the group is performative, expressed in rituals, which presume that it already exists (Appadurai 2016a, 101–123, 2016b, 17–31).

In the early stages of industrialization, in a different geography and period of history, Nietzsche also experienced himself as a "dividual," as internally split (Safranski 2002, 26–29, 184–185, 302).

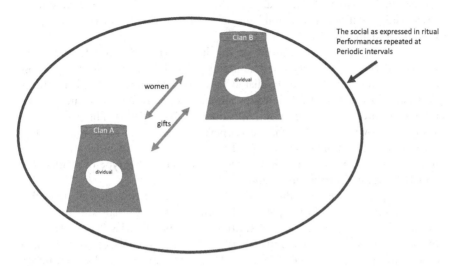

Figure 1.3 The Social as Performative

The concept of property ownership is often related to "the individual." MacPherson's concept of the "possessive individual" derives from Locke's focus on the individual as an owner of property (Butler and Athanasiou 2013, 7–8, 30–32). While the Western "individual" is typically viewed as a "separative self" (England 1993), other cultures often represent persons as inevitably part of relationships. For example, a well-regarded feminist anthropologist calls ownership a Western "root metaphor," consisting of such concepts as "the idea that persons can be less than social beings; nature as a constraint and as a resource; the kind of unitary identity implied in sex-role theory; attributes appropriated as though they were property owned; things being regarded as has having intrinsic properties; the purpose of domination being control" (Strathern 1988, 134). For example, while the "idiosyncratic Western metaphor for procreation" assigns fertility as a characteristic of women, the Melanesians see children as the result of relationships between men and women, across clans and generations (Strathern 1988, 311–318). Among these societies, the exchange of gifts enhances relationships, while in Western societies the phenomenon of "commodity fetishism" expresses relationships by the exchange of objects.

Rather than focus on relationships in the West, there is the exchange of commodities mediated by money in the market. That is, the only "relationships" are market exchanges via money. The reification of relationships by means of the commodity, as an object for sale, is possible because of the relationships of property ownership with certain kinds of commodities which can produce value "naturally" (such as the soil, the commodity of labor power, and women). These so-called "natural" processes can be acquired by the owner and "consumed" as he wishes or as will produce the most profit. In this way, the exchange of certain commodities can create value expressed in money. By the process of reification of money, the natural "growth" seems to come from money itself. Ownership itself is also "natural" and is a result of the gift of the earth from God to humankind.

By these particular definitions of the individual and property, the social seems to disappear, left only with the individual and the market for the purpose of the exchange of property mediated by money. The social, which might be understood to represent relationships among people, is now subsumed by the individual, property, and money (Appadurai 2016b, 10–11). There is a unity among the owners who exchange property via a certain currency, which is invisible because money is considered just another type of individual private property. Money is the reification of the social, an invisible type of relationship which is explored further in Chapter 2.

Drawing upon a long tradition of political commentators, Bowles states that "the economy produces people" in the sense that individuals are influenced by their period in history and institutional context (Bowles 2016, 116–122). In fact there is much conceptual debate regarding the role of consciousness as an autonomous force, according to Hegel, or the shaping by technology and the means of production, according to Marx, or the role of narratives and myth (Shiller 2019; Taylor 2004, 2016; Anderson 2006). Do theories of social and historical change also influence actual social and institutional change? Such matters remain the subject of debate among historians, sociologists, and philosophers (Szakolczai 2000). Perhaps it is only the "heroic" individual who believes that history changes one person at a time.

Supra-individual influences, such as language and culture

The recent "turns" in methodological discussions may be in part about including an analysis of important influences on individuals, as well as the meaning and salience of the term "individual" itself.

Language

Language is clearly beyond the individual while also a medium for the individual's cognition and expression, communication, and relations with others. In spite of its importance, language is often overlooked, perhaps because of the flux of disciplines (Pollock, Elman, and Chang 2015), or perhaps because of the complexity of its role (Padgett 2012, 57–58). At *fin de siècle* Vienna, there may have arisen a new salience to language, as the support for the old regime of the monarchy was eroding and new concepts and ideas were emerging. Perhaps in this context, Wittgenstein was moved to inquire regarding the nature of "language games" (Janik and Toulmin 1973) and the production of meaning.

A contemporary linguist philosopher, John Searle, argues that the "social contract" theorists of the seventeenth and eighteenth centuries ignored the importance of language (Searle 2010, 62–63, 165). That is, human institutions can be created once there is language, and only with language. Language is necessary to form agreements and commitments, and once those are formed, human actions can be coordinated and regulated to form durable institutions. For Searle, language statements are forms of contracts which the speaker implicitly promises to fulfill. A free individual who is conscious of the implications of his statements can become obliged to make these statements true, a form of "deontology" (Searle 2010, 80–85). Appadurai extends this meaning to legal and financial contracts, which he sees as the foundation of Western institutions (Appadurai 2016a, 1–10, 150–155).

The location of language centers in the brain seem to result from and to facilitate the evolution of human group formations (Kandel 2012). Language is the mechanism for memory, expression, cognition, and communication. The capacity for self-consciousness may result from the interpretation and internalization of statements about oneself made by meaningful others, a form of "recognition."

This relatively recent attention to language may help facilitate an understanding of "the individual" as a participant in symbolic communication in relation to a specific group of other human persons, without which self-awareness, much less survival, would be impossible. Taylor finds support for this understanding, in common with Habermas and Wittgenstein (Taylor 1989, 35–36, 38–39, 509).

Philosopher Charles Taylor has recently turned directly to considerations of language (Taylor 2016). He mentions the distinction between scientific language to describe objective independently existing reality, in contrast with emotional expression and narratives which provide human meaning (Hobbes-Locke-Condillac (HLC) vs. Hamann-Herder-Humbolt (HHH)). He focuses on the use of language in dialogue among humans, a form of "communion." In this context, language enables two interlocutors to focus their immediate attention on a third object of interest in the present. He mentions narratives which link the individual to the past and provide meaning and sense of self. He mentions "footings" by which language can structure the context of a relationship, such as formal and informal pronouns in some languages. Taylor's contrast of HLC to HHH is similar to Searle's distinction between ontological objectivity and ontological subjectivity. His distinction is also related to the abstract term "information," a quantitative measure without reference to human meanings (Eco 1979, 42–44). In other work (Taylor 2004), he mentions the "social imaginary," or shared narratives which provide meaning and context for national identity (Sum and Jessup 2013, 164–172).

Whether categories are timeless or influenced by history and culture remains in debate (Marder 2019). Reinhart Koselleck is a German historian who focuses on the importance of categories in social history (Sum and Jessup 2013, 107–110). Koselleck claims that language and action are always present at once in the actual event but that language takes precedence in the history of the event (Koselleck 2002, 24–31). He recounts the distinct meanings of certain terms in different cultures and the impact of these differences on the evolution of related institutions (Koselleck 1989, 657–661; Eco 1979, 79). Boltanski and co-authors examine the way in which categories are used to make judgements of worth among individuals, first in the assignment of categories and then in the relative assessment of the individuals within each (Boltanski and Thevenot 2006; Boltanski and Chiapello 2007). These judgements take place on a practical level in a variety of everyday settings.

A scholar in literary studies, Mary Poovey (1998) studies the "modern fact," a specific term which is supported by quantitative evidence to verify its scientific status. She discusses the flaws in scientific method, both induction and deduction, where the facts in themselves are not sufficient and any prior hypothesis formation would be subject to the influence of the scientists' paradigm. Scientific authority is enhanced by the distinction between "fact" and "fiction" in scientific literature and university disciplines as a way of differentiating the status of natural science (Poovey 2008). As merchants gained influence in counseling governments, the merchant's authority was enhanced, in her view, by the special role of double-entry bookkeeping. In this special format, the two sides of the ledger record the real object and the financial value, delineated separately on the same page, reflecting both concrete and abstract dimensions of the same object. This genre becomes more important in a market economy, where the exchange of objects for money becomes a key aspect of the dominant institutions. Veracity is presumably guaranteed by accurate and detailed documentary records, even while commodities and money change in value in time and location. Further, money itself is a special type of writing, covered with symbols and script in artful representation, even if on perishable paper, a new genre in the credit economy (Poovey 2008). Poovey addresses the "problematic of representation," whereby the accuracy of terms can always be questioned, in science as well as in merchant contracts.

Culture

Culture is another factor which has influence beyond the individual. The literature on the "rise of the West" seeks to address the reasons for the supremacy of Europe after the sixteenth century, also known as the "great divergence" (Pomeranz 2000). One possible explanation is the importance of culture, defined as a set of values, beliefs, and preferences (Mokyr 2016, 8–9) promoted by authorities and accepted by a given population. While culture can be subject to individual choice, it is also often the result of coercion in certain periods (Mokyr 2016, 43–56). The turn in Europe towards more attention to practical knowledge, experimentation, and openness to new ideas may have been influenced by competition among European states, long distance trade, material motivations, and the new value placed on curiosity, especially in the period from 1500 to 1700. The idea that nature was created for human use was a significant aspect of both religious and modern world views (Mokyr 2016, 14, 17, 151), facilitating the transition to a new form of expertise from religion and the ancient Greek canon to one based on scientific inquiry.

Another interpretation of Western culture is the "civilization based on property" (Satia 2018, 1–3, 8–10, 245–246), which undergirded the "military industrial state" of the eighteenth century and motivated the industrial revolution to produce war materials. Likewise, the production of armaments was important in Venice's arsenal, as well as the Harper Ferry's Armory in the US Civil War, and regimentation a legacy of war production.

In a different approach, Benedict Anderson (2006) and Charles Taylor discuss "modern social imaginaries" (Taylor 2002, 2004), while Perry Anderson (1998) and Fredric Jameson (1998) discuss the "cultural turn" from a post-modern perspective. That is, both efforts seek to discover the ways in which changing historical world views influence one's perspective of oneself and society. Eagleton (2016) discusses "culture" in a variety of forms, from traditional folk culture which formed the basis for romantic nationalism to high art and the value placed on aesthetics as separate from the mundane and quotidian. Eagleton also discusses the "culture industry," which can "colonize fantasy and enjoyment" for profit, making use of the mass media and mechanization associated with capitalism (Eagleton 2016, 143–144, 151). Jameson discusses the importance of the visual image in capitalism whereby each person is subject to the "gaze" of the other and is also bombarded with images of how one should behave in the ubiquitous advertising which permeates daily life (Jameson 1998, 103–106). Drawing upon Gramscian Marxism, Stuart Hall and others analyze forms of "hegemonic" culture (Hall et al. 1978).

Periodization

The "modern" period is often considered distinctive to historians and philosophers. Attention to the self is an important aspect of modernity for many scholars and commentators. While there was a discussion in ancient Greece, the primary focus on the individual in the modern period can be analyzed in three dimensions: the body, social relations, and "reflectivity." That is, the individual is located in a given single body and is embedded in social relations. The third aspect, "reflectivity," or awareness of oneself, requires taking oneself as an object for thought (Seigel 2005, 12–40). Using these three dimensions, Seigel traces the development of the self in Britain, France, and Germany from the seventeenth century, comparing the emphasis placed among them by various thinkers. Seigel himself prefers a balance among all three dimensions in order to maintain a stable integrated self (Seigel 2005, 651–653). This very concern reveals the fragility of the concept, as well as its geographic and temporal variation.

One can also question the notion of modernity itself and whether it inevitably means secularization and "disenchantment" of the world with modern science. Does the idea of progress inevitably derive from Christian eschatology, or can modernity generate its own criteria and dynamic based on continual questioning and learning? Is human self-realization inevitably collective rather than individual, as some recent debates indicate (Gordon 2019, 161)?

History of the self

That there might be a history of the self is surprising only to liberal theorists who assume that "the individual" is self-evident, universal, optimal, and the holder of "natural rights." The concept of the "history of the self" is one of the major areas of study inspired by Michel Foucault, according to Moyn (2009).

Corporate

Arguably, the corporate form is important in the history of social collectives (Davis 2005, 2015, 66–74, 103–105). Adam Smith refers to "freedom" as a function of membership in a guild or municipal corporation (Smith 1994, 427–434, 793–797). In this respect, the City of London may have been distinct from Paris because it was "never directly subject to the king." London was its own self-governing corporation; it had 89 guilds, 26 elected councilors, 200 council members and 12,000 taxpayers around the turn of the eighteenth century (Habermas 1989, 257, n. 7). Similarly, New York City and Philadelphia were chartered self-governing corporations in the colonial period.

The discipline of corporate forms such as communes was responsible for the notion of "equal" membership (Najemy 1982; Blaufarb 2003; Davis 2015, 2019; Bossenga 2003; Sewell 1980, 1994). Corporations like universities, guilds, and incorporated cities were also important locations for the development of new ideas and an escape from persecution for innovators (Mokyr 2016, 172–175).

Intellectual history

Ancient Greek philosophy and Christianity understand ethics in terms of what the individual "ought to do" (Geuss 2005, 40–46). In the civic republication tradition, the individual personality was "grounded" in real property, while active in the polis, and provided a model of "propertied independence." New forms of property, such as finance with variable values, constituted a threat to this stability and security (Pocock 1975).

According to Martin (1997), the combined influence of humanism and the Reformation led to the development of individual reflection. A sense of inwardness was a product of the person's relation to the deity, now more individualized than within the Catholic Church. First noted by Burckhardt in 1860, new social mobility also made the issue of role playing and normative performance relevant in the context of the rise of court culture. Greenblatt (1980) is more likely to view such "individualism" as a social product rather than an essential characteristic of human persons.

The notion of the individual as a holder of natural or human rights builds on the long history in the West. Arguably beginning with the Magna Carta in 1215, the natural rights theorists of the seventeenth century, such as Grotius, Pufendorf, and Locke, (Hunt 2007a, 114–126) viewed these rights as universal (but were opposed by Hobbes, Bentham, and Filmer; Hunt 2007b, 4–5). These ideas were later taken up in the French Enlightenment of the eighteenth century, particularly by Rousseau and Diderot (Hunt 2007a, 24–25, 2007b, 7–9). These rights were based on empathy and autonomy, and new notions of separability of individual bodies (Hunt 2007a, 26–34). The "declarations" of the American (1776) and French Revolution (1789) further announced a new source of sovereignty, the people as a collective.

> Political authority . . . derived from the innermost nature of individuals and their ability to create community through consent.
>
> (Hunt 2007a, 31)

Jonathan Israel distinguishes between a moderate and a radical Enlightenment thought, the former based on Locke and Hobbes and the latter based on Spinoza and Mandeville. The radical Enlightenment focuses on equality and the individual, represented democratically in the state with a "common good" based on political deliberation. Further, the radical Enlightenment was opposed to the power of the clergy and insisted on complete tolerance, including of various religions, as well as atheism. Freedom of belief and expression was an essential component of liberty. Israel speculates regarding the origins of the Dutch emphasis on toleration, compared with the English compromise with the monarchy and the state church. He contrasts the "land-based, parliamentary gentry" with the "city burghers" of the Dutch Republic.

> At bottom, Dutch democratic republicanism was a republicanism which pivoted on the idea of the 'common good' as the pre-eminent principle of society, envisioning merchants and wage-earners as the backbone of the citizenry.
>
> (Israel 2004, 9)

That is, the different forms of republicanism may be based on different forms of property, land vs. finance in England compared with the Dutch Republic. He further suggests that Spinoza and Mandeville had developed the concept of the "common good" before Rousseau and Diderot (Israel 2004, 30) and hence prepared the foundation of the revolutionary potential of French political thought.

Political revolutions then influenced the ideas of "freedom," such as the English Revolution of 1688 (Israel 2001, 72–73; Pincus 2009). According to Israel, the American Revolution had global revolutionary implications because of its founding on Enlightenment principles (Israel 2017, 9–10), even more than the earlier republican revolutions in Switzerland, the Dutch Republic, and the United Kingdom.

Among the many interpretations of the causes of the French Revolution, Jonathan Israel places primacy on the ideas of the Enlightenment (Israel 2001, 26–28, 2014, 714–720). Paradoxically, the so-called universal, self-evident human rights had to be "declared," based on the assumptions of universal and equal rights which were natural and the foundation of the legitimacy of all governments (Hunt 2007b, 3–4).

> Human rights are supposed to be eternal and universal, engraved, as it were, in human nature. But not everyone believes them to be inscribed in human nature, and the notion itself of human rights has a distinct history. . . . What is imagined to be universal and above history turns out to be contingent and grounded in a particular history.
>
> (Hunt 2007b, 3)

New reified concepts such as "society" indicated the human capacity for invention and self-government (Bell 2001, 25–30, 40–41, 53; Bossenga 2003, 137–138; Sewell 1980, 143–144, 2005, 325) in the eighteenth-century Enlightenment.

Cultural history

In contrast with intellectual history (Taylor 1989), Wahrman examines cultural expressions and practices to study the history of the self. Building on the work of anthropologists like Geertz and Mauss, he differentiates the notion of the self in the "ancient regime" as being more fluid and other-directed in contrast to the modern self which is distinct, inner-directed, and unique for each person. The earlier notion of "identity" builds on the category describing the person as a stereotype rather than the person claiming the category as part of his assertion of individuality in the modern period. One example of this shift is the use of standard uniforms for specific trades regulated by Sumptuary laws compared with individual choice, expression, and projection of individual identity with respect to fashion (Wahrman 2004, 59–69, 204–208; Howell 2008). The more stable, well-defined, centered modern self is rights-bearing, according to natural law.

Yet the ambiguity of the term "identity" remains as to whether it is placing the individual in a generic category like others or is claimed by the individual as a source of uniqueness and authenticity distinct from others (Wahrman 2004, xii, 276–278; Kidd 2006).

Taylor sees "recognition" as dialogic but not social or communal (Taylor 1992). Sennett sees cooperation as based on dialogue, requiring appropriate skills that are no longer cultivated in modern capitalism (Sennett 2012, 6–9).

In particular, categories with respect to gender, race, and class assumed new meanings and new salience, as the development of natural and social science arose to fill the vacuum left by the church as the organizational resource for society (Wahrman 2004, 198–202).

The sea change occurred for England during the American Revolution, creating challenges for the British, according to Wahrman 2004, 221–227). He also credits the role of religion, commerce, and empire with these changes. The decline of religion is also important for Bell (2001), and commerce for Pocock (1975), in presenting challenges for stability to the person in times of historic economic and social change. The rise of the novel permitted experiences of empathy with strangers (Hunt 2007a, 35–58), along with Smith's writings on moral theory (Hunt 2007a, 64–69).

Heightened geographic and social mobility is also a factor, as existing social hierarchies are challenged, such as the aristocracy and the monarchy.

History of sexuality

As much as sexual expression seems "natural" or merely instinctual, Foucault documents the contrast between *ars erotica* in China, India, and other geographies compared with *scientia sexualis* in the West. He also describes the evolution of an attitude towards sexuality in the West, from confession to production and incitement, and the transformation of sex into discourse (Foucault 1978, 57–64, 67–71). That is, according to Foucault, sex has a history and geography, comparative or synchronic and historical or diachronic. These various discourses of sex have an impact on identity and the formation of the "individual" by means of "objectification of sex in rational discourses" (Foucault 1978, 33–34, 155–157). These approaches to knowledge about sex then structure practices in families, as well as schools, hospitals, and other institutions.

Writing about sexuality has varied historically, including by Marque de Sade himself and commentators on his work (Hunt 1992, 124–150; Horkheimer and Adorno 1972, 94–119; Foucault 1978).

Comparative

As discussed earlier, cultural anthropologists are a strategic resource for alternative conceptions, such as "Indic dividuality" (Appadurai 2016a; Strathern 1988, 13–15, 268–278, 288).

Future

The question remains as to whether the history of the individual is linear with a steady progression towards autonomy and freedom, and irreversible, or whether it is episodic, with shifting conceptualizations across regimes. That is, is there a teleology of the individual, such as Taylor's "long march"?

Scientists can also offer new views of interpersonal interconnections, such as the "interdividual" (Bandera 2019). Drawing on the literature of the new materialisms, Appadurai offers the concept of the "progressive dividual" (Appadurai 2016a, 146).

Categories

There is a long Western tradition of universal categories, drawing from the philosophy of Plato, Aristotle, and Kant. The active citizen of the republic, *vivere civile*, is one of those concepts, which is nonetheless found in particular human histories. The Christian tradition also contains universals, such as *nunc-stans*, or "the standpoint in eternity from which God saw every moment in time as simultaneously created and present" (Pocock 1975, 7). In integrating these two world views in the Renaissance, Augustine could propose "civitas Dei, a society in communion with God," (Pocock 1975, 34), while humans would aspire to achieve a City on a Hill on earth in imitation of this transcendental model. In this way, "prophetic history" could serve as a means of "politicizing grace" and "re-sacralizing politics" (Pocock 1975, 44). In this way, political philosophers in Florence could view their citizenship as a "universal activity" and their city as a "universal community" (Pocock 1975, 68). The republics of England and the United States could see themselves in this tradition and self-consciously design their institutions to achieve a "city on a hill" (Pocock 1975, 512). The founders could glorify their efforts in this teleological tradition while also remaining completely aware of the vulnerability of their republic.

Certain central categories have overarching importance in this tradition, such as "citizen" and "republic." In the liberal state, concepts such as "the individual" and "individual private property" also have historical and institutional resonance. According to Marx, the key category of capitalism is the "commodity" (Lukacs 1971, 83–92). One could surmise that the importance of the term "commodity" is related to the role of the commodity labor power, a significant determinant of one's life chances given the importance of the institution of the labor market. The identification of certain characteristics of a person then determines the position and location of employment in the highly stratified labor institutions. That is, categories of identity are relevant to processing a person in public and private bureaucracies. The commodification of labor is a form of relationship which becomes coded by an identity category, leaving the labor market institution invisible.

Aspects of modern identity pertain to ascribing to categories of race, class, and gender, as well as nation (Scott 1986; Darity 1998; Botwinick 1993; Sewell 1994; Davis 2011; Somers 1996). Is the prominence of these categories due to the importance of administration after the decline of religion, along with "reason of state" and the rise of the "human sciences" (Martin, Gutman, and Hutton 1988, 49, 145–148, 160–162; Viroli 1992; Poovey 1998)?

For Scott, gender, although varying historically, can be a symbol of power. The core of her definition is as follows:

> Gender is a constitutive element of social relationships based on perceived differences between the sexes, and gender is a primary way of signifying relationships of power.
>
> (Scott 1986, 1067)

Drawing on Bourdieu, she further elaborates: "Concepts of gender structure perception and the concrete and symbolic organization of all social life" (Scott 1986, 1069).

Foucault describes how sexuality became an identity, a characteristic of an "individual," instead of a relationship among persons in eighteenth/nineteenth-century Europe (Foucault 1978, 33–34, 42–43, 47, 58–59, 61, 70, 146, 155–156). The irony of sexuality as an identity category is that sexuality is such a significant type of relationship among persons, now rendered merely a particular personality type.

Sometimes individuals have "identities," which are assertions of common characteristics with a specific class of other unrelated, unassociated individuals. Alternatively, "identity" can refer to the relationships among people who claim similarity to a group of other members (Calhoun 2007, 70–72). The "politics of identity" and "new social movements" can be a means to greater self-realization and self-esteem (Calhoun 2012, 249–281).

Property rights and human rights

In the Western Tradition, there is an ambiguous relationship between property rights and human rights. According to Locke, the social contract was formed by free individuals in the state of nature in order to protect their property. Property is founded by mixing one's own labor in an object; that is, labor's "property-producing" capacity (Sartori 2014, 8–20) is the origin of property. Property is an extension of the person, in this view.

The status of human rights is more contested. The notion of universal human rights has entered the global discourse through the United Nations in the 1960s, with the efforts of Eleanor Roosevelt (Meister 2011; Moyn 2018; Searle 2010; Franck 1999). Some conceptions of human rights include positive rights to subsistence, as well as political and social capacity. Rather than a moral imperative, this guarantee of positive rights is viewed as too costly (Israel 2001, 258–262, 720; Berlin 1969; Searle 2010, 184–194; Mehta 1992, 24–36; Underkuffler 2003; McKeon 2005; Geuss 2005, 67–77). That is, a commitment to positive requirements for minimum standards of life is considered too expensive relative to the negative protection of individual private property. There is an ongoing debate with regard to the conditions of implementing such a concept, whether including positive or only negative rights, and applicable to any person regardless of the status of national citizenship. One further issue is the extent to which the "incentive" system of markets requires the contingency of the conditions of life for the requisite discipline of individual efforts. That is, market discipline may require only conditional human rights to subsistence. This constraint is expressed as a trade-off between efficiency and equity in the classic work by Okun (1975).

Or do property rights for some lead to coercion for others, especially for property in the person (Pateman 1988)? The protection of property may include resistance to taxation, so that the resources for human rights are subject to budget constraints. As a result, there is a libertarian position on property which justifies inequality (Cohen 1995).

Recognizing the importance of property ownership, Habermas makes a distinction between "bourgeois" and "hommes" in his discussion of political deliberation. He recommends an extension of property ownership as a condition of reconciling effective distinctions between bourgeois and hommes (Lamoreaux 2011).

Were the seventeenth/eighteenth-century bourgeois revolutions protecting property instead of people? Does property protection entangle and limit democracy today (Polanyi 1944; Dahl 2001)? Was the protection of property understood as a proxy for human rights?

In the US, the Supreme Court expanded protections of property in the Federalist Court, with the doctrine of judicial review, asserting supremacy over the legislature (Burns 2009). The Fourteenth Amendment has been applied to protect "due process" of property protections. As suffrage has expanded historically, restrictions of campaign finance have loosened.

Have these protections for property resulted in the record levels of inequality at present (Pistor 2019)?

Interrogating "the individual"

Human communities are uniquely shaped by beliefs, values, and meanings. The notion of "the individual" emerged in the modern West after the Renaissance and the Enlightenment. Humans in families and communities have existed in a much longer historical time frame. Ironically "individual consciousness" is a social phenomenon.

The human "individual" is not self-evident but is the result of ideas and consciousness of a certain geography and time period. Is the "individual" the product of modernity, as suggested by Block and Somers (2014, 226–240)? Is this historical development irreversible, as in Taylor's "long march," eventually to be granted equally to every person? Or is this only the product of a period in history, to be replaced by other social forms?

The challenge to a contemporary reader is to examine if and how one's period in history influence one's view of oneself, norms of behavior, aspirations, and habits in daily life. Different conceptions of oneself are possible, as elaborated in fiction, dramas, biographies, and even video games. Alternate arrangements of society are possible, as articulated as early as Thomas More's Utopia in 1516. This articulation of alternatives is also the function of critique of contemporary societies. Is individual choice the appropriate frame for the analysis of social movements more broadly?

Seigel attributes Foucault's impact

> by virtue of his ability to identify practices and institutional relations within which Western individuals' sense of themselves as free agents has been constructed, so that their very sense of their freedom binds them inside the systems of discourse or power relations that form their consciousness and direct their actions.
>
> (Seigel 2005, 604)

Methodology

The wide variety of "selves" listed earlier attests to the social dimensions of one's personality and the necessary accompaniment of interpersonal association. There is no such thing as an isolated individual who would be able to survive, physically or emotionally. As only one example, Charles Taylor, who celebrates the moral dimension of the individual, also describes the "modern social imaginary" which makes that individual recognizable (Taylor 1989, 2002).

This book will treat "the individual" with the method of historical institutionalism (Davis 2015, 2017) as a discreet institutional position in the modern liberal state. That is, the concept will be treated historically and the associated institutional manifestations will be explored along with the related forms of expertise. There are in fact multiple concepts of "the individual," most commonly associated with the modern liberal nation-state. The modern disciplines of sociology and economics, as well as political science, developed in the era when this concept was emerging based on natural law theories. These social sciences were designed to answer the question regarding "the individual" and to explain the emergence of modernity (Somers and Gibson 1994, 43–46).

Considering these as three legs of a conceptual stool, the first is the history of the term, or etymology, which does have a logic to its evolution (drawing on the work of Smith, Hegel, Marx, Habermas, North; Fukuyama, Sewell); the second is language which is a social medium with which institutions are built and coordinated and with which individual cognition and interpersonal communication occurs (Searle; Wittgenstein; Austin); the third is knowledge, the criteria by which issues are framed and reliable information is generated (Foucault; Poovey; Daston). Each of the central concepts evolves, but also in relation to each other, so that the related complex or paradigm is more resilient, or "path dependent." These three aspects will be discussed further in Chapter 3.

The presumption here is that "the individual" was the outcome of the transition from tradition to modernity (Calhoun 2012, 95–102), from hereditary monarchy to republican self-government of the ideal liberal nation-state. The individual is the presumed agent and beneficiary of modernity, a conceptual innovation that is both descriptive and performative (Poovey 1998, 2008; Taylor 2002).

There is an interdisciplinary genre of classic and recent contributions to explain social change in a broader historical sweep which problematize the individual and modernity. These works will be examined (such as North, Wallis, and Weingast; Fukuyama; Taylor; Searle; Pocock; Skinner; Moyn; Marx; Polanyi; Hayek; Hardt and Negri; Streeck), and their methodologies compared. The current popularity of this genre may signal an awareness of another "Great Transformation," a new governing paradigm across academic disciplines, and entirely new "meta"-narratives of legitimation, not just "post"-modern and "neo"-liberal.

A collective turn?

Rather than see the individual in the private sphere as the ultimate expression of freedom (Berlin 1969), it is time to take the tools of modern social and natural science, such as the inquiry into language, history, and ecology, to understand the notion of the collective. According to post-modern insights, civilization is socially constructed, and "we" can reconstruct it according to "collective intentionally," Searle's term (Searle 2010). Only with such a reorientation will humankind have the capacity to assume responsibility for shaping human life on earth and to address the daunting challenges of climate change, economic instability, and political unrest.

To briefly foretell the analysis to come in the following chapters, money is the reified representation of society, which allows "the individual" to presume her own autonomy, following Thatcher. In Chapter 2, we will discuss the notion of reification in more depth.

Bibliography

"AHR Forum: Historiographic 'Turns' in Critical Perspective: Introduction," *American Historical Review*, Vol. 117, No. 3, June 2012, 698–699.

Anderson, Benedict. *Imagined Communities: Reflections on the Origin and Spread of Nationalism.* London: Verso, 2006.

Anderson, Perry. *The Origins of Postmodernity.* New York: Verso, 1998.

Appadurai, Arjun. *Banking on Words: The Failure of Language in the Age of Derivative Finance.* Chicago: University of Chicago Press, 2016a.

Appadurai, Arjun. "The Wealth of Dividuals," in Benjamin Lee and Randy Martin (eds.), *Derivatives and the Wealth of Societies.* Chicago: University of Chicago Press, 2016b, 17–36.

Bandera, Pablo. *Reflection in the Waves: The Interdividual Observer in a Quantum Mechanical World.* East Lansing: Michigan State University Press, 2019.

Barber, Lionel, Henry Foy, and Alex Barker. "Vladimir Putin says Liberalism Has Become Obsolete," *Financial Times*, June 28, 2019.

Beck, Ulrich. *Individualization: Institutionalized Individualism and Its Social and Political Consequences.* London: Sage, 2002.

Bell, David A. *The Cult of the Nation in France: Inventing Nationalism, 1680–1800.* Cambridge, MA: Harvard University Press, 2001.

Bell, David A. "The Many Lives of Liberalism," *New York Review of Books*, Vol. 66, No. 1, January 17, 2019, 24–27.

Berlin, Isaiah. *Four Essays on Liberty.* London: Oxford University Press, 1969.

Black, Antony. "The 'Axial Period:' What Was It and What Does it Signify?" *Review of Politics*, Vol. 70, No. 1, 2008, 23–39.

Blaufarb, Rafe. "Nobles, Aristocrats, and the Origins of the French Revolution," in Robert M. Schwartz and Robert A. Schneider (eds.), *Tocqueville and Beyond: Essays on the Old Regime in Honor of David D. Bien.* Newark: University of Delaware Press, 2003, 86–110.

Block, Fred L. and Margaret R. Somers. *The Power of Market Fundamentalism: Karl Polanyi's Critique.* Cambridge, MA: Harvard University Press, 2014.

Boltanski, Luc and Eve Chiapello. *The New Spirit of Capitalism.* New York: Verso, 2007.

Boltanski, Luc and Laurent Thevenot. *On Justification: Economies of Worth.* Princeton, NJ: Princeton University Press, 2006.

Bossenga, Gail. "Status, *Corps*, and Monarchy: Roots of Modern Citizenship in the Old Regime," in Robert M. Schwartz and Robert A. Schneider (eds.), *Tocqueville and Beyond: Essays on the Old Regime in Honor of David D. Bien*. Newark: University of Delaware Press, 2003, 127–154.

Botwinick, Howard. *Persistent Inequalities:Wage Disparity Under Capitalist Competition*. Princeton, NJ: Princeton University Press, 1993.

Bowles, Samuel. *The Moral Economy:Why Good Incentives are No Substitute for Good Citizens*. New Haven:Yale University Press, 2016.

Bowles, Samuel and Herbert Gintis. *Democracy and Capitalism: Property, Community and the Contradictions of Modern Social Thought*. New York: Basic Books, 1986.

Brantlinger, Patrick. *Crusoe's Footprints: Cultural Studies in Britain and America*. New York: Routledge, 1990.

Brittan, Samuel. "There's No Such Thing as Society," J.C. Rees Memorial Lecture. Swansea, SA: University College of Swansea, 1992.

Burns, James MacGregor. *Packing the Court:The Rise of Judicial Power and the Coming Crisis of the Supreme Court*. New York: Penguin Press, 2009.

Butler, Judith and Athena Athanasiou. *Dispossession:The Performative in the Political*. Cambridge, UK: Polity Press, 2013.

Calhoun, Craig. "Nationalism and Civil Society: Democracy, Diversity and Self-Determination," in Craig Calhoun (ed.), *Social Theory and the Politics of Identity*. Oxford, UK: Blackwell, 1994a, 304–336.

Calhoun, Craig (ed.). *Social Theory and the Politics of Identity*. Oxford, UK: Blackwell, 1994b.

Calhoun, Craig. *Nations Matter: Culture, History, and the Cosmopolitan Dream*. New York: Routledge, 2007.

Calhoun, Craig. *The Roots of Radicalism: Tradition, the Public Sphere, and Early Nineteenth-Century Social Movements*. Chicago: University of Chicago Press, 2012.

Carrithers, Michael, Steven Collins, and Steven Lukes (eds.). *The Category of the Person: Anthropology, Philosophy, History*. New York: Cambridge University Press, 1985.

Case, Anne and Angus Deaton. "Mortality and Morbidity in the 21st Century," *Brookings Papers on Economic Activity*, Spring 2017, 397–476.

Cohen, G. A. *Karl Marx's Theory of History: A Defense*. Princeton, NJ: Princeton University Press, 1978.

Cohen, G. A. *Self-Ownership, Freedom, and Equality*. New York: Cambridge University Press, 1995.

Cortois, Liza and Rudi Laermans. "Rethinking Individualization:The Basic Script and The Three Variants of Institutionalized Individualism," *European Journal of Social Theory*,Vol. 21, No. 1, 2018, 60–78.

Dahl, Robert A. *How Democratic is the American Constitution?* New Haven:Yale University Press, 2001.

Darity, William A. Jr. *Persistent Disparity: Race and Economic Inequality in the US Since 1945*. Cheltenham, UK: Edward Elgar, 1998.

Daston, Lorraine and Peter Galison. *Objectivity*. New York: Zone Books, 2010.

Davies, William. *The Limits of Neoliberalism:Authority, Sovereignty and the Logic of Competition*. 2nd ed.Washington, DC: Sage, 2017.

Davis, Ann E. "Property and Politics in the Hudson Valley: Continuity and Change in the Corporate Form," in Margaret Oppenheimer and Nicholas Mercuro (eds.), *Law & Economics:Alternative Economic Approaches to Legal and Regulatory Issues*. M.E. Sharpe, 2005, 131–160.

Davis, Ann E. *The Evolution of the Property Relation: Understanding Paradigms, Debates, Prospects*. New York: Palgrave MacMillan, 2015.

Davis, Ann E. *Money as a Social Institution: The Institutional Development of Capitalism*. New York: Routledge, 2017.

Davis, Ann E. "Is there a History of Property? Periodization of Property Regimes and Paradigms," in Staci M. Zavatarro, Gregory Peterson, and Ann E. Davis (eds.), *Exploring Property Rights in Contemporary Governance*. Albany: SUNY Press, 2019, 5–24. ISBN 9781438472898.

Davis, John Brian. *Individuals and Identity in Economics*. New York: Cambridge University Press, 2011.

De Vries, Jan and Ad van der Woude. *The First Modern Economy: Success, Failure and Perseverance of the Dutch Economy, 1500–1815*. New York: Cambridge University Press, 1997.

Eagleton, Terry. *Culture*. New Haven: Yale University Press, 2016.

Eco, Umberto. *A Theory of Semiotics*. Bloomington: Indiana University Press, 1979.

Eco, Umberto. *Semiotics and the Philosophy of Language*. Bloomington: Indiana University Press, 1984.

Edelstein, Dan. *On the Spirit of Rights*. Chicago: University of Chicago Press, 2019.

England, Paula. "The Separative Self: Androcentric Bias in Neoclassical Assumptions," in Marianne A. Ferber and Julie A. Nelson (eds.), *Beyond Economic Man: Feminist Theory and Economics*. Chicago: University of Chicago Press, 1993, 37–53.

Foucault, Michel. *The History of Sexuality. Volume I: An Introduction*. New York: Pantheon, 1978.

Foucault, Michel. "Governmentality," in Graham Burchell, Colin Gordon, and Peter Miller (eds.), *The Foucault Effect: Studies in Governmentality*. Chicago: University of Chicago Press, 1991, 87–104.

Franck, Thomas M. *The Empowered Self: Law and Society in the Age of Individualism*. New York: Oxford University Press, 1999.

Fukuyama, Francis. *The End of History and the Last Man*. New York: The Free Press, 1992.

Fukuyama, Francis. *Identity: The Demand for Dignity and the Politics of Resentment*. New York: Farrar, Straus, and Giroux, 2018.

Gazzaniga, Michael S. *The Consciousness Instinct: Unraveling the Mystery of How the Brain Makes the Mind*. New York: Farrar, Straus and Giroux, 2018.

Geuss, Raymond. *Outside Ethics*. Princeton, NJ: Princeton University Press, 2005.

Giddens, Anthony. *Modernity and Self-Identity: Self and Society in the Late Modern Age*. Stanford, CA: Stanford University Press, 1991.

Gordon, Peter E. "Secularization, Genealogy, and the Legitimacy of the Modern Age: Remarks on the Lowith-Blumenberg Debate," *Journal of the History of Ideas*, Vol. 80, No. 1, January 2019, 147–170.

Grapard, Ulla and Gillian Hewitson (eds.). *Robinson Crusoe's Economic Man: A Construction and Deconstruction*. New York: Routledge, 2011.

Greenblatt, Stephen J. *Renaissance Self-Fashioning: From More to Shakespeare*. Chicago: University of Chicago Press, 1980.

Habermas, Jurgen. *The Structural Transformation of the Public Sphere: An Inquiry into a Category of Bourgeois Society*. Cambridge, MA: MIT Press, 1989.

Hall, Stuart, Chas Critcher, Tony Jefferson, John Clarke, and Brian Roberts. *Policing the Crisis: Mugging, the State, and Law and Order*. London: MacMillan, 1978.

Hamilton, Darrick and William A. Darity, Jr. "The Political Economy of Education, Financial Literacy, and the Racial Wealth Gap," *Federal Reserve Bank of St. Louis Review, First Quarter*, Vol. 99, No. 1, 2017, 59–76.

Haraway, Donna J. "A Cyborg Manifesto: Science, Technology, and Socialist-Feminism in the Late Twentieth Century," in *Manifestly Haraway*. Minneapolis: University of Minnesota Press, 2016 [first published in *Socialist Review*, No. 80, 1985, 65–108].

Harvey, David. *A Brief History of Neoliberalism*. New York: Oxford University Press, 2005.

Hayek, Friedrich A. *Individualism and Economic Order*. Chicago: University of Chicago Press, 1948.

Horkheimer, Max and Theodor W. Adorno. *Dialectic of Enlightenment*. New York: Seabury Press, 1972.

Howell, Martha C. "The Gender of Europe's Commercial Economy, 1200–1700," *Gender and History*, Vol. 20, No. 3, September 2008, 519–538.

Huddy, Leonie. "From Group Identity to Political Cohesion and Commitment," in Leonie Huddy, David O. Sears and Jack S. Levy (eds.), *Political Psychology*. 2nd ed. New York: Oxford University Press, 2013, 737–773.

Hunt, Lynn. *The Family Romance of the French Revolution*. Berkeley: University of California Pres, 1992.

Hunt, Lynn. *Inventing Human Rights: A History*. New York: W.W. Norton & Company, 2007a.

Hunt, Lynn. "The Paradoxical Origins of Human Rights," in Jeffrey N. Wasserstrom, Greg Grandin, Lynn Hunt, and Marilyn B. Young (eds.), *Human Rights and Revolutions*. 2nd ed. New York: Rowman & Littlefield Publishers, Inc., 2007b, 3–20.

Hunt, Lynn. "The Global Financial Origins of 1789," in Suzanne Desan, Lynn Hunt, and William Max Nelson (eds.), *The French Revolution in Global Perspective*. Ithaca, NY: Cornell University Press, 2013, 32–43.

Israel, Jonathan I. *Radical Enlightenment: Philosophy and the Making of Modernity 1650–1750*. New York: Oxford University Press, 2001.

Israel, Jonathan I. "The Intellectual Origins of Modern Democratic Republicanism (1660–1720)," *European Journal of Political Theory*, 2004, 7–36.

Israel, Jonathan I. *Revolutionary Ideas: An Intellectual History of the French Revolution from the Rights of Man to Robespierre*. Princeton, NJ: Princeton University Press, 2014.

Israel, Jonathan I. *Expanding the Blaze: How the American Revolution Ignited the World, 1775–1848*. Princeton, NJ: Princeton University Press, 2017.

Jainchill, Andrew. "1685 and the French Revolution," in Suzanne Desan, Lynn Hunt, and William Max Nelson (eds.), *The French Revolution in Global Perspective*. Ithaca, NY: Cornell University Press, 2013, 57–72.

Jameson, Fredric. *The Cultural Turn: Selected Writings on the Postmodern, 1983–1998*. New York: Verso, 1998.

Janik, Allan and Stephen Toulmin. *Wittgenstein's Vienna*. New York: Simon and Schuster, 1973.

Kandel, Eric R. *The Age of Insight: The Quest to Understand the Unconscious in Art, Mind, and Brain, From Vienna 1900 to the Present*. New York: Random House, 2012.

Kidd, Colin. "Identity Before Identities: Ethnicity, Nationalism, and the Historian," in Julia Rudolph (ed.), *History and Nation*. Lewisburg: Bucknell University Press, 2006, 9–44.

Konings, Martijn. *The Emotional Logic of Capitalism: What Progressives Have Missed*. Stanford, CA: Stanford University Press, 2015.

Koselleck, Reinhart. "Linguistic Change and the History of Events," *Journal of Modern History*, Vol. 61, No. 4, December 1989, 649–666.

Koselleck, Reinhart. *The Practice of Conceptual History: Timing History, Spacing Events*. Stanford: Stanford University Press, 2002.

Kranton, Rachel. "The Devil is in the Details: Implications of Samuel Bowles's *The Moral Economy* for Economics and Policy Research," *Journal of Economic Literature*, Vol. 57, No. 1, March 2019, 147–160.

Lamoreaux, Naomi R. "The Mystery of Property Rights: A U.S. Perspective," *Journal of Economic History*, Vol. 71, June 2011, 275–306.

Lemert, Charles. "Dark Thoughts About the Self," in Craig Calhoun (ed.), *Social Theory and the Politics of Identity*. Oxford, UK: Blackwell, 1994, 100–130.

Lukacs, Georg. *History and Class Consciousness: Studies in Marxist Dialectics*. Cambridge, MA: MIT Press, 1971.

Lukes, Steven. *Individualism: Key Concepts in the Social Sciences*. Oxford, UK: Basil Blackwell, 1973.

Marder, Michael. *Political Categories: Thinking Beyond Concepts*. New York: Cambridge University Press, 2019.

Marglin, Stephen A. *The Dismal Science: How Thinking Like an Economist Undermines Community*. Cambridge, MA: Harvard University Press, 2008.

Martin, John. "Inventing Sincerity, Refashioning Prudence: The Discovery of the Individual in Renaissance Europe," *American Historical Review*, December 1997, 1308–1342.

Martin, Luther H., Huck Gutman, and Patrick H. Hutton (eds.). *Technologies of the Self: A Seminar with Michel Foucault*. Amherst: University of Massachusetts Press, 1988.

McKeon, Michael. *The Secret History of Domesticity: Public, Private and the Division of Knowledge*. Baltimore, MD: Johns Hopkins University Press, 2005.

Mehta, Uday Singh. *The Anxiety of Freedom: Imagination and Individuality in Locke's Political Thought*. Ithaca, NY: Cornell University Press, 1992.

Meister, Robert. *After Evil: A Politics of Human Rights*. New York: Cambridge University Press, 2011.

Mokyr, Joel. *Culture of Growth: The Origins of the Modern Economy*. Princeton, NJ: Princeton University Press, 2016.

Moyn, Samuel. "The Assumption by Man of His Original Fracturing: Marcel Gauchet, Gladys Swain, and the History of the Self," *Modern Intellectual History*, Vol. 6, No. 2, 2009, 315–341.

Moyn, Samuel. *Not Enough: Human Rights in an Unequal World*. Cambridge, MA: Harvard University Press, 2018.

Najemy, John M. *Corporatism and Consensus in Florentine Electoral Politics*. Chapel Hill: University of North Carolina Press, 1982.

Okun, Arthur. *Equality and Efficiency: The Big Tradeoff*. Washington, DC: Brookings, 1975.

Padgett, John F. "Organizational Genesis, Identity, and Control: The Transformation of Banking in Renaissance Florence," in James E. Rauch and Alessandra Casella (eds.), *Networks and Markets*. New York: Russell Sage Foundation, 2001, 211–257.

Padgett, John F. "Autocatalysis in Chemistry and the Origin of Life," in John F. Padgett and Walter W. Powell (eds.), *The Emergence of Organizations and Markets*. Princeton, NJ: Princeton University Press, 2012, 33–69.

Pateman, Carole. *The Sexual Contract*. Stanford, CA: Stanford University Press, 1988.

Pierson, Christopher. *Just Property: A History in the Latin West. Volume One: Wealth, Virtue, and the Law*. New York: Oxford University Press, 2013a.

Pierson, Christopher. "Rousseau and the Paradoxes of Property," *European Journal of Political Theory*, Vol. 12, No. 4, 2013b, 409–424.

Pierson, Christopher. *Just Property: Volume Two: Enlightenment, Revolution, and History*. New York: Oxford University Press, 2016.

Pincus, Steve. *1688: The First Modern Revolution*. New Haven: Yale University Press, 2009.

Pistor, Katharina. *The Code of Capital: How the Law Creates Wealth and Inequality*. Princeton, NJ: Princeton University Press, 2019.

Pocock, J. G. A. *The Machiavellian Moment: Florentine Political Thought and the Atlantic Republican Tradition*. Princeton, NJ: Princeton University Press, 1975.

Polanyi, Karl. *The Great Transformation*. Boston: Beacon Press, 1944.

Pollock, Sheldon, Benjamin A. Elman, and Ku-ming Kevin Chang (eds.). *World Philology*. Cambridge, MA: Harvard University Press, 2015.

Pomeranz, Kenneth. *The Great Divergence: Europe, China, and the Making of the Modern World Economy*. Princeton, NJ: Princeton University Press, 2000.

Poovey, Mary. *A History of the Modern Fact: Problems of Knowledge in the Sciences of Wealth and Society*. Chicago: University of Chicago Press, 1998.

Poovey, Mary. "The Liberal Civil Subject and the Social in Eighteenth-Century British Moral Philosophy," *Public Culture*, Vol. 14, No. 1, 2002, 125–145.

Poovey, Mary. *Genres of the Credit Economy: Mediating Value in Eighteenth-and Nineteenth-Century Britain*. Chicago: University of Chicago Press, 2008.

Raworth, Kate. *Donut Economics*. White River Junction: Chelsea Green, 2017.

Riesman, David. *Individualism Reconsidered and Other Essays*. Glencoe, IL: The Free Press, 1954.

Riesman, David, with Reuel Denney and Nathan Glazer. *The Lonely Crowd: A Study of Changing American Character*. New Haven: Yale University Press, 1950.

Rorty, Richard. *Achieving our Country: Leftist Thought in Twentieth-Century America*. Cambridge, MA: Harvard University Press, 1998.

Safranski, Rudiger. *Nietzsche: A Philosophical Biography*. New York: W.W. Norton & Company, 2002.

Sartori, Andrew. *Liberalism in Empire: An Alternative History*. Oakland, CA: University of California Press, 2014.

Satia, Priya. *Empire of Guns: The Violent Making of the Industrial Revolution*. New York: Penguin Press, 2018.

Scott, Joan W. "Gender: A Useful Category of Historical Analysis," *American Historical Review*, Vol. 91, No. 5, December 1986, 1053–1075.

Searle, John R. *Making the Social World: The Structure of Human Civilization*. New York: Oxford University Press, 2010.

Seigel, Jerrold. *The Idea of the Self*. Cambridge, UK: Cambridge University Press, 2005.

Sennett, Richard. *Together: The Rituals, Pleasures and Politics of Cooperation*. New Haven: Yale University Press, 2012.

Serna, Pierre. "Every Revolution is a War of Independence," in Suzanne Desan, Lynn Hunt, and William Max Nelson (eds.), *The French Revolution in Global Perspective*. Ithaca, NY: Cornell University Press, 2013, 165–182.

Sewell, William H. Jr. *Work and Revolution in France: The Language of Labor from the Old Regime to 1848*. New York: Cambridge University Press, 1980.

Sewell, William H. Jr. *A Rhetoric of Bourgeois Revolution: The Abbe Sieyes and What is the Third Estate?* Durham, NC: Duke University Press, 1994.

Sewell, William H. Jr. *Logics of History: Social Theory and Social Transformation*. Chicago: University of Chicago Press, 2005.

Sewell, William H. Jr. "Economic Crises and the Shape of Modern History," *Public Culture*, Vol. 24, No. 2, 2012, 303–327.

Shiller, Robert J. *Narrative Economics: How Stories Go Viral and Drive Major Economic Events*. Princeton, NJ: Princeton University Press, 2019.

Siedentop, Larry. *Inventing the Individual: The Origins of Western Liberalism*. Cambridge, MA: Harvard University Press, 2014.

Smith, Adam. *An Inquiry into the Nature and Causes of the Wealth of Nations*. Ed. Edwin Cannan. New York: The Modern Library, 1994.

Somers, Margaret R. "Where is Sociology After the Historic Turn? Knowledge Cultures, Narrativity, and Historical Epistemologies," in Terrence J. McDonald (ed.), *The Historic Turn in the Human Sciences*. Ann Arbor: The University of Michigan Press, 1996, 53–90.

Somers, Margaret R. and Gloria D. Gibson. "Reclaiming the Epistemological 'Other': Narrative and the Social Constitution of Identity," in Craig Calhoun (ed.), *Social Theory and the Politics of Identity*. Oxford, UK: Blackwell, 1994, 37–99.

Strathern, Marilyn. *The Gender of the Gift: Problems with Women and Problems with Society in Melanesia*. Berkeley: University of California Press, 1988.

Strathern, Marilyn. *Kinship, Law and the Unexpected: Relatives Are Always a Surprise*. New York: Cambridge University Press, 2005.

Sum, Ngai-Ling and Bob Jessup. *Towards a Cultural Political Economy: Putting Culture in its Place in Political Economy*. Cheltenham, UK: Edward Elgar, 2013.

Szakolczai, Arpad. *Reflexive Historical Sociology*. New York: Routledge, 2000.

Taylor, Charles. *Sources of the Self: The Making of Modern Identity*. New York: Cambridge University Press, 1989.

Taylor, Charles. *Multiculturalism and the Politics of Recognition: An Essay*. Ed. Amy Gutmann. Princeton, NJ: Princeton University Press, 1992.

Taylor, Charles. "Modern Social Imaginaries," *Public Culture*, Vol. 14, No. 1, 2002, 91–124.

Taylor, Charles. *Modern Social Imaginaries*. Durham, NC: Duke University Press, 2004.

Taylor, Charles. *The Language Animal: The Full Shape of the Human Linguistic Capacity*. Cambridge, MA: Harvard University Press, 2016.

Underkuffler, Laura S. *The Idea of Property: Its Meaning and Power*. New York: Oxford University Press, 2003.

Viroli, Maurizio. "The Revolution in the Concept of Politics," *Political Theory*, Vol. 20, No. 3, August 1992, 473–495.

Wahrman, Dror. *The Making of the Modern Self: Identity and Culture in Eighteenth-Century England*. New Haven: Yale University Press, 2004.

Weber, Marx. *Economy and Society: An Outline of Interpretive Sociology*. Berkeley: University of California Press, 1978.

White, Harrison C. *Identity and Control: How Social Formations Emerge*. 2nd ed. Princeton, NJ: Princeton University Press, 2008.

Yergin, Daniel and Joseph Stanislaw. *The Commanding Heights: The Battle Between Government and the Market Place That is Remaking the Modern World*. New York: Simon & Schuster, 1998.

Yuran, Noam. *What Money Wants: An Economy of Desire*. Stanford, CA: Stanford University Press, 2014.

Zaretsky, Eli. "Identity Theory, Identity Politics: Psychoanalysis, Marxism, Post-Structuralism," in Craig Calhoun (ed.), *Social Theory and the Politics of Identity*. Oxford, UK: Blackwell, 1994, 198–215.

Zaretsky, Eli. *Political Freud: A History*. New York: Columbia University Press, 2015.

2 Property and reification

Introduction

The goal of this chapter is to explore the connection between the individual and property. In contrast to monarchical methods of governance, the individual and property become the foundation of a new system of modern governance based on natural law theory in the seventeenth century. This analysis will help us to understand how Margaret Thatcher could claim in 1987 that there is no such thing as society (Brown 2019, 28, 115), by examining the concept of reification. In decrying the abstraction of the concept of "society," Thatcher sought to resolve it into its constituent components, individuals (Brittan 1992). Another strategy will be pursued here, making use of the analysis of language in Chapter 1, which is both beyond the individual and helps relate the individual to larger units.

The individual and property – reifying abstractions

We will argue that "property" and "the individual" are also reifying abstractions, not just "society," contrary to Hayek, Thatcher's mentor (Brown 2019, 30–39). There is a history of property contrary to the notion that property is simply a natural object (Davis 2019, 2015a; Novak 2009). The legal and institutional foundations of property are necessary for permanence, transferability, and the durability that makes the institution of "property" seem material (Pistor 2019, 42–46).

Concept of property

The conventional meaning of property is that it is self-evident and invariant; it is a concrete tangible object in the world. Yet a recent legal studies text cites five alternative theories of property and four key debates (Alexander and Penalver 2012).

There are certain paradoxes regarding property, in spite of its presumed self-evident character, such that it is both individual and social, while the latter social dimension is frequently denied. Ownership of property is viewed as a bulwark for the individual against the social, while property is also social, requiring recognition and enforcement of others (Singer 2000, 37–38, 130–139; Underkuffler 2002, 144–145; Yuran 2014). In this case, property is "paradoxical" (Davis 2015a, 35–37, 38–42, 49–50, 206–208; Gordon 1996). There is a "paradigm of property," based on the rational individual, maximizing utility, in the context of a free market, in which this paradoxical dimension of property is ignored. Some would consider this an "ideology" (Singer 2000, 8–9; Gordon 1996, 95, 101).

According to Gordon, Blackstone's famous image of absolute dominium for the individual owner was not even applicable to forms of property at the time of his writing, such as the corporation, the credit contract, or the mortgage (Gordon 1996; Singer 2000, 101; Davis 2019). The persuasiveness of Blackstone's metaphor of absolute property as the individual's castle is based on reification (Gordon 1996, 100–101, 106–108) such that the collective nature of property is suppressed.

Justifications of property include efficiency, maximizing utility, and fairness, as well as a requirement for personal development (Peterson 2019, 148–150; Singer 2000, 105–130; Sonenscher 2008). Yet explanations for income distribution are notably inconsistent, and the recent trends towards increasing inequality cannot be justified by performance or merit.

Transition period

In seventeenth-century England, the hereditary monarch was justified and supported by the church. In the period of civil wars, there was an interrogation of both the source of authority and truth (McKeon 2005, 342–357). In developing a right of revolution, the natural law theorists developed the concept of property as a mediation between God, who created the earth, and humans, who were authorized to make use of it. The formation of the state was among individuals, by social contract, who were creatures of God, for the sake of protection of the property which was obtained from working on the earth. This has been called the "workmanship" model of property, where humans are imitating God, capable of creation. And as creations of God, each person has a right to consume resources from the earth in order to perpetuate his own life (Pierson 2013a, 208–245). This is a "conjectural history," not based on ancient custom (Pocock 1975), a new genre to justify a new era of a nondenominational state. One could even mention the term "paradigm" related to discourse and values of a newly acceptable commercial society (Pocock 2009, xii–xiv, 72–81).

Following Grotius in the early seventeenth century (Pierson 2013a, 165–171), Locke's origin story can be understood as a rationale for self-government, the formation of a state by social contract to protect property while also maintaining a link to a Christian deity who is no longer necessary to designate the hereditary monarch as ruler. According to natural law theories, the earth is given to humans in common, with individual private property created by labor in the state of nature. The naturalness of property is linked to the deity, while also designed to recognize and reward individual activity. The labor theory of value of Locke and Smith becomes a new justification of property as well as a new rationale for the state. Property in the state of nature is also a limit to the state and authorizes a right to revolution.

McKeon sees the "devolution" of the notion of the absolute monarch to the absolute dominion of individual private property. As a consequence, the monarch becomes depersonalized, and property owners form the new "civil society," separate from the monarchy and the commoners (McKeon 2005, 16–18, 32–33). From the sovereign as a person, there developed the abstract concept of sovereignty as residing in the populace, associated with a right of self-government. The conceptual separation of public and private was debated in the decades prior to the French Revolution; there was a separation of public office, such as jurisdiction by feudal sovereigns and tax farmers, and now assigned to the functions of the head of state. Property was designated as fully private, with no duties or service associated with it (Blaufarb 2016).

According to Poovey (Poovey 1998, 2008, 139–144), "naturalization" is a strategy to make a given institution seem immutable and beyond challenge, even as natural law theorists were proposing a new logic for justifying governance arrangements. Given the enormous prestige of natural philosophy (Poovey 1998, 183), and the presumption that the study of nature is the study of God's work (Poovey 1998, 194–195), natural law could be used to establish presumptions about human nature, such as "homo economicus" and the naturalness of self-interest, and led to the foundation of a new science of political economy (Poovey 1998, 174–175). There was a conceptual separation of natural from social science (Latour 1993) and then a justification of novel social and political arrangements based on their presumed "naturalness."

At the same time, the appropriate methods of natural science were also being debated by Bacon, Boyle, as well as Locke (Poovey 1998; Daston and Galison 2010; Shapin and Schaffer 1985), such as deduction from amassing quantitative evidence. The first scientists were gentlemen hobbyists, then founding the Royal Society and separating laboratories as neutral spaces in a period of intense political strife. Methods of government were also developing which considered varieties of individual interests and opinions to form a general "public opinion" (McKeon 2005).

While Locke is the most-cited English-speaking writer on the topic of property (Pierson 2013a, 208), there were also property "radicals" (Pierson 2013a, 189–207; Israel 2001; Pierson 2013b). In the long history of the concept of property from Ancient Greece and Rome, including early Christian thinkers (Pierson 2013a, 5–20), there is often a stress on property as a means to the end of human flourishing, compared with Locke's emphasis on a natural right to property per se.

Critiques of Locke

Locke's presumptions were that the earth was a gift to humankind as a commons; nonetheless, enclosure of property increased productivity, and money facilitated accumulation beyond the "spoilage limit" and beyond a person's immediate needs.

The commons proviso is well known among discussions of Locke, authorizing the appropriation of nature only if "leaving enough and as good for others." The requirement that land be enclosed and used intensively is also known as the "waste" provision because enclosed land was considered more productive. As a consequence, Native American land-use practices were considered inferior, meriting acquisition by the European settlers in the early exploration phases of the fifteenth, sixteenth, and seventeenth centuries.

There are other issues as well. First, Locke famously describes the property-creating aspect of labor but also includes one's own servant's property, clearly indicating status differentials among various types of workers. Second, he does not address the lack of access or control of the worker to his own product in the context of the division of labor so typical of industrial economies. Locke also presumes "consent" to the resulting inequality by users of money (Pierson 2013a, 219, 240–245). Third, his concept of "self-ownership" implies the existence of a "self" separate from one's body and one's person (Pierson 2013a, 233; Balibar 2006).

Reification

While "property" may seem to be a self-evident, natural object, we will explore the concept of reification using property and several other examples. Because language is a public medium of communication, as well as a private medium of cognition, it is often taken for granted (Searle 2010), like the air we all breathe, which is a necessity of life. Recent theoretical attention has brought the role of language under greater scrutiny, which we will explore throughout this book. For example, there is a type of use of language whereby a noun can refer to a human institution, with the metaphor of an object. The object metaphor conveys a sense of concreteness, or materiality, which may be difficult to grasp in an institution consisting of norms, rules, and practices. The human institutions then can be symbolized by that object, with the association of permanence and objectivity. This is a form of reification.

According to Searle (2010, 64, 79–80), there is a generativity to language. If a word can refer to a thing, such as the word "property" refers to "land," then "property" has a concrete meaning. But a representation like "property" can also have a representation. In this case, the term "property" can refer to a legal code which conveys a legal right to that piece of property and its future return (Pistor 2019, 2–21). But when the term "property" refers both to the legal code and to the piece of land, the distinction disappears and the conventional use of the term refers to both. Reification is particularly important in capitalism when relationships are referred to as objects, like "property."

Interpersonal relationships are particularly important in modern industrial economies, characterized by markets and division of labor. Such relationships are invisible, nonetheless, due to reification, or the naming of human relationships as objects. These objects symbolize these relationships, which then become invisible. For example, in capitalist market economies, where commodities become so important, the idea that the value of these commodities stands for the relationships among the workers who produced them, becomes significant in the operation of the system. These "dead" objects stand for living relationships, which become invisible. The living workers seem superfluous, depending on the market for access to the commodities that they themselves have produced. These expendable workers then must search for other jobs, which become increasingly contingent and insecure, while the commodities stand for "wealth," the goal and measure of nations. That is, there is a reversal of dead and living and a reversal of valuation, or objects over persons (Davis 2017b).

The contention here is that reification is a significant factor in the use of language in modern economies, and in modern economics, which renders human institutions invisible. A critique of abstractions is found before Hayek and Thatcher, with Hegel, Marx, Nietzsche, and Stirner in the nineteenth century (Safranski 2002, 122–132), but with a focus on history rather than language. That is, a human person can challenge the meaning of "the social" while using a language that always already indicates the importance of the social dimension to her single life.

Reification of property

Natural law theory is subject to reification by its claim that there is property in a state of nature, prior to the state. All that is required is for an individual to "mix his labor" with the soil. There is ostensibly no need for other individuals to respect this property or for a state to protect it. A second reason for the ease of reification is the usual assumption that language merely refers to natural objects, not institutions. According to recent analytic philosophy (Searle 2010), institutions are created by "status function declarations" which create a status at the same time as describing it. For example, the chair of the meeting can declare it adjourned by merely stating that it is adjourned, and the couple is married as soon as the presiding official declares them so. For some, these institutions which are socially constructed seem less real than natural objects, although much of "civilization" can be described in these terms (Berger and Luckmann 1966).

For example, the same term, "property," can refer both to the natural object and the institution. Such an elision then reinforces reification.

The use of language in the first example in row (1) in Table 2.1 is merely a referral of words to "things," such as natural objects like land and the earth. The second use of language row (2) in Table 2.1 requires an understanding of the capacity to create institutions with language. According to Searle (2010), declarations from authorities can create institutions by assigning functions to certain objects, which can also include institutions (Davis 2015a, 28–30). For example, the ownership of an object such as a parcel of land requires a title

Table 2.1 Language Uses: Property

Term	Institutions	Object
(1) Property	Work of the Creator; pre-political re: natural law theory	Land; earth
(2) Property	Public institutions of the judiciary and the police to interpret and protect property	Discrete parcel of land, marked by boundaries and GPS coordinates by formal survey in official documents

and formal recognition, such as registry and verification (Singer 2000, 28–32). These institutional procedures are easily ignored in conventional use of the term "my property," until there is some damage or competing claim. In this way, social institutions are part of the meaning of property, while often ignored or misunderstood. That is, property can seem merely "self-evident," merely based on possession of an object.

According to this reasoning, there are several fallacies with regard to property (Davis 2015a, 40):

1) Property appears to be individual, but it is social.
2) The object of property appears to be concrete, but it can be abstract.
3) Property seems to be self-evident, but it relies on the state for definition and enforcement.
4) Property appears to be self-evident, but it is inscribed and documented in language, which is social.
5) The relationship of ownership is not individual, but it is social, requiring recognition by others.

In spite of the metaphor of property as an object, self-evident and tangible like land, the legal concept of property has been remarkably fluid (Rosser 2015).

Reification of the individual

With natural law theory, there is a similar reification of "the individual." The category of "the individual" is deemed natural, a product of the deity, without requiring institutional enforcement. The concept of the individual apparently refers to a unique natural human body, but legal and institutional contexts can include other meanings. The institutional framework is less visible; the liberal nation-state has slots or positions which any person can fill, based on competition and merit, once the functions of military, finance, and welfare have been internalized, instead of professional mercenaries, tax farms, or parish Poor Laws (Davis 2015a, 2017c; Pierson 2007; Garland 2014). That is, the modern state is characterized by bureaucracy, with general categories of positions to serve discreet functions, filled on an impersonal, competitive basis (Weber 1978; North, Wallis, and Weingast 2009).

Table 2.2 Language Uses: The Individual

Term	Institutions	Object
(1) Individual	Work of the Creator; pre-political re: natural law theory	Human person
(2) Individual	Abstract individual as an institutional position in the liberal nation-state: for example, citizenship in the public sphere; employee in the private sphere; chartered corporation	Unique human person in a role such as specific voter or employee; other entities which can have the legal status of a human person, such as the private business corporation

In natural law theory, the individual is the chief protagonist of the liberal state, its agent, while property is its object. These two concepts represent the two essential poles around which society and the state are structured and are mutually constituted. Adam Smith's "invisible hand" is their mysterious relationship.

For the category of "the individual" to have meaning and agency, nonetheless, the institutional context must be specified and traced historically. In natural law theory, such an individual can seem self-evident, sprung like mushrooms from the ground, according to Hobbes (Somers and Gibson 1994, 48), without accounting for the labor of birthing or the institutions of the family, education, socialization, or employment or governance.

Reification of money

In Locke's formulation, the role of money is to avoid the spoilage limit so that unlimited accumulation is then possible, even beyond a person's immediate consumption. He ignores the requirement that someone else be producing the fresh produce to exchange for the money at some future time. That is, Locke presumes that money itself is productive, obfuscating the condition that production take place to provide the commodities for which it can be exchanged after its accumulation. This assignment of productivity to money itself is a form of reification. Further, Locke assumes that money is created by contract among freely associated individuals, without acknowledging the role of the state (Desan 2014, 351–353, 372–375).

According to Marx, money is the reification of the collective product of labor, which renders invisible the institutional relationships which are the origin of profit. The existence of the wage labor force presumes already the separation of the worker from the means of production and means of subsistence; in that sense, the worker is a non-owner (Yuran 2014, 52–53). The worker is "free" in a double sense, mobile but also needing to offer himself for employment to obtain necessities. In this context, the worker is separated from his product, which belongs to the owner, contrary to Locke. The individual

Table 2.3 Language Uses: Money

Term	Institutions	Object
(1) Money	Guild; mint; long-distance trade	Stamped metal coins
(2) Money	Interlinked markets in a liberal state based on wage labor	Inscribed engraved paper; exchangeable for all commodities, including necessities and luxuries and human labor; legal tender

worker spends his entire working day to earn a wage, a sum of money which can purchase any other product but in limited quantity. The products for sale have use value or utility, and their exchange value or price reflects the value of social cooperation and division of labor for the economy as a whole. The characteristic of the value of the commodity seems stamped on the object itself, nonetheless, rather than resulting from this particular social organization. The value produced by living labor is reified in money so that workers do not recognize the value of products as the result of their own work (Davis 2017c). That is, the money object or symbol has value only because of living labor, another form of an object representing human relationships. The "ownership" relationship does not create value; rather it excludes the worker from conditions of independence and so enforces the financial circuit as a matter of necessity, what Polanyi (1944) called the "prod of hunger" (Davis 2015b). That is, the discipline of capitalism is a matter of life and death for those most vulnerable.

There is an exchange of time for money, for the worker and consumer, as well as saver and investor, by means of financial markets. Although measured in objective, abstract time, these are the personal lifetimes of the individual protagonists. Other theorists assume that money stands for types of relationships, such as credit/debt and taxes (Ingham 2004; Wray 2015). What is unique to Polanyi and Marx is the assumption that there is coercion, not volition, due to the initial conditions of the labor force, understood as "free" ironically.

Reification of the state

Drawing upon Latour, one can argue that the state itself is a reified social relation.

> Hobbes invents the naked calculating citizen, whose rights are limited to possessing and to being represented by the artificial construction of the Sovereign. . . . The Republic is a paradoxical artificial creature composed of citizens united only by the authorization given to one of them to represent them all. . . . The Leviathan is made up only of citizens, calculations, agreements or disputes. In short, it is made up of nothing but social relations.
> (Latour 1993, 26–28)

Table 2.4 Language Uses: The State

Term	Institutions	Object
(1) Nation	Divine right of kings	Hereditary monarch; the sovereign
(2) Nation	Popular sovereignty, with recognized institutional representation, elections	Collective population in bounded territory

A similar point was made elsewhere by this author regarding the corporate form of the state as a reification of the power of the collective (Davis 2015a).

The importance of reification

In the context of the devolution of authority from the monarch to the self-governing republic, the conventional acceptance is based on the understanding that the republic represents freedom for the individual. This meaning is declared in the US Declaration of Independence and the rhetoric of the French Revolution. These new governmental arrangements pledge to protect individual freedom by the guarantee of the security of individual private property. There are two ways to represent this property-owning individual: in the private sphere as owner and in the public sphere as citizen (for further discussion see Chapter 3). Representation was generally not allocated by class or by designed to avoid factions based on property (importance of labor for political influence and representation (Sewell 1994, 75–94, 102–108; Madison Federalist Paper #10). The continuing development of the market economy in the late eighteenth century was also providing new opportunities for the exchange of property and labor.

The very necessity for a governing authority, nonetheless, is inconsistent with this definition of freedom. These institutional relationships remain "invisible" in Adam Smith's articulation and are reified in the "free market." These concepts of "sovereignty," "property," "the individual," and the "market" are "reifying abstractions," according to Poovey (2002). These terms refer to new institutional arrangements which are established by public and private law and governmental bureaucracy, which give these new concepts meaning. Yet the terms themselves appear to convey all the efficacy needed without fully comprehending the complex institutional infrastructure which gives them authority and operational capacity.

This dilemma between property and freedom is discussed in MacPherson. He notes the "collectivism" which is inherent in Locke, in spite of his "individualism." As long as property is protected, the individual submits to the majority will. The agreement of the individual with the majority is assured by the exclusive political enfranchisement of property owners, who then share this perspective in common. These contradictions come to the fore when there is significant inequality and when wage workers are enfranchised with different interests (MacPherson 1962, 247–262, 271–277).

In this way, the freedom of the individual can be claimed while always necessitating institutional arrangements which provide interpretation and enforcement. Any coercion associated with these institutions or authorities can be denied or blamed on governmental interference with the market, according to laissez faire principles. The market can be claimed as the embodiment of self-organization, the perfect expression of freedom. Any law or regulation can be interpreted as unnecessary intervention between the individual and her private property, for whom no interpersonal relationships appear to be necessary as a result of the reification of both.

In the process of founding and organizing these institutions, there is a shift in perspective. Instead of the view from the deity as interpreted by the church, there developed the view of social science and other types of experts, with a focus on the "social." These new experts, such as merchants and lawyers, develop a "view from nowhere," as if the "social" were an object of scrutiny and observation by these newly empowered expert subjects. This new perspective is based on several regular characteristics of "society," such as the autonomous, predictable practices of individuals, as well as the lawful, systemic features of their interactions, which are capable of representation by concepts and numbers, according to the scientific method (Poovey 2002, 129–131). This new subject/object relationship of these experts to the general population develops along with "the economy" as an abstract concept, the public sphere, and the codification of methods of "liberal governmentality" (Poovey 2002, 135–136). Such objectification becomes a seemingly natural part of the modern "social imaginary," to use Taylor's term for the necessary background for knowledgeable participation in modern institutions (Taylor 2002).

What had been viewed as the sovereign authority of the monarch is now represented as a natural, "invisible" relationship between the individual and private property, no longer political but essential, self-evident, and eternal. These new terms carry authority, along with the associated institutions and expertise, which can be analyzed with what we can call the method of historical institutionalism (Davis 2015a, 2017c, 158–162).

The individual and property ownership

Self-ownership has been an important concept across the political spectrum, including liberal, libertarian, and Marxist. One issue is whether this concept can stabilize either the notion of "the individual" or the notion of "individual private property," while bringing each pole into more direct relationship with each other. Another issue is whether the notion of "self-ownership" is part of a strategy to universalize property, to declare all as owners. A third issue is whether self-ownership is a form of alienation instead of freedom.

The concept of "ownership" typically means the capacity to exclude, as well as to make use of the object, to sell, to acquire the rents from its sale.

Similarly, self-ownership would mean the capacity to make use of oneself, including one's own sale, as well as the right to exclude others from using oneself. While self-enslavement is illegal after widespread abolition in the nineteenth century, the temporary sale of one's capacity to work becomes the normal method of participation in the economy. This self-ownership is a requirement for one's participation in the wage labor force. This capacity, if unused, renders the person without means of subsistence. One's "own" body becomes a burden without regular means of subsistence. The primary objective of a member of the labor force is to obtain employment, to "get a job."

For libertarians, "self-ownership" is a further bulwark of the self, protecting returns to one's own labor and preserving autonomy against the claims of government. For Cohen (1995, 68–69, 214), the concept of self-ownership is straight forward, like the slave owner owns the slave. But in fact there are different types of ownership (Cohen 1978, 63–87), and self-ownership has wider implications of feasibility and equality for all self-owners (Cohen 1995, 210–228).

The logic of this position of individual self-ownership has been criticized in turn for not fully taking into account the social aspects of the return to labor in a market economy characterized by the division of labor and the need to access public goods such as education for meaningful "autonomy" to be achieved (Cohen 1995, 68–72, 236–238). Further, Kant's critique of self-ownership claims that humans cannot be owned, only things can be owned. Humans cannot be an end for others, only an end in themselves (Cohen 1995, 211–213, 238–243). That is, any meaningful concept of self-ownership does not merely protect the individual as an isolated entity in society or government. The complementary relationship between the individual and individual private property relies on concepts which are unstable on both ends (Davis 2015a, 14–16).

Both Locke and Marx take self-ownership seriously, but this concept operates like a transitional one to a different state. For example, Locke's analysis of self-ownership is only in the state of nature, and Marx's analysis of self-ownership is only in the sphere of circulation. This particular status is changed in the social contract with money, for Locke, and in the sphere of production for Marx.

Table 2.5 The Concept of Self-Ownership

	Self-Ownership	
Political Theorist	*Yes*	*No*
Locke	State of nature	Social contract with money
Marx	Sphere of circulation	Sphere of production

The mind/body problem

Another issue is whether the self is one unit or split into two. That is, is the "self" which is the owner less material than the body which is the object owned? There are both interpretations in various periods of history and types of philosophy.

In Ancient Greece, there was a separation of the realm of necessity, the *oikos*, occupied by women, children, and slaves, from the realm of freedom, the polis of free expression and deliberation among free men. There was a further separation of the "ideal," the realm of perpetual universal concepts vs. the real.

From religious tradition and from Enlightenment philosophy, there is a view that the soul is separate from the body, or the rational mind is immaterial, such as a Cartesian self. By contrast, the view in this book is similar to Searle, who posits that consciousness, rationality, and intentionality are all characteristics of the same world as physics and biology. There is only one world (Searle 2010) which can explain social and intellectual phenomena by reference to neurons and brain chemistry. The human person is embodied and can persist through time. One can almost paraphrase Descartes: "I eat therefore I am." A basic imperative for self-preservation is a common characteristic of consciousness from animals to humans (Gazzaniga 2018), made explicitly legitimate in Locke.

Human persons experience themselves as *having* a body with its own needs and desires, as well as *being* a body (Berger and Luckmann 1966, 50–51). That is, after secularization, most modern persons understand that their existence is not separate from the organic material of one's own body. The use of the term "own" seems appropriate, even if there is no actual separation of self from body. Yet human interdependence, and the impossibility of survival of a truly isolated human, can lead to the paradox that humans can, and indeed must, produce a social institutional world which seems external to each individual (Berger and Luckmann 1966, 60–61).

For an analysis of the social, political, and economic organization of modern society, are cognition and linguistic expression sufficient, as discussed earlier, with terms, institutions, and expertise? That is, is the method of historical institutionalism in need of a "material turn" (Bennett and Joyce 2010)? Searle insists that language is both ideal and real, subjective and objective. Words create meaning in the minds of interlocutors, which are stored in the brain and documented in writing. Laws and institutional rules have associated "extra-linguistic" rules of behavior (Searle 2010, 109–115). That is, the behavior is concrete and material, even if the rules are abstract and ideal.

Language is an evolved capacity for communication among humans. Even internal soliloquy and dialogue take place by means of language, with explicit reasoning and articulate memories. With distinct language centers in the brain (Kandel 2006, 121–124, 2018, 10–13), it is difficult to differentiate mind vs. body or material vs. symbolic with respect to language. Although not all mental processes are conscious, or retrievable by memory, nonetheless, all are arguably stored in discrete structures in neuronal networks.

The notion of an "individual" body is most ambiguous with the example of the pregnant female (Strathern 2005, 29–30, 155–156). The relative status of the fetus or the mother is much debated with respect to the legality of contraception and abortion, with highly contested rights claims between individual self-determination for the mother vs. the rights of the fetus after conception. According to the notion of individual responsibility, pregnancy is attributed to the woman as a "property" of the female gender, with no assignment of responsibility to the male inseminator in some recent anti-abortion laws.

The role of women is complex in several contexts (Davis 2017a). In psychological theory, the relationship of mother and child is expressed in terms consistent with the dominant property paradigm, or "object relations" (Winnicott 1987; Chodorow 1978; Klein 1984), where the mother offers herself to the child as an object in order to nurture the child's developing subjectivity. The mother's role is often dismissed as merely "natural," nonetheless, without requiring incentives or professionalization. The value of "caring labor" has been articulated by feminists and its proper conditions and compensation (Folbre 1994; Hochschild 2000, 2002). There is also much debate regarding women's labor force participation and the flexibility of the workplace vs career motivation and determination by the female worker (Sandberg 2013; Williams and Dempsey 2014).

"Fictional commodities"

There is debate regarding whether labor is a "fictional" commodity, in Marx and Polanyi. Marx is very clear in Chapter 6 of Volume I of *Capital* that the worker must own himself, in contrast to the slave, in order to have the legal authority to contract for its sale to the employer. The worker "must be the untrammeled owner of his capacity for labour (i.e. of his person). . . . He must constantly look upon his labour-power as his own property" and sell it only for a limited period of time (Marx 1967, Vol. I, Chapter 6, 168). It is on this basis of equal ownership that the buyer and seller of the commodity labor power are equal in the eyes of the law (Marx 1967, Vol. I, Chapter 6, 176).

The apparent equality of the owner of labor power marks the "sphere of circulation," or the labor market, which is the "Eden of the innate rights of man."

> On leaving this sphere of simple circulation . . . we think we can perceive a change in the physiognomy of our dramatis personae. He, who before was the money-owner, now strides in front as the capitalist; the possessor of labour-power follows as his labourer. The one with an air of importance, smirking, intent on business; the other, timid and holding back, like on who is bringing his own hide to market and has nothing to expect but – a hiding.
>
> (Marx, Vol. I, Chapter 6, 176)

That is, this legal "equality" in the sphere of circulation contrasts with the sphere of production, where the owner of the factory has property rights in the space, in the worker, and in the worker's product and can command the worker to make use of his body in ways specified by the owner.

The apparent equality of property owners before the law can have different impacts de jure and de facto. For example, the concept of "freedom of contract" can reduce the workers' bargaining power if collective bargaining is not allowed (Cohen 1978, 242–243).

Marx's language refers to the stage, the theater, where the worker and the capitalist make their performances. While these enactments are real, they are roles adopted temporarily, bounded by the working day. These games are played while the players temporarily suspend disbelief to follow the proper scripts. The scene is a familiar one, and the audience knows that its turn will come soon.

Morality of self-ownership

According to Cohen (1995, 211–212, 238–243), Kant questioned the morality of self-ownership, since humans are ends in themselves, never means. According to Taylor (2002), there is a moral foundation of individualism, based on rights, new forms of sociality based on the economy, and mutual benefit.

According to Wolff, Marx's use of the idea of "self-ownership" was ironic, hinting at the duplicity of the equality of property owners in the sphere of circulation vs. the coercion of the worker in the sphere of production (Marx 1967, Vol. I, Chapter 6; Wolff 1988). The description of the scene, like the context of the stage of the theater, with changing "dramatis personae" before the audience, suggests a dual dimension to "self-ownership," theatricality, or even "performativity."

For Wolff, "irony is a mode of communication that employs an utterance with a double meaning" (Wolff 1988, 28). "Eventually I shall want to argue that Marx's complex vision of the reality and mystifying appearance of capitalist society can be rendered literarily only by the ironic discourse that we in fact find in *Capital*" (Wolff 1988, 31). "The principal verb of the opening sentence of *Capital* Is *erscheinen als*, "appears as." Marx chooses to begin his analysis of capitalism, and the theories of capitalism advanced by his predecessors, at the level of appearances, thereby invoking the distinction between appearance and reality on which his entire theoretical enterprise depends" (Wolff 1988, 36–38, 42–60, 82).

The role of doubles in capitalism

There is a distinction between appearance and reality in capitalism (Jameson 2011, 27–46). These dual levels of meaning in capitalism make the formation of consciousness of the working class more difficult (Jackson 2017).

There is much "doubling" in capitalism, related to the following dual levels of meaning.

Double-entry bookkeeping which keeps track of the same object or commodity, including its use value as well as its exchange value, and ownership at a given time and place. The object and its financial value are recorded in opposite sides of the page.

(Brine and Poovey 2017)

The commodity has two types of value, use value and exchange value.

The difference between the use value of the commodity labor power and its exchange value is the actual source of surplus.

(Jameson 2011, 100–101)

The worker is "free in a double sense" with mobility to sell itself as well as the lack of anything else to sell.

(Marx 1967, Vol. I, Chapter 6, 169)

The claim of equal rights of property, compared with the difference between ownership of capital and ownership of labor.

(Davis 2017b)

Commodity fetishism, where the commodities represent the value of the workers' labor.

(Jameson 2011, 43–46)

Double counting in credit. The asset exists in real form as the tangible means of production and as paper form as a claim to the surplus produced in the future.

(Beckert 2016)

> Titles of ownership to public works, railways, mines, etc., are indeed, as we have also seen, titles to real capital. But they do not place this capital at one's disposal. It is not subject to withdrawal. They merely convey legal claims to a portion of the surplus- value to be produced by it. But these titles likewise become paper duplicates of the real capital. . . . They come to nominally represent non-existent capital. For the real capital exists side by side with them and does not change hands as a result of the transfer of these duplicates from one person to another.
>
> (Marx 1967, Vol. III, Chapter 30, p. 477)

Unintended consequences; According to Smith and Mandeville, individuals pursue self-interest and achieve public good, via the market.

(McKeon 2005, 18–21, 32)

The Public Private Divide

The unity of the medieval economy is evident from the political role of corporations, such as guilds and communes. This clarity is replaced by doubling in the modern economy. The state is separate from civil society, the citizen from the bourgeois, the general interest from the private interest (Marx 1978, 34–36, 44–46).

> Where the political state has attained to its full development, man leads, not only in thought, in consciousness, but in *reality*, in *life*, a double existence – celestial and terrestrial. He lives in the *political community*, where he regards himself as a *communal being*, and in *civil society* where he acts simply as a *private individual*, treats other men as means, degrades himself to the role of mere means.
>
> (Marx 1978, 34, italics in original)

There is a separation between *bourgeois* and *citoyen*, even in the same person (Marx 1978, 41). Such divisions will continue until "political emancipation" becomes "human emancipation" (Marx 1978, 46).

Is the ownership of the commodity labor power, or "property in the person" (Pateman 1988) the foundation of the public/private divide? The citizen subject in the public sphere is also the object of ownership in the private sphere (McKeon 2005, 12–13, 48).

The body

Is there a single body, or a divided one? Is there a single person, or an aggregate population? Is there a single body politic, or a public/private divide? What are the techniques of "governmentality" of this complex entity (Foucault 1991, 100–104)?

Biopolitics

Foucault has developed a concept, "biopolitics," with which the science of government, or "governmentality," focuses on the individual body and the population (Foucault 1978; Paras 2006). There is a foundation for such a focus on the body, given the role of labor in production, stressed by Smith, which is of increasing importance in the new industrial economy compared with the agrarian economy. Such an economic logic is more typical of Marx, nonetheless, while Foucault generally eschews that type of explanation (Foucault 1991, 103). Further, political economy becomes part of the art of government, the associated knowledge and expertise, as a way of managing both the individual and the macro dimensions (Foucault 1991).

In Foucault's analysis, there is a focus on the body and sexuality to form individual identity. From the priest's confessional to the analyst's couch, the translation of sexuality into discourse enables a relationship with authority (Foucault 1978). There is also a focus on the population as a resource for political economy, value, and production. Since the seventeenth century, the focus of political economy has been the individual, the social contract, and the protection of private property (Pierson 2013a).

Foucault was also interested in Gary Becker's notion of "human capital," that is, enhancing the body as part of the opportunities of self-ownership and self-investment (Repo 2018). One could invest in the body, and the self, to enhance one's own "human capital" (Bourdieu 1986). One can construct a unique self and perfect one's own "presentation of self" in daily life (Goffman 1959). Or is this the ultimate alienation from oneself, commodification, and personal branding (Hochschild 2013, 3, 101–110)?

Centrality of the individual

Is "the individual" the link between the body, the population, and the economy? Considering Figure 2.1, it can be argued that the individual is the central pivot of both the state and the economy. The individual counts in elections, given particular suffrage criteria, and the individual counts at work and at the bank, where performance and repayment of loans are monitored carefully for each person.

Is the modern consumer economy the ultimate expression of this set of individual values? Is Foucault's concept of "biopolitics" a useful way to understand the motivations and "incitements" for individuals who are otherwise alienated from their work product through the detailed division of labor? Does

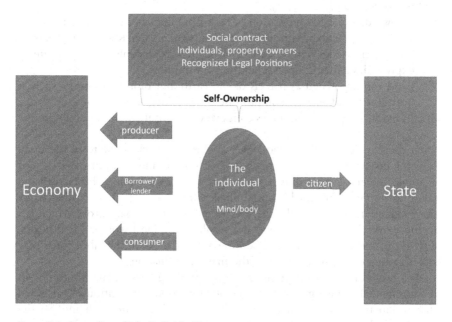

Figure 2.1 Centrality of "the Individual"

the individual benefit from the immense productivity from the division of labor to enjoy the cornucopia of pleasures? Or does pursuit of intensification of pleasures become fatal (such as the obesity, the HIV, or the opioid epidemics)?

Divisions and separations

In summary, since the seventeenth century, innovations in political economy, individual private property, and the social contract have been the foundation of the system. The capitalist system is based on such divisions, such as Smith's division of labor, and separations, such as the public/private divide (McKeon 2005).

Consider the following list of such separations, for example.

1)   The worker from his product, contra Locke.
2)   The factory space, compared with the household, where the factory owner can command the organization of work and the motions of the workers' bodies.
3)   Public space, such as city squares, compared with private space, such as residential abodes; the intermediate spaces of retail are then subject to competing imperatives, open access vs. privacy restrictions.
4)   Time, wherein the worker sells only part of his day, or his lifetime, in employment.
5)   Speech and communication; speech is free, as a matter of right, but can be censored for hate speech or for political or religious views which are not tolerated in a given society.
6)   Knowledge, and the separation of tacit from explicit knowledge, to codify workplace practices without reliance on workers (McKeon 2005; Marglin 2008); knowledge which can be protected, by patents, or can be freely expressed, such as in open scientific communities.
7)   Land can be owned as parcels of the earth, but mobile resources such as heat, water, and air may compromise the viability of particular uses.
8)   Individual, separable bodies vs cohesive work, family, or community groups.

Such divisions can be less productive, in certain aspects, in spite of the usual case for productivity gains from the specialization and division of labor. For example, the employer is only interested in the worker's time in his factory and takes no responsibility for his home life, leisure, or family. On the other hand, the productivity of the worker is determined by such social factors, which left to the worker's own choices, may not result in the ideal worker. Or if health, education, and nutrition are not addressed, the quality of the labor force may suffer, reducing competitiveness of the firm or the nation.

As a result of such overlapping issues, or "public goods," Adam Smith (1994) recommended that the government provide for worker's education and assumed that productivity gains will improve the workers' standard of living. So the choice of relatively narrow or broad definitions of such divisions of public and private goods, for example, becomes a choice by the state and the employers as a whole in a given country.

Conclusion

Given reification, separations, and divisions, the coherence of "society" seems beyond conceptual reach, and the public interest is difficult to discern. As a result of reification of the individual, private property, money, and the state, there seems to be no separate entity of "society." Even the state is divided into two separate parts, as we will explore further in Chapter 3.

Bibliography

Alexander, Gregory S. and Eduardo M. Penalver (eds.). *Property and Community*. New York: Oxford University Press, 2010.

Alexander, Gregory S. and Eduardo M. Penalver (eds.). *An Introduction to Property Theory*. New York: Cambridge University Press, 2012.

Balibar, Etienne. "My *Self* and My *Own*: One and the Same?" in Bill Maurer and Gabriele Schwab (eds.), *Accelerating Possession: Global Futures of Property and Personhood*. New York: Columbia University Press, 2006, 21–44.

Beckert, Jens. *Imagined Futures: Fictional Expectations and Capitalist Dynamics*. Cambridge, MA: Harvard University Press, 2016.

Bennett, Tony and Patrick Joyce (eds.). *Material Powers: Cultural Studies, History and the Material Turn*. New York: Routledge, 2010.

Berger, Peter L. and Thomas Luckmann. *The Social Construction of Reality: Treatise in the Sociology of Knowledge*. New York: Doubleday & Company, 1966.

Blaufarb, Rafe. "Nobles, Aristocrats, and the Origins of the French Revolution," in Robert M. Schwartz and Robert A. Schneider (eds.), *Tocqueville and Beyond: Essays on the Old Regime in Honor of David D. Bien*. Newark: University of Delaware Press, 2003, 86–110.

Blaufarb, Rafe. *The Great Demarcation: The French Revolution and the Invention of Modern Property*. New York: Oxford University Press, 2016.

Bourdieu, Pierre. "Forms of Capital," in J. Richardson (ed.), *Handbook of Theory and Research for Sociology of Education*. New York: Greenwood Press, 1986, 241–258.

Brine, Kevin R. and Mary Poovey. *Finance in America: An Unfinished Story*. Chicago: University of Chicago Press, 2017.

Brittan, Samuel. "There's No Such Thing as Society," J.C. Rees Memorial Lecture. Swansea, SA: University College of Swansea, 1992.

Brown, Wendy. *In the Ruins of Neoliberalism: The Rise of Antidemocratic Politics in the West*. New York: Columbia University Press, 2019.

Canfield, John V. *The Looking-Glass Self: An Examination of Self-Awareness*. New York: Praeger, 1990.

Chodorow, Nancy. *Reproduction of Mothering: Psychoanalysis and the Sociology of Gender*. Berkeley: University of California Press, 1978.

Cohen, G. A. *Karl Marx's Theory of History: A Defense*. Princeton, NJ: Princeton University Press, 1978.

Cohen, G. A. *Self-Ownership, Freedom, and Equality*. New York: Cambridge University Press, 1995.

Daston, Lorraine and Peter Galison. *Objectivity*. New York: Zone Books, 2010.

Davis, Ann E. *The Evolution of the Property Relation: Understanding Paradigms, Debates, Prospects.* New York: Palgrave MacMillan, 2015a.

Davis, Ann E. "The Process of Provisioning: The Halter for the Workhorse," *Journal of Economic Issues*, Vol. XLIX, No. 2, June 2015b, 449–457.

Davis, Ann E. "Paradoxical Positions: The Methodological Contributions of Feminist Scholarship," *Cambridge Journal of Economics*, Vol. 41, No. 1, 2017a, 181–201.

Davis, Ann E. "Fetishism and Financialization," *Review of Radical Political Economics*, Vol. 49, No. 4, December 2017b, 551–558.

Davis, Ann E. *Money as a Social Institution: The Institutional Development of Capitalism.* New York: Routledge, 2017c.

Davis, Ann E. "Is There a History of Property? Periodization of Property Regimes and Paradigms," in Staci M. Savattaro, Gergory R. Peterson, and Ann E. Davis (eds.), *Property Rights in Contemporary Governance.* Albany: State University of New York Press, 2019, 5–24.

Desan, Christine. "From Blood to Profit: Making Money in the Practice and Imagery of Early America," *Journal of Policy History*, Vol. 20, No. 1, 2008, 26–46.

Desan, Christine. *Making Money: Coin, Currency, and the Coming of Capitalism.* New York: Oxford University Press, 2014.

Desan, Christine. "Money as a Legal Institution," in David Fox and Ernst Wolfgang (eds.), *Money in the Western Legal Tradition: Middle Ages to Bretton Woods.* New York: Oxford University Press, 2016, 18–35.

Desan, Christine. "The Constitutional Approach to Money: Monetary Design and the Production of the Modern World," in Nina Bandelj, Frederick F. Wherry, and Viviana A. Zelizer (eds.), *Money Talks: Explaining How Money Really Works.* Princeton, NJ: Princeton University Press, 2017, 109–130.

Doran, 'Nob'. "Re-Writing the Social, Re-Writing Sociology: Donzelot, Genealogy and Working-Class Bodies," *The Canadian Journal of Sociology*, Vol. 29, No. 3, Summer 2004, 333–357.

Folbre, Nancy. *Who Pays for the Kids? Gender and the Structures of Constraint.* New York: Routledge, 1994.

Foucault, Michel. *History of Sexuality. Volume I: An Introduction.* New York: Pantheon Books, 1978.

Foucault, Michel. "Governmentality," in Graham Burchell, Colin Gordon, and Peter Miller (eds.), *The Foucault Effect: Studies in Governmentality.* Chicago: University of Chicago Press, 1991, 87–104.

Garland, David. "The Welfare State: A Fundamental Dimension of Modern Government," *European Journal of Sociology*, Vol. 55, No. 3, December 2014, 327–364.

Gazzaniga, Michael S. *The Consciousness Instinct: Unraveling the Mystery of How the Brain Makes the Mind.* New York: Farrar, Straus and Giroux, 2018.

Geuss, Raymond. *Outside Ethics.* Princeton, NJ: Princeton University Press, 2005.

Goffman, Erving. *Presentation of Self in Everyday Life.* Garden City, NY: Doubleday, 1959.

Gordon, Robert W. "Paradoxical Property," in John Brewer and Susan Staves (eds.), *Early Modern Conceptions of Property.* New York: Routledge, 1996, 95–110.

Hochschild, Arlie Russell. "Global Care Chains and Emotional Surplus Value," in W. Hutton and A. Giddens (eds.), *On the Edge: Living with Global Capitalism.* London: Jonathan Cape, 2000, 131–146.

Hochschild, Arlie Russell. "Love and Gold," in B. Ehrenreich and A. R Hochschild (eds.), *Global Woman: Nannies, Maids and Sex Workers in the New Economy.* New York: Metropolitan Books, 2002, 15–30.

Hochschild, Arlie Russell. *So How's the Family? And Other Essays*. Berkeley: University of California Press, 2013.

Ingham, Geoffrey K. *The Nature of Money*. Cambridge, UK: Polity Press, 2004.

Israel, Jonathan I. *Radical Enlightenment: Philosophy and the Making of Modernity 1650–1750*. New York: Oxford University Press, 2001.

Jackson, Robert P. "Lebowitz, Lukacs and Postone: Subjectivity in *Capital*," *Science and Society*, Vol. 81, No. 2, April 2017, 248–278.

Jameson, Fredric. *Representing Capital: A Commentary on Volume One*. New York: Verso, 2011.

Kahneman, Daniel. *Thinking, Fast and Slow*. New York: Farrar, Straus and Giroux, 2011.

Kandel, Eric R. *In Search of Memory: The Emergence of a New Science of Mind*. New York: W.W. Norton & Company, 2006.

Kandel, Eric R. *The Disordered Mind: What Unusual Brains Tell Us About Ourselves*. Farrar, Straus, and Giroux, 2018.

Klein, Melanie. *Envy and Gratitude and Other Works*. New York: The Free Press, 1984.

Latour, Bruno. *We Have Never Been Modern*. Cambridge, MA: Harvard University Press, 1993.

MacPherson, C. B. *The Political Theory of Possessive Individualism: Hobbes to Locke*. Oxford: Clarendon Press, 1962.

Madison, James, Federalist Paper #10 in Alexander Hamilton, James Madison, John Jay, The Federalist Papers, New York: Penguin Putman, 1961, 45–52.

Marglin, Stephen A. *The Dismal Science: How Thinking Like an Economist Undermines Community*. Cambridge, MA: Harvard University Press, 2008.

Marx, Karl. *Capital*. New York: International Publishers, 1967.

Marx, Karl. "On the Jewish Question," in Robert C. Tucker (ed.), *The Marx-Engels Reader*. 2nd ed. New York: W.W. Norton & Company, 1978, 26–52.

McKeon, Michael. *The Secret History of Domesticity: Public, Private, and the Division of Knowledge*. Baltimore: The Johns Hopkins University Press, 2005.

Milonakis, Dimitris. "The Dynamics of History: Structure and Agency in Historical Evolution," *Science & Society*, Vol. 61, No. 3, Fall 1997, 303–329.

North, Douglass Cecil, John Joseph Wallis, and Barry R. Weingast. *Violence and Social Orders: A Conceptual Framework for Interpreting Recorded Human History*. New York: Cambridge University Press, 2009.

Novak, William J. "Public-Private Governance: A Historical Introduction," in Jody Freeman and Martha Minow (eds.), *Government by Contract: Outsourcing and American Democracy*. Cambridge, MA: Harvard University Press, 2009, 23–40.

Paras, Eric. *Foucault 2.0: Beyond Power and Knowledge*. New York: Other Press, 2006.

Pateman, Carole. *The Problem of Political Obligation: A Critical Analysis of Liberal Theory*. New York: John Wiley & Sons, 1979.

Pateman, Carole. *The Sexual Contract*. Stanford, CA: Stanford University Press, 1988.

Peterson, Gregory R. "Intellectual Property and Fairness Across Borders: Capabilities Account," in Staci M. Zavattaro, Gergory R. Peterson, and Ann E. Davis (eds.), *Property Rights in Contemporary Governance*. Albany: State University of New York Press, 2019, 145–162.

Pierson, Christopher. *Beyond the Welfare State? The New Political Economy of Welfare*. University Park, PA: The Pennsylvania State University Press, 2007.

Pierson, Christopher. *Just Property: A History in the Latin West. Volume One: Wealth, Virtue, and the Law*. New York: Oxford University Press, 2013a.

Pierson, Christopher. "Rousseau and the Paradoxes of Property," *European Journal of Political Theory*, Vol. 12, No. 4, 2013b, 409–424.

Pierson, Christopher. *Just Property: Volume Two: Enlightenment, Revolution, and History*. New York: Oxford University Press, 2016.

Pistor, Katharina. *The Code of Capital: How the Law Creates Wealth and Inequality*. Princeton, NJ: Princeton University Press, 2019.

Pocock, J. G. A. *The Machiavellian Moment: Florentine Political Thought and the Atlantic Republican Tradition*. Princeton, NJ: Princeton University Press, 1975.

Pocock, J. G. A. *Political Thought and History: Essays on Theory and Method*. New York: Cambridge University Press, 2009.

Polanyi, Karl. *The Great Transformation*. Boston: Beacon Press, 1944.

Poovey, Mary. *A History of the Modern Fact: Problems of Knowledge in the Sciences of Wealth and Society*. Chicago: University of Chicago Press, 1998.

Poovey, Mary. "The Liberal Civil Subject and the Social in Eighteenth-Century British Moral Philosophy," *Public Culture*, Vol. 14, No 1, 2002, 125–145.

Poovey, Mary. *Genres of the Credit Economy: Mediating Value in Eighteenth-and Nineteenth-Century Britain*. Chicago: University of Chicago Press, 2008.

Repo, Jemima. "Gary Becker's Economics of Population: Reproduction and Neoliberal Biopolitics," *Economy and Society*, Vol. 47, No. 2, 2018, 234–256.

Rosser, Ezra. "Destabilizing Property," *Connecticut Law Review*, Vol. 48, No. 2, December 2015, 397–472.

Safranski, Rudiger. *Nietzsche: A Philosophical Biography*. New York: W. W. Norton & Company, 2002.

Sandberg, Sheryl. *Lean In: Women, Work, and the Will to Lead*. New York: Alfred A. Knopf, 2013.

Searle, John R. *Making the Social World: The Structure of Human Civilization*. New York: Oxford University Press, 2010.

Sewell, William H. Jr. *A Rhetoric of Bourgeois Revolution: The Abbe Sieyes and What is the Third Estate?* Durham, NC: Duke University Press, 1994.

Shapin, Steven and Simon Schaffer. *Leviathan and the Air-Pump: Hobbes, Boyle, and the Experimental Life*. Princeton, NJ: Princeton University Pres, 1985.

Singer, Joseph William. *Entitlement: The Paradoxes of Property*. New Haven: Yale University Press, 2000.

Skocpol, Theda and Alexander Hertel-Fernandez. "The Koch Network and Republican Party Extremism," *Perspectives on Politics*, Vol. 14, No. 3, September 2016, 681–699.

Smith, Adam. *An Inquiry into the Nature and Causes of the Wealth of Nations*. New York: The Modern Library, 1994.

Somers, Margaret R. and Gloria D. Gibson. "Reclaiming the Epistemological 'Other': Narrative and the Social Constitution of Identity," in Craig Calhoun (ed.), *Social Theory and the Politics of Identity*. Oxford, UK: Blackwell, 1994, 37–99.

Sonenscher, Michael. *Sans-Culottes: An Eighteenth-Century Emblem in the French Revolution*. Princeton, NJ: Princeton University Press, 2008.

Strathern, Marilyn. *Kinship, Law and the Unexpected: Relatives are Always a Surprise*. New York: Cambridge University Press, 2005.

Taylor, Charles. "Modern Social Imaginaries," *Public Culture*, Vol. 14, No. 1, 2002, 91–124.

Underkuffler, Laura S. *The Idea of Property: Its Meaning and Power*. New York: Oxford University Press, 2002.

Weber, Max. *Economy and Society: An Outline of Interpretive Sociology*. Berkeley: University of California Press, 1978.

Williams, Joan C. and Rachel Dempsey. *What Works for Women at Work: Four Patterns Working Women Need to Know*. New York: New York University Press, 2014.

Winnicott, Donald Woods. *Babies and Their Mothers*. Reading, MA: Addison-Wesley, 1987.

Wolff, Robert Paul. *Moneybags Must Be So Lucky: On the Literary Structure of Capital*. Amherst, MA: University of Massachusetts Press, 1988.

Wray, L. Randall. *Modern Money Theory: A Primer on Macroeconomics for Sovereign Monetary Systems*. New York: Palgrave MacMillan, 2015.

Yuran, Noam. *What Money Wants: An Economy of Desire*. Stanford, CA: Stanford University Press, 2014.

3   The public/private divide

Introduction

This chapter will review the institutional foundations for the individual and property to better understand the divisions within an overall unity. Ultimately these divisions become more visible than the unity, with a significant impact on the self-understanding of these participating "individuals."

The historical institution method

As discussed briefly in Chapter 1, the historical institutional methods consist of three elements: the term ("the individual"); the related institutions; and knowledge/expertise (economics). These elements can vary historically, with a key term or category depending on a distinctive period in history.

The "individual" emerged in the modern period in association with the concept of absolute individual private property (Pistor 2019, 29–35). Rather than overlapping types of property in the early modern period, the clear demarcation facilitated trade and mobility (Blaufarb 2016). The associated institutions are the market and the liberal state. The forms of expertise include political philosophy, as well as economics, political science, psychology, and management (with its consideration of marketing, human resource management, and production efficiency). These three aspects, the term, the institutions, and the expertise, are interrelated and mutually reinforcing in a given period.

In this case, the term, "the individual," affects the self-concept and self-consciousness, as well as aspirations and expectations, of each contemporary human. And, in turn, each individual is judged by her accomplishments, acquisitions, and achievement of authentic individuality. That is, "the individual" is a term which is both normative and descriptive, as well as performative, which varies historically. Each human person is influenced by a term and meanings that are part of a new paradigm emerging at a particular period of history. That is, the concept of "the individual" is social, paradoxically.

Key terms like "the individual" can be the building blocks of institutions and are often related to a larger narrative or "Background" (Searle 2010, 31–32,

155–160). As articulated by Blyth (2002), ideas such as "the individual" can provide a tool for organizing collective action and coalitions and for reinforcing institutions, reducing uncertainty. Ideas can provide blueprints and can be used in contests among competing ideas.

The typical interpretation of "the individual" is a form of freedom, according to liberal theory (Berlin 1969). On the other hand, critics emphasize the coercive dimensions (MacPherson 1962; Pateman 1988; Polanyi 1944). The association with freedom provides a legitimating device and helps to justify restrictions on the range of choices based on notions of individual responsibility.

History of the individual

The notion of the individual and human rights emerged in the eighteenth century in a revolutionary period in the context of natural law theorists (Hunt 2007). The contemporary discussions of the individual and "identity" presume the naturalness of this category.

I propose that the "individual" is a salient category in the context of the modern state theorized by Locke, Hegel, Marx, and Polanyi (Habermas 1989, Kreitner 2007, Hardt and Negri 2017, 85–105; MacPherson 1962). That is, the "individual" is not an isolated monad but holds a discreet normal position in the liberal state. As discussed in Chapter 2, "the individual" and "individual private property" are key terms around which society and the state are structured in the modern period. The importance of "the individual" as the owner of property is associated with the rise of "individualism" (Harvey 2014, 40–43). These abstract terms may apply to a variety of persons and objects, with the impersonality and impartiality associated with a rational bureaucracy (Weber 1978; North, Wallis, and Weingast 2009). Yet the concrete features are relevant to the bureaucratic processes, whether institutions of the state or market, as specified in each context. The presumed generality often conflicts with the specifics of the selection process, which can be considered a form of corruption in application of the general principles of impartiality, equality, and fairness.

As indicated in Table 3.1, the individual and property have both abstract and concrete characteristics.

Table 3.1 Key Concepts: Individual and Property

	Individual	*Property*
Abstract	Agent: Human person or corporate entity	Object: Land, commodity, worker, or corporate entity; ownership relation by law
Concrete	Unique personality, skills, knowledge, experience, capacities	Particular physical characteristics, material composition, instrumentality, location

The rational individual of the modern liberal state is a property owner, as is fitting for a nation whose primary objective is "wealth." There is a consonance between this individual and the nation, both conceived as unitary, coherent, self-contained objects (Calhoun 2007, 87–88, 1994, 315–316).

The relationship of ownership between individual and property becomes "invisible" in the liberal state, assigned to the object itself, with the market assuming the role of "the invisible hand." There is a shift in focus from social or kin relationships to categories in which collections of individuals can be identified by prescribed characteristics, such as nationality or ethnic group (Calhoun 2002, 160–161, 2007, 70–72). As relationships become reified, categories regarding "'objects" and "identities" assume greater relevance.

This self-evident dichotomy between "the individual" and "individual private property" in Table 3.1 is most unambiguous when the individual is a specific human person and the property is a discrete parcel of land. Once the abstract category of "the individual" can include a corporation, or the abstract category of "property" can include a corporation, the clarity is disrupted and the dichotomy becomes more problematic. Once the "individual" is a self-owner, and the corporation can "employ" human persons, the categories are potentially reversible. These free-standing abstract categories which apparently preclude institutional interconnections must be specified, without which the terms become ambiguous.

When clearly specified as a particular human person in a modern liberal state, the individual is a "self-owner" within a discreet body (circumscribed by skin, powered by nutrition, and controlled by conscious and autonomic processes in the brain). The individual is aware of his own continuity and his own history, with memory and ongoing social relationships which were and are formative. The individual self-awareness is influenced by the period of history and location in social groups. There is a combination of individual initiative and autonomy as well as normative, socioeconomic competitive pressures and requirements.

The relation of "ownership" has evolved historically. From the monarch whose being incorporated the entire kingdom, to the lord who owned the manor, to the merchant who owned the commodity en route to market, to the bourgeois who owns the factory and its product, to the worker who owns himself.

The relationship of the owner is recognized and operationalized within the state in its various forms, the monarchy, the medieval manor, the merchant's city-state or city-league, and the modern liberal state.

Unlike the monarchy, the modern liberal state is no longer a unity but is typically divided into civil society, the state, and the public sphere (Hegel 1952; Marx 1967; Habermas 1989). The modern state internalizes finance and military, leading to a bureaucratization and rationalization of functions.

> The modern state was basically a state based on taxation, the bureaucracy of the treasury the true core of its administration. The separation precipitated

thereby between the prince's personal holdings and what belonged to the state was paradigmatic of the objectification of personal relations of domination. . . . [Public authority] assumed objective existence in a *permanent* administration and a *standing* army. . . . Civil society came into existence as the corollary of a depersonalized state authority.

(Habermas 1989, 17, 18, 19; italics in original)

From the personal authority of the sovereign, represented in the king's own body and his own lands, there emerged the reifying abstraction of sovereignty based on association of equal owners of individual private property (Blaufarb 2016). Among this new public, functional "categorical identities" referring to equivalent individuals replaced "direct social relations" (Calhoun 2002, 161).

The presumed clarity of the definition of independent private property, free from obligations and public functions, was accomplished by the "great demarcation" of the French Revolution (Blaufarb 2016). This clear-cut separation depends on considering "property" as an object, not a relationship (Yuran 2014, 50–65). This presumably clear division is complicated by the role of the state in the definition and enforcement of property (Alexander 2006, 2–6; Fried 1998). Further, money is a type of public power which can be owned by a single person, used to exchange commodities, and is capable of compelling the labor of other persons (Davis 2017b).

As indicated in the left column in Table 3.2, in fact there are two types of ownership, the bourgeois factory owner, or capitalist, and the worker as self-owner, or "homme," for Habermas, or "proletarian." As capitalism develops, there is a third owner of financial capital, the financier, or "rentier." The member of the public sphere, the civil society, is an "individual," according to Calhoun's reading of Habermas, an owner of property sufficient to provide independence, education, and the capacity for rational deliberation and debate regarding the public interest (Calhoun 2012, 124–128). Especially when there are property requirements for suffrage, one could inquire whether the *citoyen* only represented the bourgeois, not the homme. That is, the state may represent the property, not the person.

According to Pateman (1988), there are two private spheres, one for the worker, whose body is owned by the bourgeois during the working day, and the other is the family, where the body of the wife is owned by the husband (literally under the doctrine of coverture). These two relationships of ownership, or

Table 3.2 Public/Private Divide (Adapted from Habermas 1989, 30)

Private	Public Sphere	State
Firm (*bourgeois*)	Critical press	Public officials
	Free speech and assembly	
Household (*homme*)	Informed electorate (*citoyen*)	Bureaucracy

Source: (modified from Davis 2017a)

"property in the person," are governed by contracts, which cannot be voluntary given the coercion involved in that type of property.

There are two spheres of freedom, according to the ideal liberal state. The individual is free, equal, and autonomous in the public sphere, with recognized legal rights of citizenship. The so-called freedom in the private sphere is constrained by the labor and marriage contracts, which involve control of the body of another person. That is, the freedom in the private sphere is for the owners, the bourgeois and the *patria potestas*. These freedoms or realms of subjectivity and agency in the public sphere presume to offset the forms of objectification in the private sphere of the workplace and the household.

The discussions in contemporary literature assume that any individual can assume any identity of choice. There are three issues with this position, in my view. First, the choice of identity is related to the type of property with which one is associated in terms of family of origin and social position. Second, some identities are assigned by bureaucratic functionaries without the consent of the individual. Third, there is a historical institutional context within which "the individual" is recognized and can operate (Calhoun 2012, 122–123; Shapiro, Skowronek, and Galvin 2006).

These assigned categories indicate functions within the state and the market, and its various interrelationships, often related to the conceptual prominence of property and ownership in the modern liberal state.

For example, the salience of race recalls the legacy of slavery. The importance of gender suggests the subordinate role of women in the household. The history of wage labor suggests the salience of class, or those who were unable to accumulate sufficient property across the generations of the family. These status categories indicate social standing since ownership provides more autonomy and more control over others. In fact, greater resources do provide more autonomy for a given household, in terms of education, leisure activities, and social links with other more empowered individuals. That is, the concept of "intersectionality" is the legacy of types of property (Crenshaw 2020), in my view.

The assertion of equality appeals to the de jure relationships in the sphere of circulation, the public sphere. The difficulties with these claims rest with the de facto inequalities in the private spheres of the household and the factory, based on the ownership of "property in the person." In fact, the claims of equality, while having some salience in law, are actually duplicitous given the different types of property and their respective associated rights. For example, the owner can exclude the worker from the factory and can prevent access to the means of production. The workers' rights to organize and to strike are more restricted by "anti-combination" laws historically (Smith 1994; Marx 1967) and by "right to work" laws and "freedom of contract" interpretations of the Constitution.

The clear distinction between the spheres was "transformed" almost immediately by commercialization of the public media and unequal distribution of property with the implied further divergence of the status of "bourgeois" and 'homme" (Habermas 1989), as well as shifting boundaries of public responsibilities (Novak 2009). There may be multiple public spheres, with concrete characteristics such as gender, race, and class, which challenge the generality of the category of the abstract "individual" (Calhoun 1992; Fraser 2013; Calhoun 2002, 163–168; O'Mahoney 2019). The presumed rationality and open debate were assumed to rest on property ownership and urban social foundations like coffee houses (Calhoun 2012). Other transgressions include support for non-workers by means of the welfare provisions (Pierson 2007; Garland 2014) and unequal suffrage requirements in the representation of the citizens. Further erosion of the boundaries of the public/private divide occurred with the removal of campaign finance laws and the treatment of private business corporations as persons with free speech. The role of public debt as the cornerstone of financial markets relies on national cohesion (Davis 2017b), which became more problematic after the global financial crisis of 2008. And in fact national cohesion has been under duress recently with the divisive appeals of "populism" and the contingencies of "identity politics" (Fukuyama 2018, 140–162).

The basic assumption of the property-owning liberal state was that independence of the individual was assured through property ownership. This idea is found in Locke, the civic republican tradition (Pocock 1975), and even Habermas. In the late nineteenth century, the rational calculating individual was theorized as the owner of property, capable of voluntary promises that were the foundation of contracts (Kreitner 2007). The notion that ownership of land provides self-sufficiency is belied by other forms of property, such as finance, which involves the owner in interdependent relationships of division of labor and the market. James Madison worried about the "faction" based on property ownership, nonetheless, and Lessig documents a "dependence" based on the interests of property, a form of corruption (Lessig 2018, 17–25). While Madison and the Founders relied on checks and balances, as well as a large scale to dilute any particular set of interests, the concentration of income in the twenty-first century, if not also the nineteenth, certainly makes those provisions less effective.

When one speaks of "democracy" in the contemporary context, these limitations are seldom discussed, as if these institutional constraints were nonexistent. For example, Gutmann (2003) compares the identity groups with the isolated individual. Davis (2011) sees identity as social but does not position the available options within the historical institutional context. Fukuyama (2018, 93–104) sees identity politics as the outcome of the therapeutic society of the 1960s and 1970s, which sought to express the true "inner self." The contemporary discussion of "democracy" assumes that rights belong to persons equally. They do not address the protection of property in the liberal state and the notion that property can consist of persons, a form of domination.

The institutions of liberal governmentality

Even though the liberal state is one society, there is an important internal division. As illustrated in Table 3.2, the logic of the abstract state separate from its citizens leads to the public/private divide, according to Habermas (1989).

Polanyi

A different explanation is offered by Polanyi (1944) for the same institutional characteristic. Polanyi differentiates between "genuine" commodities, produced for sale for profit, and "fictitious" commodities, consisting of land, labor, and money. In a commercial society, all of the requirements of industry must be available for sale, including land, labor, and money, even though these fictitious commodities were obviously not produced for sale for profit (Polanyi 1944, 72–76). A self-regulating free market would require these elements to be available, nonetheless, without which the market could not smoothly control production. Yet subjecting these fictitious commodities to the requirements of the market endangers their existence. In particular, humans cannot live without employment, if the means of subsistence are entirely contingent upon money wages. As a result of this inconsistency, there is a separation of the market from society and a periodic "double movement" by which the rest of society resists these market imperatives. "A self-regulating market demands nothing less than the institutional separation of society into an economic and political sphere" (Polanyi 1944, 71) so that the market can be the dominant institution, subordinating the rest of society.

> Indeed, human society would have been annihilated but for the protective countermoves which blunted the action of this self-destructive mechanism. Social history in the nineteenth century was thus the result of a double movement: the extension of the market organization in respect to genuine commodities was accompanied by its restriction in respect to fictitious ones ... a deep-seated movement sprang into being to resist the pernicious effects of a market-controlled economy.
>
> (Polanyi 1944, 76)

The requirements of the commodification of land, labor, and money may help to explain the peculiar characteristics of the liberal nation-state. As the state has internalized the functions of defense, finance, and welfare, it has become more complex and more bureaucratic. Regular laws and institutions rely on rules formed by deliberation by representative organs of the state. The state relies on experts, who provide qualitative and quantitative evidence to support their recommendations, according to the scientific method.

In addition, the liberal state is formed on the principle of the protection of individual private property and the support of the market. The associated commodification of land, labor, and money required the passage of specific laws and their enforcement. For example, the Poor Law Reform of 1834 instituted a market economy, which led to the discovery of "society" to try to explain poverty in the midst of plenty (Polanyi 1944, 86–103). Rather than acknowledge that the laws of the market were not the same as human laws, there was an even greater faith placed in the "liberal creed" of self-regulating markets (Polanyi 1944, 125, 135–150; Block and Somers 2014). Forms of social solidarity were destroyed to make the "prod of hunger" effective and were replaced by "atomistic" and "individualist" ones (Polanyi 1944, 163–166). Laissez faire was enforced by the state, which required an enormous increase in administrative organs (Polanyi 1944, 139–141).

Ultimately the organization of labor within corporations also required an immense bureaucracy (Marglin 2008; Gordon 1996). The protection of property was also contentious and required the intervention of the legal profession (Pistor 2019). Ironically, the expansion of the market society required an expansion of the state. These linguistic rules and regulations were required by the management of the economy and imposed by the state, rather than being self-regulating.

Marx

Marx's analysis can be used to explain the division of society into public and private spheres. According to Marx, the commodity has two dimensions: use value and exchange value. The two dimensions are typically complementary. While commodities must be useful to be sold on the market, their exchange value reflects the conditions of production and the profit potential. The more useful it is, the greater the profit potential. But these two dimensions can be contradictory. For example, in a crisis there may be unmet needs and surplus commodities. Their sale may not take place, nonetheless, if there is insufficient demand or insufficient profit, as may occur in a crisis.

These two dimensions of the commodity can be managed by the two sides of the state, the human side representing use value in the public sphere, and the exchange value and profit requirements in the private sphere. Just like the whole commodity, the society consists of a single whole, but divided to manage contradictory relationships.

Integration of "self" and "society"

With a set of moves based on interdisciplinary scholarship, one could explore the apparent strangeness of both terms, "self" and "society." Both terms are apparently self-standing and autonomous, although they are defined by relationships which have become invisible. These relationships are represented by objects which are symbols, understood by participants in the given "society."

One important object is property, created by the worker. That is, Locke's definition of property is created by labor. Yet this link is broken in the wage labor system of modern industrial capitalism, as the worker is separated from his product (MacPherson 1962). The creator and the process of creation of the product are invisible in the commodity for sale on the market. Yet Locke's ideas continue to structure the modern state based on "individuals" in the state of nature forming a state by consent, a "social contract." The purpose of the state is the protection of their individual property, which is already separated from the worker. The owners who form the state are rationalized by the existence of property, which is always already removed from the producer. The consent of those initial contractors is always already presumed by existing state institutions, along with the right of revolution.

The ability to exchange such products on the market is one key characteristic of modern societies. Yet, according to Thatcher, this "society," formed of consenting individuals, is a strange object whose existence is denied, as discussed in Chapters 1 and 2.

This denial of society may be due to the ubiquitous splits. First, it is not commonly acknowledged that the principle of capitalism is the separation of the worker from his product. Instead, the employment relation is considered voluntary and fully compensated with a wage payment (Bell 1978). Locke instead discusses the desirable characteristics of money as beyond the "spoilage limit" and so arguably better than one's own product. The wage payment further provides the worker with access to a range of commodities, potentially more useful than his own product, and more convenient than barter, according to that logic.

Second, the "self" that is characteristic of modern industrial capitalist countries is "possessive" (MacPherson 1962), "calculative," (Kreitner 2007), and "separative" (England 1993). This "self" is willing to separate from one's own product and one's own relationships. Yet this self is defined by its acquisition and possession of objects of property, a type of relationship that constitutes autonomy instead of dependence. This "ownership" of objects may not even be considered to be a "relationship," except consisting of one person's exclusive "dominion" over objects, according to Blackstone (Alexander 2006, 3–4).

Third, this willingness to separate is further differentiated by gender (Chodorow 1978; Gilligan 1993) in relationship to one's own mother. The modern family, so important as a foundation for modern industrial society, even in Thatcher's account, is based on the exchange of women (Levi-Strauss 1969; Rubin 1975) and the incest taboo (Freud 1918). That is, one must relinquish the desire for one's own mother and substitute an appropriate (heterosexual) partner upon maturity. According to Lacan (1981), the Oedipus complex is installed in the foundation of one's own personality, symbolized by the phallus and the breast. The importance of symbols in modern societies is arguably founded on the nature of one's own (gendered) body.

Fourth, the "recognition" so memorably analyzed by Hegel is in the context of ownership and the object of property. That is, the struggle between the master and the slave is over the recognition of mastery, which is denied by the material dependence of the master on the slave for access to the object. This struggle and the potential for reversal is built in to the need for constant recognition and affirmation. Further, the desire for the product is always ongoing, as the object is separated, acquired, consumed, and desire reconstituted (Butler 1987; Yuran 2014). The replication of this drama in sexual relations is analyzed by Simone de Beauvoir and in the context of love relationships by

Jessica Benjamin (1988, 1998). The importance of visual recognition (the Look) is analyzed by Sartre and (the Gaze) by Foucault, along with the replication of images in mass media and consumer culture (Jameson 1998)

Fifth, the denial of these relationships is symbolized by objects, accessible by money, even if never fully possessed or controlled (Yuran 2014). The ostensible possession of desirable objects can be a source of status and recognition, another form of relationship, even if anonymous (Howell 2010; Veblen 1934).

Finally, in modern capitalism, money is the ultimate object, a symbol for all social relationships, and the potential for ultimate fulfillment of every desire. Money can master time, providing for desires in the future, or even providing assurance of an afterlife, according to Weber's famous thesis regarding the origin of capitalism in the Protestant ethic (Weber 2001).

Representation

The basic principle of morality in modernity is "equality" (Menke 2006), which can be interpreted as opposed to "individuality." That is, the claim that all persons are equal can be understood as erasing the unique characteristics of each person. The position argued here is that the presumed equality is abstract and within the boundaries of specific spheres. That is, the "equality" of each person is de jure, such that laws and procedures apply equally, and need not require the same uniform garments or same physical body types, skills, or personalities. Within and across each sphere, there are unequal practices which are formally condemned in modern liberal states, subject to Taylor's "long march." Given the principles of the separation of powers and constitutional protection of individual private property, nonetheless, the individual voter has little control over the economy (Polanyi 1944) and the polity (Dahl 2001). The division of political powers in the state is intended to limit the power of any given person, another form of "equality."

Forms of representation

In modern society, there are multiple forms of representation, such as language, images, and public deliberative bodies. Representation can also refer to a relationship, such as the legal counsel/client relationship or employment contract. While interactive and processual, such relationships can also be documented in language and in symbols; the production of the documents or symbols may also be invested with the power of the relationship, like illuminated manuscripts. The physical symbol may represent the importance of the relationship by the value of its material composition (such as gold or the royal seal) or labor requirement. In the case of money where speed of turnover is relevant, there may be dematerialization, as long as the documents are objectively verifiable. In such manifestations, the symbol can be taken as the relationship, and the interpersonal dimension becomes invisible, or reified. There are few occasions for the direct presentation of one's own unique body, in immediacy and unadorned (Goffman 1959), except in the private sphere or mass transportation infrastructure. The collective presence of various persons, such as protest marches, celebrations, and parades (Ehrenreich 2007), or direct assemblies (Hardt and Negri 2017), is rare and may be an occasion of challenging routine practices.

Equality

The modern representation of the "equal individual" is located within each separate sphere. For example, there is equality among property owners in their representation in the organs of the state. There is equality among creditors in their application for loans. There is equality in the protection of individual private property in their own homes, businesses, and financial assets. Yet in each case this is de jure bureaucratic equality, which can be violated in distinct ways in each sphere, such as voter suppression, distorted credit allocation, and uneven police protection in a given city. There is a presumption of global equality based on human rights, with actual hierarchy based on the nation of origin, such as metropole and periphery (Mehta 1999).

The presumed realm of unique personal expression is in the multiple organizations of civil society, where voluntary association is an important principle (North, Wallis, and Weingast 2009). In the sphere of civil society, the arts provide for multiple means for self-expression and identity without restraint. Given official tolerance and freedom of association, one can participate in different religious beliefs and practices without fear. In spite of a particular position in the private sphere, women are de jure equal citizens recognized with freedoms in public (Ryan 1990; Bloch 2005).

The liberal form of government, with freedom and equality for each person, remains the ideal. Each of these presumed freedoms is preserved in each sphere, imperfectly, with notable violations, even while the principle of equality remains the purported foundation for the polity. The very divisions may constrain freedom, as much as manifest it, a possibility which is not acknowledged in many discussions of the liberal model. That is, the structure of the liberal state is divided, perhaps with the effect of limiting freedom to the designated sphere as a form of buffering and balancing of powers across spheres. The division of the spheres also requires the division of the person, who behaves differently in each context (Bell 1978).

That is, the liberal state is not as "equal" as its critics or its advocates claim.

Money and property as representation

The individual is represented by his "own" property and vice versa in liberal governance. Money is a representation of the social whole, although understood as independent private property by the individual holder. This form of social representation, money, is widely misunderstood; if money were not actually social, the individual would have no access to the means for sustenance based on the division of labor and advanced technical knowledge which he need not personally acquire.

"Property rights"

The importance of "property rights" in New Institutional Economics (Davis 2015, 42–54) illustrates the focus on objects instead of relationships. Of course, "property," as an object, cannot have "rights;" this concept apparently refers to the owners' rights over the object. This phrase is characteristic of animation or personification, as if the object were a person, as discussed further in Chapter 7. As a result, even the owner becomes invisible in this typical formulation, and the object represents the entire economy.

"Property rights," as a core of both the economy and the political sphere, are protected by the courts. This provides the sufficient and appropriate incentives for individuals (Milhaupt and Pistor 2008, 4–8), whose role it is to maximize the value of property so that the economy can "grow."

The economy is centered on property and the goal of increasing its value rather than on the relationships. It is a unified system focused on one object, regardless of the apparent division into public and private spheres. It is not clear who is served by this system, whether the consumer who can consume the object, or the owner of the property itself, who benefits from its own growth.

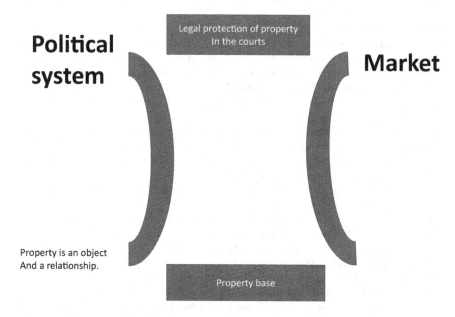

Figure 3.1 Structure of the Liberal State

Summary

Does the public/private divide enable the bourgeois public to maintain scrutiny of the state, according to Habermas? Does the public/private divide reflect different types of property, according to Pateman? Does it help protect society from the market, according to Polanyi? Does it reflect the dual dimensions of the commodity, according to Marx? Does this division make the system more resilient or more fragile? Do these divisions make the unity of society invisible, the truth of Thatcher's declaration?

These issues will be addressed after an account of the emergence of the liberal state in Chapter 4.

Bibliography

Alexander, Gregory S. *The Global Debate over Constitutional Property: Lessons for American Takings Jurisprudence*. Chicago: University of Chicago Press, 2006.

Beck, Ulrich and Elisabeth Beck-Gernsheim. *Individualization: Institutionalized Individualism and its Social and Political Consequences*. New York: Sage, 2002.

Bell, Daniel. *The Cultural Contradictions of Capitalism*. New York: Basic Books, 1978.

Benjamin, Jessica. *The Bonds of Love: Psychoanalysis, Feminism, and the Problem of Domination*. New York: Pantheon, 1988.

Benjamin, Jessica. *The Shadow of the Other: Intersubjectivity and Gender in Psychoanalysis*. New York: Routledge, 1998.

Bennett, Tony and Patrick Joyce (eds.). *Material Powers: Cultural Studies, History and the Material Turn*. New York: Routledge, 2010.

Berlin, Isaiah. "Two Concepts of Liberty," in *Four Essays on Liberty*. New York: Oxford University Press, 1969, 118–172.

Blaufarb, Rafe. "Nobles, Aristocrats, and the Origins of the French Revolution," in Robert M. Schwartz and Robert A. Schneider (eds.), *Tocqueville and Beyond: Essays on the Old Regime in Honor of David D. Bien*. Newark: University of Delaware Press, 2003, 86–110.

Blaufarb, Rafe. *The Great Demarcation: The French Revolution and the Invention of Modern Property*. New York: Oxford University Press, 2016.

Bloch, Ruth H. "Inside and Outside the Public Sphere," *William and Mary Quarterly*, Vol. 62, No. 1, January 2005, 99–106.

Block, Fred L. and Margaret R. Somers. *The Power of Market Fundamentalism: Karl Polanyi's Critique*. Cambridge, MA: Harvard University Press, 2014.

Blyth, Mark. *Great Transformations: Economic Ideas and Institutional Change in the Twentieth Century*. New York: Cambridge University Press, 2002.

Butler, Judith P. *Subjects of Desire: Hegelian Reflections in Twentieth Century France*. New York: Cambridge University Press, 1987.

Calhoun, Craig J. (ed.). *Habermas and the Public Sphere*. Cambridge, MA: MIT Press, 1992.

Calhoun, Craig J. "Imagining Solidarity: Cosmopolitanism, Constitutional Patriotism, and the Public Sphere," *Public Culture*, Vol. 14, No. 1, 2002, 147–171.

Calhoun, Craig J. *Nations Matter: Culture, History, and the Cosmopolitan Dream*. New York: Routledge, 2007.

Calhoun, Craig J. *The Roots of Radicalism: Tradition, the Public Sphere, and Early Nineteenth-Century Social Movements*. Chicago: University of Chicago Press, 2012.

Crenshaw, Kimberle. *On Intersectionality: Essential Writings*. New York: The New Press, 2020.

Dahl, Robert A. *How Democratic is the American Constitution?* New Haven: Yale University Press, 2001.

Davis, Ann E. *The Evolution of the Property Relation: Understanding Paradigms, Debates, Prospects.* New York: Palgrave MacMillan, 2015.

Davis, Ann E. "Paradoxical Positions: The Methodological Contributions of Feminist Scholarship," *Cambridge Journal of Economics*, Vol. 41, No. 1, 2017a, 181–201.

Davis, Ann E. *Money as a Social Institution: The Institutional Development of Capitalism.* New York: Routledge, 2017b.

Davis, John Bryan. *Individuals and Identity in Economics.* New York: Cambridge University Press, 2011.

Ehrenreich, Barbara. *Dancing in the Streets: A History of Collective Joy.* New York: Metropolitan Books, 2007.

England, Paula. "The Separative Self: Androcentric Bias in Neoclassical Assumptions," in Marianne A. Ferber and Julie A. Nelson (eds.), *Beyond Economic Man: Feminist Theory and Economics.* Chicago: University of Chicago Press, 1993, 37–53.

Fraser, Nancy. *Fortunes of Feminism: From State-Managed Capitalism to Neoliberal Crisis.* New York: Verso, 2013.

Fraser, Nancy. "Contradictions of Capital and Care," *New Left Review*, 100, July/August 2016, 99–117.

Freud, Sigmund. *Totem and Taboo: Resemblances Between the Psychic Lives of Savages and Neurotics.* New York: Moffat, Yard, and Company, 1918.

Fried, Barbara H. *The Progressive Assault on Laissez Faire: Robert Hale and the First Law and Economics Movement.* Cambridge, MA: Harvard University Press, 1998.

Fukuyama, Francis. *Identity: The Demand for Dignity and the Political of Resentment.* New York: Farrar, Straus, and Giroux, 2018.

Garland, David. "The Welfare State: A Fundamental Dimension of Modern Government," *European Journal of Sociology*, Vol. 55, No. 3, December 2014, 327–364.

Giddens, Anthony. *Modernity and Self-Identity: Self and Society in the Late Modern Age.* Stanford, CA: Stanford University Press, 1991.

Gilligan, Carol. *In a Different Voice: Psychological Theory and Women's Development.* Cambridge, MA: Harvard University Press, 1993.

Glendon, Mary Ann. *The Transformation of Family Law: State, Law, and Family in the United States and Western Europe.* Chicago: University of Chicago Press, 1989.

Goffman, Erving. *Presentation of Self in Everyday Life.* Garden City, NY: Double Day, 1959.

Gordon, David M. *Fat and Mean: The Corporate Squeeze of Working Americans and the Myth of Managerial Downsizing.* New York: The Free Press, 1996.

Gutmann, Amy. *Identity in Democracy.* Princeton, NJ: Princeton University Press, 2003.

Habermas, Jurgen. *The Structural Transformation of the Public Sphere: An Inquiry into a Category of Bourgeois Society.* Cambridge, MA: MIT Press, 1989.

Hardt, Michael and Antonio Negri. *Assembly.* New York: Oxford University Press, 2017.

Harvey, David. *Seventeen Contradictions and the End of Capitalism.* New York: Oxford University Press, 2014.

Hegel, Georg Wilhelm Friedrich. *Philosophy of Right.* Chicago: Encyclopedia Britannica, 1952.

Hegel, Georg Wilhelm Friedrich. *Phenomenology of Spirit.* Trans. Terry Pinkard. Cambridge, UK: Cambridge University Press, 2018.

Heuer, Jennifer Ngaire. *The Family and the Nation: Gender and Citizenship in Revolutionary France, 1789–1830.* Ithaca, NY: Cornell University Press, 2005.

Howell, Martha C. *Commerce Before Capitalism in Europe 1300–1600.* New York: Cambridge University Press, 2010.

Hunt, Lynn. *Inventing Human Rights: A History*. New York: W. W. Norton & Company, 2007.

Israel, Jonathan I. *Radical Enlightenment: Philosophy and the Making of Modernity 1650–1750*. New York: Oxford University Press, 2001.

Jameson, Fredric. *The Cultural Turn: Selected Writings on the Postmodern, 1983–1998*. New York: Verso, 1998.

Joyce, Patrick (ed.). *The Social in Question: New Bearings in History and the Social Sciences*. New York: Routledge, 2002.

Joyce, Patrick. *The State of Freedom: A Social History of the British State Since 1800*. New York: Cambridge University Press, 2013.

Kidd, Colin. "Identity Before Identities: Ethnicity, Nationalism, and the Historian," in Julia Rudolph (ed.), *History and Nation*. Lewisburg, PA: Bucknell University Press, 2006, 9–44.

Kreitner, Roy. *Calculating Promises: The Emergence of Modern American Contract Doctrine*. Stanford, CA: Stanford University Press, 2007.

Lacan, Jacques. *Language of the Self*. Baltimore: Johns Hopkins University Press, 1981.

Lessig, Lawrence. *America, Compromised*. Chicago: University of Chicago Press, 2018.

Levi-Strauss, Claude. *Elementary Structures of Kinship*. Boston: Beacon Press, 1969.

MacPherson, C. B. *The Political Theory of Possessive Individualism: Hobbes to Locke*. Oxford: Clarendon Press, 1962.

Marglin, Stephen A. *The Dismal Science: How Thinking Like an Economist Undermines Community*. Cambridge, MA: Harvard University Press, 2008.

Marx, Karl. *Capital*. New York: International Publishers, 1967.

Mehta, Uday Singh. *Liberalism and Empire: A Study in Nineteenth Century British Liberal Thought*. Chicago: University of Chicago Press, 1999.

Menke, Christopher. *Reflections of Equality*. Stanford, CA: Stanford University Press, 2006.

Milhaupt, Curtis J. and Katharina Pistor. *Law and Capitalism: What Corporate Crises Reveal About Legal Systems and Economic Development around the World*. Chicago: University of Chicago Press, 2008.

North, Douglass Cecil, John Joseph Wallis, and Barry R. Weingast. *Violence and Social Orders: A Conceptual Framework for Interpreting Recorded Human History*. New York: Cambridge University Press, 2009.

Norton, Peter D. *Fighting Traffic: The Dawn of the Motor Age in the American City*. Cambridge, MA: MIT Press, 2008.

Novak, William J. "Public-Private Governance: A Historical Introduction," in Jody Freeman and Martha Minow (eds.), *Government by Contract: Outsourcing and American Democracy*. Cambridge, MA: Harvard University Press, 2009, 23–40.

O'Brien, Karen. *Women and Enlightenment in Eighteenth-Century Britain*. New York: Cambridge University Press, 2009.

O'Mahoney, Patrick. *The Contemporary Theory of the Public Sphere*. 2nd ed. New York: Peter Lang, 2019.

Pateman, Carole. *The Sexual Contract*. Stanford, CA: Stanford University Press, 1988.

Pierson, Christopher. *Beyond the Welfare State? The New Political Economy of Welfare*. 3rd. ed. University Park, PA: The Pennsylvania State University Press, 2007.

Pierson, Christopher. *Just Property: A History in the Latin West. Volume One: Wealth, Virtue, and the Law*. New York: Oxford University Press, 2013.

Pistor, Katharina. *The Code of Capital: How Law Creates Wealth and Inequality*. Princeton, NJ: Princeton University Press, 2019.

Pocock, J. G. A. *The Machiavellian Moment: Florentine Political Thought and the Atlantic Republican Tradition*. Princeton, NJ: Princeton University Press, 1975.

Polanyi, Karl. *The Great Transformation*. Boston: Beacon Press, 1944.

Rubin, Gayle. "'The Traffic in Women' Notes on the 'Political Economy' of Sex," in Rayna R. Reiter (ed.), *Toward an Anthropology of Women*. New York: Monthly Review Press, 1975, 157–210.

Ryan, Mary P. *Women in Public: Between Banners and Ballots, 1825–1880*. Baltimore: Johns Hopkins University Press, 1990.

Searle, John R. *Making the Social World: The Structure of Human Civilization*. New York: Oxford University Press, 2010.

Sewell, William H. Jr. *A Rhetoric of Bourgeois Revolution: The Abbe Sieyes and What Is the Third Estate?* Durham, NC: Duke University Press, 1994.

Shammas, Carole. *A History of Household Government in America*. Charlottesville: University of Virginia Press, 2002.

Shapiro, Ian, Stephen Skowronek, and Daniel Galvin (eds.). *Rethinking Political Institutions: The Art of the State*. New York: New York University Press, 2006.

Shiller, Robert J. *Narrative Economics: How Stories Go Viral and Drive Major Economic Events*. Princeton, NJ: Princeton University Press, 2019.

Smith, Adam. *The Wealth of Nations*. New York: Modern Library, 1994.

Taylor, Charles. *The Language Animal: The Full Shape of the Human Linguistic Capacity*. Cambridge, MA: Harvard University Press, 2016.

Veblen, Thorstein. *Theory of the Leisure Class: An Economic Study of Institutions*. New York: Modern Library, 1934.

Weber, Max. *Economy and Society: An Outline of Interpretive Sociology*. Berkeley: University of California Press, 1978.

Weber, Max. *Protestant Ethic and the Spirit of Capitalism*. Chicago: Fitzroy Dearborn, 2001.

Yuran, Noam. *What Money Wants: An Economy of Desire*. Stanford: Stanford University Press, 2014.

4 The shaping of the modern liberal state

Introduction

This chapter traces the emergence of the ideas of liberalism, as well as the liberal form of the modern state. Contradictory pressures will be identified, to be further explored in Chapter 5.

What is the ideal liberal state?

Thatcher (Chapter 1) claimed that there is no such thing as society. Her mentor, Hayek, belonged to the Austrian School of economics, whose members were aware of the socialist experiment of "Red Vienna" in the 1920s (Rabinbach 1985) and were explicitly anti-union, pro-globalization, and pro-monetarism. Members of this school explicitly separated facts from norms and values in the study of economics, and economic theory from history (Slobodian 2018b). They wished to defend the economy from democracy (Slobodian 2018a, 4–5, 12, 14, 30–34, 42–48, 267). Or perhaps Thatcher understood very well the power of rhetoric to change beliefs and behavior, and so to alter and weaken the institutions which she disliked, which would include all forms of "collectivism." It would be the height of irony to call Thatcher a "social constructionist," perhaps aware of the capacity of prominent leaders to change ideas and institutions by such declarative statements, which can then alter political alignments and public conventional wisdom.

Neoliberal epistemology

In fact, there was a distinctive understanding of knowledge among Hayek and his followers (Slobodian 2018a, 223–235, 259, 264). He believed that human knowledge is surpassed by the market price system, an approach that Mirowski calls "agnotology" (Mirowski 2013, 227–230, 239, 296–298, 300, 344; Slobodian 2018a, 83, 231–232, 235; Rosenboim 2017, 157–165). That is, human persons can and should respond to the price system, without question, to achieve efficiency. This was an epistemological position, as well as a moral one. The neoliberals did not proclaim "the individual" until after 1931, which was later defended in terms of property rights, with the market as a steering mechanism (Slobodian 2018a, 24, 118, 121–123, 232–235, 238, 270, 277–280).

In promoting this view, Hayek used the term "society" but argued that the knowledge communicated by the decentralized system of the market is superior to that of any individual or group of experts (Hayek 1945). He suggested that the market system is superior to expert knowledge because of "how little the individual participants need to know in order to be able to take the right action" (Hayek 1945, 526–527). He chastised the planners for naïve "constructivism," a form of hubris regarding human rationality (Slobodian 2018a, 258–262). While Hayek primarily lauded the market system for its ability to communicate information by rules and symbols which individuals may not understand, he also mentions the "inducements" for the individual, "while seeking his own interest, to do what is in the general interest (Hayek 1945, 527, 529). Hayek at times sounded like an institutionalist, such as when he emphasizes the "social process" needed to make mathematical models accurately reflect reality (Hayek 1945, 520, 530). Whether he believed that individuation improves the effectiveness of these inducements, like his contemporary (Polanyi 1944), is not addressed in this context except to insist on decentralization and competition (Hayek 1945, 521, 524). Rather than "conscious direction," Hayek quoted Alfred Whitehead that "civilization advances by extending the number of important operations which we can perform without thinking about them" (Hayek 1945, 528).

Model of the liberal state

It is tempting to see a teleology towards the model of the liberal state, with principles of the protection of property rights, free speech, constitutions with separation of powers, and multi-party elections for representative bodies. The principles of liberalism have varied historically, nonetheless, and even the term itself has been used only since the beginning of the nineteenth century in France and Germany (Rosenblatt 2018, 3). Equality and free markets were not always part of the definition (Pitts 2005, 3). To be "liberal" first meant to be considerate and moral before it meant the priority of individual rights.

The origin of the term liberalism is the Latin term, "liber," meaning free. This term differentiated a person from a slave in terms of being free from domination and possessing citizenship. But a person was only considered truly free with a "republican constitution . . . and a government focused on the common good, the *res publica* . . . [and] a noble and generous way" of behavior (Rosenblatt 2018, 9; italics in the original). During the Renaissance, a "liberal arts education" was designed to train the elite men for public service (Rosenblatt 2018, 12–15). That is, the original meaning of liberalism was associated with property and status.

The so-called liberal state was often characterized by compromise, such as the recognition of property rights (Maier 2016, 146–164) in return for legitimate procedures for taxation. Extension of suffrage in the public sphere was another mechanism to balance the enforcement of property rights in the labor market in the private sphere. Equality before the law eliminated the influence of aristocracy by birth but was replaced by property requirements for suffrage in nineteenth-century Europe (Rosenblatt 2018, 50–52). Electoral competition gave voice to various constituencies, but elected representative bodies had limited power.

What is termed "democracy" in contemporary literature focuses on elections rather than on the powers of the representative bodies or the strength of protection of property (Berman 2019). That is, there tends to be insufficient attention to the structure of the public/private divide (see Chapter 3).

Importance of historicizing money, property, and the nation-state

So-called liberal principles have varied historically, along with the concept of property and the form of the nation.

The Austrian school believed that the principles of property and money were neutral, apolitical, in spite of their personal awareness of the socialism of *fin de siècle* Vienna (Slobodian 2018a, 46, 119, 212–213, 265, 275). In their view, the "rule of law" could be an instrument for removing politics from economics, according to the principle of the protection of property, and by ruling workers' organizations illegal. In order to understand the historical evolution of the liberal state, which integrates both politics and economics, one must see the relationship between them in terms of "political economy." That is, meanings of property and the state co-evolved (Davis 2015) with various schools of thought in law and economics.

According to Schmitt's analysis, in a global world order there is a need for symmetry between the internal structure of each nation and the global international structure. In the Holy Alliance, for example, the common international principle was respect for dynastic succession in each nation. By contrast, one common principle for modern states is the distinction between the public/private divide, or between the state and the market. That is, there is a form of "double government," consisting of a government of the people, the *imperium*, and government of the territory or property, the *dominium* (Slobodian 2018a, 10–16, 21, 22–24, 104–112, 118–119, 123, 214, 2018b; Schmitt 2006, 46–47, 235). The role of "property" may be to make an immediate connection between the individual owner and the discreet parcel of land, according to domestic laws in the liberal state. Alternatively, there could be forms of collective property, such as the *ejido* in Mexico. Respect for individual property is also a principle of international liberal alliances, such as the International Monetary Fund and the World Trade Organization.

The notion of "Double Government" may relate to the public/private divide (Chapter 3). That is, the market is conceptually distinct from the state in spite of the fact that the entire nation is both market and state (Slobodian 2018a, 10–16, 21, 23–24, 104–112, 118–119, 123, 214, 2018b). The public/private divide was important to Hayek (Rosenboim 2017, 163), as well as to Searle

(2010, 170–171). There is a symmetry with the global order as well, with an international market among a set of nation-states whose boundaries are then permeable to flows of capital and commodities.

These associated ideas of property and governance have varied historically. A cursory review of the notion of property historically provides evidence for wide variation. For example, in the feudal period, property was used by serfs, governed by lords of the manor, associated with a monarch and the church. The enclosures of these lands in England took place by change of legal forms, with little recognition of prior claims to use rights (Marglin 2008; North, Wallis, and Weingast 2009). The French Revolution established unitary ownership, consolidating rights to each parcel to a single owner, so-called allodial rights (Blaufarb 2016). In the twentieth-century US, the legal realists understood property as a "bundle of sticks" which could be assigned separately (Banner 2011; Fried 1998). The law and economics movement after the 1980s in the US reestablished the "natural" unity of property and extended economic principles into jurisprudence (Epstein 1985; Posner 1972; Medema 1997).

These historical institutions related to property have evolved along with forms of the state. This process should be historicized, re-politicized, and subject to question and debate rather than reified and naturalized (Pistor 2019). For example, environmental implications of property could be added, such as "greenwood in the bundle of sticks" (Goldstein 2005). Public trust could be used to gage the environmental implications of property regimes (Blumm and Wood 2013).

The shift in governance principles from hereditary monarchy to representative government was accomplished over centuries and may constitute another "Great Transformation." The establishment of markets in labor and land tended to destabilize other forms of government (Polanyi 1944; Maier 2016, 146–148). The development of new ideas for the legitimation of authority coincided with the rise of the market, whether or not there is any causal relationship between these two phenomena (Davis 2015).

Early forms of self-government were expressed in corporate bodies, such as communes, city-states, and chartered municipalities, on a small geographic scale. In the monarchies, the body of the king represented the nation and the people (Kantorowicz 1957). After the revolutions in England (1640–1688), the United States (1776), and France (1789), there was considerable debate and experimentation regarding the methods of "representation" of the population as a whole, of individual members, in what balance, and who "counts" in the electorate. For example, in opposition to the crown and Parliament, the Levellers in the 1640s claimed rights for individuals as self-owners (Sabbadini 2016, 178–186).

Changing ideas of governance and authority may have been driven by the twin dynamic of the Enlightenment and the Industrial Revolution (Israel 2017; Mokyr 2016), with rationality a key principle of both, with a feedback loop accelerating the entire complex. That is, ideas, such as natural science, and institutions, including the state, may have a mutually reinforcing dialectic relationship.

Further, liberalism may be more consistent with capitalism, with its focus on the mobile individual, property rights including the right to alienate, the public/private divide, and the privilege of the private sphere for consumption, along with checks and balances (Berlin 1969; Hirschman 1977). Protection of property would serve the accumulation of capital against claims for redistribution. Protection of property can also legitimate the use of violence and rationalize the limits of suffrage by property requirements. In this case, a key term like "property" can provide an integration across spheres, as well as rationalize their separation; it provides a common discourse for law, administration, economics, and political rhetoric and provides a long-standing sense of stability to both the government and the economy.

Turning points in the evolution of the liberal state

There has been long-term evolution of the forms of the state in the West, which can illustrate the importance of considering historical variation.

Long-distance trade in the Mediterranean

Prior to the participation of European city-states, there existed long-distance trade in the Mediterranean (Abu-Lughod 1989; Bisaha 2004; Bavel 2016).

Peasant mode of production

Prior to the rise of the market, the peasant model with family ownership of small plots and production for use was predominant throughout the world (Maier 2012). There is some debate about the timing of the rise of individual private property in England, whether in the thirteenth or the seventeenth century, and the rise of the "individual" as sole owner, with no obligation to heirs (Macfarlane 1978). The timing of the transition matters with respect to classic explanations of the rise of the market, as to whether individualism is the cause or the result, as argued by Marx, Weber, and Polanyi, among others.

The emergence of factor markets, first in land and the development of capitalist agriculture, were important turning points in the rise of individualism and the transition to capitalism (Brenner 2003; Allen 2009; Bavel 2016).

The notion of English exceptionalism has been attributed to its unique form of feudalism (Macfarlane 2002), its early unification, its position as an island separated from the continent, as well as Anglo-Saxon love of liberty (Rosenblatt 2018, 253–259).

Communes

The first organized communities in the West after the fall of Rome had the form of the corporation, a collective with sworn allegiance by its members for mutual protection. The corporate form itself was an important means of organization in the medieval period (Black 1984; Ogilvie 2019).

City-states

The city-states had republican forms with collective decision-making, to which some attribute the rise of public debt (Stasavage 2003).

Competing forms in Europe

In the early modern period, there were several competing models of state, including city leagues like the Hanseatic League and small principalities in the Holy Roman Empire (Spruyt 1994; Poggi 1978).

The first "modern" economy was the Dutch Republic, the wealth of which was notable to visitors. It was an extension of the urbanization and commercial development which originated in Northern Italy from the fifteenth century and into the Low Countries and England. Among their notable innovations was long-term public debt available in secondary markets from the seventeenth century (Davids and Lucassen 1995, 1–25). The existence of markets for both commodities and factors of production, high agricultural productivity, an effective state protecting property rights, freedom of movement and contract, and attaining a high level of technology were considered other factors relevant to its "modernization." The Dutch Republic was also highly urbanized, relatively tolerant of religious diversity, with a modern fiscal system and a comprehensive program of poor relief, all before the Industrial Revolution in England (de Vries and van der Woude 1997, 693, 711–718).

Pincus describes the Glorious Revolution 1688 in England as the first "modern" revolution, as a contest of competing visions of political economy, one based on finite land (Tory) and the other based on infinite productivity of labor in manufacturing (Whig), which he characterizes as a "bourgeois revolution" (Pincus 2009, 483–486). The adoption of the Dutch model with the invasion of William of Orange enabled the establishment of the Bank of England in 1694 and the financial resilience for England's ultimate victory in war with France. The competing visions of political economy facilitated the emergence of a modern bureaucratic state, rather than a traditional patrimonial one, and the ascendance of mercantile values.

There were frequent wars contesting the succession of the hereditary monarchies, according to maintaining the balance of power within Europe. After discoveries of the New World, there were also wars of colonial expansion and intense competition for trade (Cheney 2010). These continual and increasing costs may have increased pressure for revenue and for more efficient fiscal systems. These pressures led to the centrality of public finance, with tax collection bureaucracies and approval of public expenditures by representative bodies (Davis 2015, 128–129).

Pressures of trade, colonization and war

The importance of government bond holders in the mid-eighteenth century was important enough to merit the term "capitalist" (Sonenscher 2007, 2, 74). Writing in 1752, Hume anticipated the problem of public debt used to finance war, and the risk to the population for taxes to support foreign ventures. The worry was that the requirement to secure public credit may reduce the capacity to address the "social question" of inequality. Such problems would face both republican and monarchical governments, and French theorists like Montesquieu and Abbe Sieyes sought to formulate a representative government to offset this risk (Sonenscher 2007, 4–5, 11, 41–67). Montesquieu's recommendations included elected government, constitutional decision-making, and separation of powers, along with a tax system, public expenditures, and public debt. Whether these provisions would be sufficient without a strong moral foundation in the populace remained an important question (Sonenscher 2007, 56–57).

Eighteenth-century liberal revolutions

American Founders were familiar with liberal theorists like Locke and the "rights of free-born Englishmen," as well as the structure of the British "constitution."

According to Blaufarb (2016), the French Revolution of 1789 remade the system of property, what he called "the Great Demarcation." Theorists of the French Revolution drew upon the legacy of republican thought beginning in fifteenth-century Florence, and the property theorists of seventeenth-century England (Sonenscher 2007, 33–41, 2008; Pocock 1975; Soll 2014). The *sans-culottes*, important supporters of the Revolution, believed in the dignity of labor, in contrast with privileged elites who did not work with their hands. They inspired concepts of complete unity of the nation, "one and indivisible," based on equality. Rather than use Lockean rhetoric to represent property owners in government, the sans-culottes wished to represent labor directly rather than indirectly (Sewell 1980, 109–113, 120–133).

Once the corporate bodies were declared illegal on August 4, 1789, including guilds as well as nobility and the clergy, workers became individuals, bargaining directly with employers. Faced with the lack of support of the collective work forms of the *ancien regime*, workers became more conscious of their common experience as a class and began to develop new forms of worker organization (Sewell 1980, 133–142, 194–218). These new worker corporations, often using the same rhetoric and organizational practices as the guilds, were an important source of the Revolutions of 1848, which began in France and Italy (Sperber 2005). The worker organizations were like mini-republics, which saw themselves as the foundation of the nation, with labor as a universal principle (Sewell 1980, 277–284). The Revolutions in France of 1830 and 1848 were repressed with force and replaced with an emperor and a subsequent number of republics.

After the Revolutions of 1830 and 1848, the liberals sought to find a middle ground between the revolutionaries and the conservatives. Their support for property rights and limited suffrage was intended to enfranchise a propertied middle class to provide ballast among these conflicting pressures (Rosenblatt 2018, 89–95, 132–138).

Pressures of the labor movement

The 1848 revolutions occurred throughout Europe, and liberal ideas of individual and property rights challenged monarchies at the same time as warfare continued among these same states.

In Marx's own writings, he mentions the variations of class during the mid-nineteenth century period, including factory workers, artisans, peasants, nobles, and the bourgeoisie. In the wave of unrest across continental Europe in this period, there were outbreaks including some or all of these constituencies. The period of the 1840s was characterized by increasing unrest due to poor harvests and inefficient economic infrastructure, as well as the mechanization of textile mills. In Silesia, the region of textile production, unrest, and poverty, Wilhelm Wolff produced a critical analysis that Marx himself admired (Clark 2006, 450–458) (the person to whom Volume I of *Capital* was dedicated). The peasants were still the most numerous in this period (Sperber 2005, 5–20), but they did not yet form a class in terms of unity and self-consciousness, in Marx's view (Tucker 1978, 608).

Exceptional Eastern Europe

The states in Eastern Europe were not simply shaped by the liberal model emerging in France and England. With lower levels of urbanization, the strong influence of the Ottoman Empire and the Russian Empire, and less access to coastal and river transportation, the role of large land owners remained significant in shaping the polity.

The Hapsburg Empire

After engaging in war with France for 20 years, the Austro-Hungarian Empire was faced with fiscal restraint and the challenge of the ideas of the Revolution. The industrial workers were restive, along with the peasants. In this context, the liberals in cities like Vienna pushed for reforms, including increasing representation and extending suffrage. Yet the reforms of the General Civil Law Code of 1811 and the "liberal" constitution of 1867 were limited. Individuals were equal in terms of the law, which aided peasants in relations with nobles and helped to create loyalty to the central state. But juridical equality did not necessarily change social or economic relations. While respecting property rights and mobility after the end of feudalism, and improving education, there was still censorship and a state religion. The reforms were implemented by a centralized state bureaucracy, which was no longer the exclusive province of the nobility, but open to the educated middle class. There were differential classes of citizenship based on property requirements (Judson 1996, 49–58, 2016, 51–53, 227–230, 238–239, 262–268, 288–290).

In addition to equal citizenship and protection of property, the principle of nationalism was also very important in the Austrian Empire, partly due to historic circumstances. As a far-flung hereditary monarchy from the thirteenth century, the Hapsburg Empire expanded partly from marriage alliances and partly from continuous war, including wars of succession. A separate ruling allowed a woman to succeed to the throne of the Holy Roman Empire, called the "Pragmatic Sanction" (Judson 2016, 22–27). When Maria Theresa ascended to the throne in 1741, she sought support from the newly acquired territories of Hungary. Subsequently she was particularly solicitous of the requirements of the Hungarian nobility, including their resistance to taxation, liberation of the peasantry, and imposition of consistent bureaucratic procedures, such as the use of the German language throughout the empire. The nobles who claimed to represent the entire population resisted the centralizing strategies, using language and common heritage as one defense. Hungarian nationalism was a potent force through the period, and similar assertion of "national" prerogatives was used by other acquired territories. Rather than a "natural right for nations," the political use of this strategy did effectively compromise the centralizing administrative practices of subsequent monarchs (Judson 2016, 24–36, 42–46, 48–49, 85–89, 109, 151–154, 161, 198–214, 270–275).

Prussia

The hereditary monarchs were unprepared to deal with these challenges and sometimes vacillated between repression and concession. For example, in Prussia, the king's hesitation led to some unnecessary violence, but ultimately a liberal constitution was adopted. While formally curtailing the king's power, it represented the public with suffrage based on three tiers of property ownership. The press censorship was reduced but not eliminated. The bureaucracy was rationalized, but the power of land owners remained substantial. Yet the unrestrained absolute power of the monarch was no longer acceptable, and a new class of bourgeoisie supported "liberal" reforms like equal treatment under the law (in contrast to aristocracy by birth). A new synthesis was forged among the large land owners and the new bourgeoisie to support taxes directed towards modernization and to reduce feudal dues in the countryside (Clark 2006, 500–509). Leaders like Bismarck played a significant role by mediating among the various constituencies and developing pragmatic alliances to consolidate and stabilize power (Clark 2006; Steinberg 2011; Judson 2016; Sperber 2005). The monarchies made reforms, partly influenced by liberal ideas from France and England, partly due to the industrializing economy and its impact, as well as the needs for fiscal efficiency and in response to overt class conflict. In this turbulent period, Bismarck as Chancellor used economic growth and military power to consolidate Germany in 1871 with a new imperial constitution (Clark 2006, 518–552, 556–562; Anievas 2015, 99–126). The Prussian three-class suffrage system was preserved in the German constitution of 1871, assuring political influence for the Junkers and agrarian conservatives against liberal reform throughout the new German state (Clark 2006, 559–562).

Bismarck used expansion of the scale of the state to avoid compromise with a liberal parliament to assure taxation. With a customs union, tariff revenue was a substitute for taxes approved by formal constitutional provisions, preserving the monarch's privilege. Then with a federal form of government, the newly united German nation could recognize the monarchies of the formally independent German states, consolidating support for unification. Unification also won the support of the liberal bourgeoisie seeking access to the larger German market and the ambitious German leaders aspiring to the "great leader" status in Europe, compared with France, the United Kingdom, and Italy (Ziblatt 2006).

German liberals compromised with Bismarck, arguing that he had successfully founded a unified state which would then have the capacity to implement reforms. They supported Bismarck in his attack on Catholicism and his anti-socialist laws, which then made the unification of a strong liberal party more difficult (Rosenblatt 2018, 182–193).

Ironically, the first welfare provisions (other than seventeenth-century Poor Laws in England) were by "Caesarist" leaders, with the trappings of popular sovereignty and representative government, but censorship and propaganda, Napoleon III in the 1850s and Bismarck in the 1870s (Rosenblatt 2018, 136–139, 220–221).

Liberal reaction

Liberalism may have been a progressive force compared with feudal and monarchical regimes in the nineteenth century. While these liberal reforms originated in the Dutch Republic, England, the US, and France, the application of these ideas was inhibited in some countries by the persistence of feudalism, with nobles having a significant role in government in the Habsburg Empire. In Prussia the centralization and bureaucratization had reduced the power of the towns and the bourgeoisie. The persistent power of the Junkers was able to resist land reforms, a partial explanation of German exceptionalism or "*sonderweg*" (Blackbourn and Eley 1984; Clark 2006, xiii, 149, 155–167, 327–330, 518–523; Steinberg 2011, 72–95).

The principles of liberalism posed a particular threat to existing dynastic states, whose governance principles were hereditary succession, not representation of the sovereign public by rational deliberation in the public sphere. There was an increase in suffrage and other "liberal" reforms, like equality under the law and protection of property rights. For example, the Reform of 1832 expanded suffrage in England, as well as the Constitution of 1867 in Austria. Centralized bureaucratic reform prior to industrialization in Prussia may have been more extensive, improving its fiscal resilience, military strength and popular cohesion, even without liberalization (Brophy 1998).

In spite of the liberal reforms in the wake of the revolutions of 1848, the leading powers in Europe in the early twentieth century were still monarchies with imperial authority to appoint ministers and to lead the military. Only France was a republic (Clark 2013, 170–185). It was only after World War II that the US was in a position to impose liberal republican constitutions on Germany and Japan, as an occupying power with allies.

Nationalism

To replace the cohesion of the corporations of the *ancien régime* (clergy, nobility, and commoners), nationalism can reintegrate a population newly divided into "individuals" who may be more mobile than the stationary communities of the past.

As an alternative form of association, nationalism was "conservative," embedded in a glorified past, tied to specific geographies and peoples. Nationalism was a pragmatic strategy to unite the nobles and peasants against workers and the bourgeoisie, new classes who were emerging from the new market economy (Judson 2016, 85–89, 109, 151–154, 161, 198–214, 270–275; Steinberg 2011). Nationalism was part of the "romantic" resistance to industrialization (Herder; Judson 2016, 199). Nationalism was also promoted in resistance to Napoleonic occupation in the early nineteenth century in Austria and Germany and helped to unite the principalities of the German Confederation. In the challenge to the Austro-Hungarian Empire in the late nineteenth century, nationalism was a pragmatic method to form new nations who could claim their independence in the form of newly independent peoples. The development of railroads as the first capitalist industry which provided the capacity to unify larger territories, but which required more public subsidy, fostered the development of a national frame of mind, along with modern financing by public taxes and private corporations (Maier 2016, 188–200; Clark 2006, 458–462).

> The turn to cultural arguments [in Austria-Hungary] developed because politics after 1867 became increasingly popular and more democratic . . . [with] an expansion of suffrage. . . . Nationalist activists turned increasingly to broad cultural-nationalist arguments partly to unify voters from different social classes for their programs. . . . This language made cultural commonalities the basis for group identification. It appealed to imperial fairness to achieve redress for past and present victimization.
>
> (Judson 2016, 273)

Individualism may be compatible with nationalism when considered as a shared narrative to facilitate cohesion and commitment (Calhoun 2007, 3, 124–129, 140–144).

Liberalism and empire and its contradictions

In the 1870s, the European states again scrambled for territories in intense competition with each other (Maier 2012, 183–202, 2016, 214–229). Liberals in Britain, France, and Germany were able to reconcile this domination of foreign territories for the benefit of their own progress (Rosenblatt 2018, 247–252; Pitts 2005, 2018). Mehta finds the confluence of the terms liberalism and empire as simultaneous with the first emergence of the popular use of the term "liberalism" in 1818 (Mehta 1999, 11). Rather than accidental, he locates this apparent contradiction in Locke's thought. For Locke, nature contributes nothing of value to the product of one's labor, which is the origin of ownership. This "worthless" empty nature belies the origin of community from territory and from sharing the commons. For Locke, the only source of political community is the voluntary contract for preservation of property by rational owners. As a result, territory has no meaning except as it relates to the land owned by these individual workers who combine their labor with it, who then contract for a state. Locke thus erases the history of "military conquest, matrimonial alliances, language, ethnicity, geographical delineation" and other uses of power to acquire territory (Mehta 1999, 131).

> For Locke, the parceling of nature into private units is the condition for the possibility of political unity, because no such unity is deemed to exist by virtue of the experience of nature itself.
>
> (Mehta 1999, 132)

Thus liberalism's universal assumption of rationality and equality is true only of property owners (Mehta 1999, 51–56), who have the requisite capacity for representative self-government. The West can advance "universal" histories which can account for "stages of development" with their own leadership based on science, rationality, and progress (Mehta 1999, 82–87).

Sartori also locates the foundation of liberalism on Locke but sees its revolutionary potential by recognition of the property-constituting capacity of labor. For example, small proprietors in colonial Bengal can make claims to land on this basis. On the other hand, the routine operation of capitalism removes the product of the worker from his control and explicitly assigns ownership to the capitalist. At the same time, this provides the possibility of critique of capitalism (Sartori 2014, 8–25).

While there is a large literature which finds liberalism logically incompatible with empire, there are others which see this empire as a method for bringing "civilization" and "progress" to underdeveloped countries. This line of thought follows Fukuyama and Huntingdon to celebrate the role of the West in providing models for effective government (Bowden 2009).

World Wars I and II

The period of World Wars in Europe can be considered another "Thirty Years' War" (1914–1944) which succeeded in restructuring the modern state

(Anievas 2015). After World War I, empires were dismantled, such as the Tsarist, Habsburg, and Ottoman Empires, while the Chinese empire was subject to civil war. After World War II, American hegemony was clearly established (Tooze 2014).

According to Rosenblatt, the turn to individual rights was a post-World War II phenomenon, so that the liberals could differentiate themselves more decisively from totalitarian socialists. Further, the liberals split between an endorsement of laissez faire, on the one hand, and government intervention, particularly to aid the poor, on the other. Rights were defined in the negative, such as protection of property from interference, and the emphasis on public good was lost (Rosenblatt 2018, 271–274).

Methodology

Reviewing the long-term history of the modern liberal state, "property" as a concept and principle provides a common element, along with "individualism," while the meaning of both terms has continually changed. It is important to recognize, nonetheless, that there are many contested issues with respect to historiography and method (Sewell 2005). There are important questions and challenges: did liberalism emerge due to its fit with capitalism? There are pitfalls to arguments by teleology and functionalism.

Drawing upon Sewell's discussion of the "turns" in historiography (Sewell 2005), there are implications for methodology. It is important to recognize path dependence, imitation, and competition among states. Ideas and institutions are co-constituted and mutually interactive; historical contingency is also important. The operation of "capitalism" as a system, nonetheless, helped to shape both states and markets, which in turn helped alter and reinforce capitalism.

At key turning points there are new ideas, institutions, and expertise. The state is an institution, and so forms of the state evolve with changing ideas. Ideas emerge to address new challenges, which then influence the structure of emerging institutions, as illustrated in Table 4.1.

There are separate disciplines such as intellectual history, history of economic thought, and the history of particular nations. Yet if human institutions are

Table 4.1 Periodization of Ideas and Institutions

Period	Ideas	Institutions
Pre-modern	Collective	Communes
Monarchies	Hereditary succession	Church, family
Liberal state	Enlightenment; rationality; property; the individual	Constitutions; formal public representation; checks and balances; fiscal and monetary system
Empire	Nationalism; civilization	Territory
Global systems	Capitalism	Money; international law; markets; colonies; private business corporations

constituted by language statements, ideas are expressed in those institutions and enacted in human behavior. The ideas and the institutions are co-constituted and so evolve together and are mutually interactive.

Definition of "capitalism"

In contrast with some observers (Hodgson 2014, 2015, 2016; Bavel 2016), I argue that when considering factors of economic production, "capital" has a different ontology. "Capital" is a social relation, not an object like even land or labor, although often reified. As a definition here, "capital" is an ownership relation, with the right to exclusion, use, alienation, and return. In that sense, "capital" is like property, with certain associated rights (Pistor 2019). The capitalist can use money to purchase equipment, tools, hire labor, engage in commodity production, and money lending, all for the purposes of profit. The importance of the profit motive, and its priority over other motives, is one distinguishing feature of capitalism as a system. The importance of the legal definitions of capital based on the ownership of property involves the state and so may have an impact on the forms of the state and the associated alliances which support it. Because of the importance of property in the financial circuits of capitalism, there is typically constitutional protection of property in most liberal states (Harvey 2014, 39–40), along with consistent international laws.

The development of capitalism benefitted from the integration of long-distance merchants with the state in organizational innovations in the Dutch Republic and Britain in 1688 (Pincus 2009). Political parties and compromises across class were necessary to form a political coalition and to modify the role of religion and patriarchy (Adams 2005) compared with reason and science.

The emergence of the liberal state occurred with an alliance of merchants and landlords in England and the Dutch Republic. The establishment of merchant monopoly corporations in the early seventeenth century enabled the state to gain an advantage from global trade and to stabilize its domestic finances. These financial arrangements in turn facilitated the expansion of territory and trade by means of military strength.

There was an integration of capitalism and the state (Arrighi 1994, 11–20) with an organizational revolution (Arrighi 1994, 144–158). The merchant monopoly corporations, such as the English East India Company and the Dutch East India Company (VOC), were consolidated into public finance. The founding of the Bank of England and the "financial revolution" of 1688–1720 (Davis 2017b) further established this new form. These innovations were then imitated by other states, what David Harvey calls the "state-finance nexus" (Harvey 2014, 44–47).

In these two important models, the circuit of global trade for spices and slaves was integrated by means of the corporation, by issuing stock to the public and sharing returns by means of speculation in the financial markets in Amsterdam and London. The trade in financial assets rendered opaque the brutal conquest of natives and nations by the VOC. In the case of the Bank of England, the corporation acquired public debt as an asset and issued currency as a liability while also trading its stock on the London financial market. The issue of currency further provided liquidity to domestic as well as global trade. Based on the monopoly of these global trades, the British currency, the pound sterling, became a global currency and enabled Britain to manage global financial markets.

Rather than competition among equals, the management of global trade by its key currency, and a strong navy enabled England to become the global hegemon (Polanyi 1944, 207–208)

Capital, as a social relation among related institutions, enabled the nation to finance its military and global expansion, as well as domestic infrastructure for trade. "Capital" is not an object but a legal right to acquire types of property with money, both of which are defined and enforced by the state, to sell at a price higher than its cost. These objects of property, whether natural resources like land, or global commodities like spices, or domestically manufactured commodities like textiles, provided expanded value to reward investors with financial assets.

After the "revolutionary upheaval of 1776–1848," the rhetoric of protection of property was a new "universal" principle for the formation of a new form of the state, particularly the United Kingdom (Arrighi 1994, 53–56). The liberal nation-state could claim to protect property and individual rights, as well as represent the public in government to support the claim of government by consent. After World War II, the US was more likely to stress human rights and national self-determination (Arrighi 1994, 66–74) in defense of "Pax Americana."

Fault lines/contradictions

The key concepts of protection of property, equality, and individual rights are historically the foundation of liberalism, a compromise program which arose after the French Revolution.

The relation of liberalism to capitalism has been ambivalent, enabling popular sovereignty and representation to balance the duality of property and stabilize public finance.

There are regimes, nonetheless, which represent the tendencies towards "counter movements."

There are some contradictions of liberalism, such as the following:

> It is not clear whether Lockean principles represent the worker or the property owner. That is, labor constitutes property, but the property owner seeks representation and protection in the state.
>
> Further, liberalism often emphasizes the rational individual choice vs. the "agnotology" and the naiveté of "constructivists," according to Hayek.
> (Hayek 1945; Slobodian 2018a)

The role of protection of private property, widely endorsed among liberal states, also has a dilemma. A state strong enough to protect property is strong enough to seize it, a challenge addressed by modern economists such as Lamoreaux, Shleifer, and North.

The fiscal/military state, based on a liberal form of government, can be more resilient, yet there is a danger of allowing too much power to the bond holders and financiers (Adams 2005; Arrighi 1994).

There is a discreet delineation of border/boundary/geography of territory and population vs. the global flows of investment and finance. The private business corporation is a proxy global agent for the territorial state but can also undermine the nation-state.

Property can be considered a neutral principle of government, according to Hayek vs. the foundation of "faction" (Madison in Federalist Paper #10), with class-based governance and increasing political/economic inequality.

The following chapter considers the implications of capitalism more fully.

Bibliography

Abu-Lughod, Janet. *Before European Hegemony: The World System A.D. 1250–1350*. New York: Oxford University Press, 1989.

Adams, Julia. *The Familial State: Ruling Families and Merchant Capitalism in Early Modern Europe*. Ithaca, NY: Cornell University Press, 2005.

Allen, Robert C. *The British Industrial Revolution in Global Perspective*. New York: Cambridge University Press, 2009.

Anievas, Alexander. "Marxist Theory and the Origins of the First World War," in *Cataclysm 1914: The First World War and the Making of Modern World Politics*, 96–143. Boston: Brill, 2015.

Arrighi, Giovanni. *The Long Twentieth Century: Money, Power, and the Origins of our Times*. New York: Verso, 1994.

Banner, Stuart. *American Property: A History of How, Why, and What We Own*. Cambridge, MA: Harvard University Press, 2011.

Bavel, Bas J. P. Van. *The Invisible Hand? How Market Economies Have Emerged and Declined Since 500 AD*. New York: Oxford University Press, 2016.

Beck, Hermann. *The Origins of the Authoritarian Welfare State in Prussia: Conservatives, Bureaucracy, and the Social Question, 1815–70*. Ann Arbor: The University of Michigan Press, 1995.

Bell, David A. "The Many Lives of Liberalism," *The New York Review of Books*, Vol. 66, No. 1, January 17, 2019, 24–27.

Berlin, Isaiah. "Two Concepts of Liberty," in *Four Essays on Liberty*. New York: Oxford University Press, 1969, 118–172.

Berman, Sheri. *Democracy and Dictatorship in Europe: From the Ancient Regime to the Present Day*. New York: Oxford University Press, 2019.

Bisaha, Nancy. *Creating East and West: Renaissance Humanists and the Ottoman Turks*. Philadelphia: University of Pennsylvania Press, 2004.

Black, Antony. *Guilds and Civil Society in European Political Thought from the Twelfth Century to the Present*. Ithaca, NY: Cornell University Press, 1984.

Blackbourn, David and Geoff Eley. *The Peculiarities of German History: Bourgeois Society and Politics in Nineteenth Century Germany*. New York: Oxford University Press, 1984.

Blaufarb, Rafe. *The Great Demarcation: The French Revolution and the Invention of Modern Property*. New York: Oxford University Press, 2016.

Blumm, Michael C. and Mary Christina Wood. *The Public Trust Doctrine in Environmental and Natural Resources Law*. Durham, NC: Carolina Academic Press, 2013.

Bourke, Richard and Quentin Skinner (eds.). *Popular Sovereignty in Historical Perspective*. New York: Cambridge University Press, 2016.

Bowden, Brett. *The Empire of Civilization: The Evolution of an Imperial Idea*. Chicago: University of Chicago Press, 2009.

Brenner, Robert. *Merchants and Revolution: Commercial Change, Political Conflict, and London's Overseas Traders, 1550–1653*. New York: Verso, 2003.

Brophy, James M. *Capitalism, Politics and Railroads in Prussia, 1830–1870*. Columbus: Ohio State University Press, 1998.

Calhoun, Craig. *Nations Matter: Culture, History, and the Cosmopolitan Dream*. New York: Routledge, 2007.

Cheney, Paul. *Revolutionary Commerce: Globalization and the French Monarchy*. Cambridge, MA: Harvard University Press, 2010.

Clark, Christopher M. *Iron Kingdom: The Rise and Downfall of Prussia, 1600–1947*. Cambridge, MA: Harvard University Press, 2006.

Clark, Christopher M. *The Sleepwalkers: How Europe Went to War in 1914*. New York: HarperCollins, 2013.

Davids, Karel and Jan Lucassen (eds.). *A Miracle Mirrored: The Dutch Republic in European Perspective*. New York: Cambridge University Press, 1995.

Davis, Ann E. *The Evolution of the Property Relation: Understanding Paradigms, Debates, Prospects*. New York: Palgrave MacMillan, 2015.

Davis, Ann E. "Paradoxical Positions: The Methodological Contributions of Feminist Scholarship," *Cambridge Journal of Economics*, Vol. 41, No. 1, 2017a, 181–201.

Davis, Ann E. *Money as a Social Institution: The Institutional Development of Capitalism*. New York: Routledge, 2017b.

Deak, John. *Forging a Multinational State: State Making in Imperial Austria from the Enlightenment to the First World War*. Stanford, CA: Stanford University Press, 2015.

De Vries, Jan and Ad van der Woude. *The First Modern Economy: Success, Failure and Perseverance of the Dutch Economy, 1500–1815*. New York: Cambridge University Press, 1997.

Epstein, Richard A. *Takings: Private Property and the Power of Eminent Domain*. Cambridge, MA: Harvard University Press, 1985.

Fried, Barbara H. *The Progressive Assault on Laissez Faire. Robert Hale and the First Law and Economics Movement*. Cambridge, MA: Harvard University Press, 1998.

Goldstein, Robert J. *Greenwood in the Bundle of Sticks*. Burlington, VT: Ashgate, 2005.

Harvey, David. *Seventeen Contradictions and the End of Capitalism*. New York: Oxford University Press, 2014.

Hayek, F. A. "The Use of Knowledge in Society," *American Economic Review*, Vol. 35, No. 4, September 1945, 519–530.

Hirschman, Albert O. *The Passions and the Interests: Political Arguments for Capitalism Before its Triumph*. Princeton, NJ: Princeton University Press, 1977.

Hodgson, Geoffrey M. "What is Capital? Economists and Sociologists Have Changed Its Meaning: Should It Be Changed Back?" *Cambridge Journal of Economics*, Vol. 38, 2014, 1063–1086.

Hodgson, Geoffrey M. *Conceptualizing Capitalism: Institutions, Evolution, Future*. Chicago: University of Chicago Press, 2015.

Hodgson, Geoffrey M. "Varieties of Capitalism: Some Philosophical and Historical Considerations," *Cambridge Journal of Economics*, Vol. 40, 2016, 941–960.

Israel, Jonathan I. *Expanding the Blaze: How the American Revolution Ignited the World, 1775–1848*. Princeton, NJ: Princeton University Press, 2017.

Judson, Pieter M. *Exclusive Revolutionaries: Liberal Politics, Social Experience, and National Identity in the Austrian Empire, 1848–1914*. Ann Arbor: The University of Michigan Press, 1996.

Judson, Pieter M. *The Habsburg Empire: A New History*. Cambridge, MA: Harvard University Press, 2016.

Kantorowicz, Ernst H. *The King's Two Bodies: A Study in Mediaeval Political Theology*. Princeton, NJ: Princeton University Press, 1957.

Macfarlane, Alan. *The Origins of English Individualism: The Family, Property and Social Transition*. New York: Cambridge University Press, 1978.

Macfarlane, Alan. *The Making of the Modern World: Visions from the West and East*. New York: Palgrave, 2002.

Magdoff, Fred and Chris Williams. *Creating an Ecological Society: Towards a Revolutionary Transformation*. New York: Monthly Review Press, 2017.

Maier, Charles S. *Leviathan 2.0: Inventing Modern Statehood*. Cambridge, MA: Harvard University Press, 2012.

Maier, Charles S. *Once Beyond Borders. Territories of Power, Wealth, and Belonging Since 1500*. Cambridge, MA: Harvard University Press, 2016.

Marglin, Stephen A. *The Dismal Science: How Thinking Like an Economist Undermines Community*. Cambridge, MA: Harvard University Press, 2008.

Medema, Steven G. *Economics and the Law: From Posner to Post-Modernism*. Princeton, NJ: Princeton University Press, 1997.

Mehta, Uday Singh. *Liberalism and Empire: A Study in Nineteenth-Century British Liberal Thought*. Chicago: University of Chicago Press, 1999.

Mirowski, Philip. *Never Let a Serious Crisis Go to Waste*. New York: Verso, 2013.

Mokyr, Joel. *Culture of Growth: The Origins of the Modern Economy*. Princeton, NJ: Princeton University Press, 2016.

Narizny, Kevin. "Anglo-American Primacy and the Global Spread of Democracy: An International Genealogy," *World Politics*, Vol. 64, No. 2, April 2012, 341–373.

North, Douglass Cecil, John Joseph Wallis, and Barry R. Weingast. *Violence and Social Orders: A Conceptual Framework for Interpreting Recorded Human History*. New York: Cambridge University Press, 2009.

Ogilvie, Sheilagh C. *The European Guilds: An Economic Analysis*. Princeton, NJ: Princeton University Press, 2019.

Pincus, Steve. *1688: The First Modern Revolution*. New Haven: Yale University Press, 2009.

Pistor, Katharina. *The Code of Capital: How Law Creates Wealth and Inequality*. Princeton, NJ: Princeton University Press, 2019.

Pitts, Jennifer. *A Turn to Empire: The Rise of Imperial Liberalism in Britain and France*. Princeton, NJ: Princeton University Press, 2005.

Pitts, Jennifer. *Boundaries of the International: Law and Empire*. Cambridge, MA: Harvard University Press, 2018.

Pocock, J. G. A. *Machiavellian Moment: Florentine Political Thought and the Atlantic Republican Tradition*. Princeton, NJ: Princeton University Press, 1975.

Poggi, Gianfranco. *The Development of the Modern State: A Sociological Introduction*. Stanford, CA: Stanford University Press, 1978.

Polanyi, Karl. *The Great Transformation*. Boston: Beacon Press, 1944.

Posner, Richard A. *Economic Analysis of the Law*. Boston: Little Brown and Company, 1972.

Rabinbach, Anson (ed.). *The Austrian Socialist Experiment: Social Democracy and Austromarxism, 1918–1934*. Boulder: Westview Press, 1985.

Rosenblatt, Helena. *The Lost History of Liberalism: From Ancient Rome to the Twenty-First Century*. Princeton, NJ: Princeton University Press, 2018.

Rosenboim, Or. *The Emergence of Globalism: Visions of World Order in Britain and the United States, 1939–1950*. Princeton, NJ: Princeton University Press, 2017.

Sabbadini, Lorenzo. "Popular Sovereignty and Representation in the English Civil War," in Richard Bourke and Quentin Skinner (eds.), *Popular Sovereignty in Historical Perspective*. New York: Cambridge University Press, 2016, 164–186.

Sartori, Andrew. *Liberalism in Empire: An Alternative History*. Oakland, CA: University of California Press, 2014.

Schmitt, Carl. *The Nomos of the Earth: In the international Law of the Jus Publicum Europaeum*. New York: Telos Press, 2006.

Searle, John R. *Making the Social World: The Structure of Human Civilization*. New York: Oxford University Press, 2010.

Sewell, William H. Jr. *Work and Revolution in France: The Language of Labor from the Old Regime to 1848*. New York: Cambridge University Press, 1980.

Sewell, William H. Jr. *A Rhetoric of Bourgeois Revolution: The Abbe Sieyes and What Is the Third Estate?* Durham, NC: Duke University Press, 1994.

Sewell, William H. Jr. *The Logics of History: Social Theory and Social Transformation*. Chicago: University of Chicago Pres, 2005.

Slobodian, Quinn. *Globalists: The End of Empire and the Birth of Neoliberalism*. Cambridge, MA: Harvard University Press, 2018a.

Slobodian, Quinn. "Perfect Capitalism, Imperfect Humans: Race, Migration and the Limits of Ludwig von Mises's Globalism," *Contemporary European History*, Vol. 28, No. 2, May 2019, 143–155.

Smith, Adam. *An Inquiry into the Nature and Causes of the Wealth of Nations*. New York: Modern Library, 1994.

Soll, Jacob. *The Reckoning: Financial Accountability and the Rise and Fall of Nations*. New York: Basic, 2014.

Sonenscher, Michael. *Before the Deluge: Public Debt, Inequality, and the Intellectual Origins of the French Revolution*. Princeton, NJ: Princeton University Press, 2007.

Sonenscher, Michael. *Sans-Culottes: An Eighteenth-Century Emblem in the French Revolution*. Princeton, NJ: Princeton University Press, 2008.

Sperber, Jonathan. *The European Revolutions, 1848–1851*. 2nd ed. New York: Cambridge University Press, 2005.

Spruyt, Hendrik. *The Sovereign State and Its Competitors: An Analysis of System Change*. Princeton, NJ: Princeton University Press, 1994.

Stasavage, David. *Public Debt and the Birth of the Democratic State: France and Great Britain, 1688–1789*. New York: Cambridge University Press, 2003.

Steinberg, Jonathan. *Bismarck: A Life*. New York: Oxford University Press, 2011.

Tooze, J. Adam. *The Deluge: The Great War, America, and the Remaking of the Global Order, 1916–1931*. New York: Viking, 2014.

Tucker, Robert C. (ed.). *The Marx-Engels Reader*. New York: Norton, 1978.

Ziblatt, Daniel. *Structuring the State: The Formation of Italy and Germany and the Puzzle of Federalism*. Princeton, NJ: Princeton University Press, 2006.

Ziblatt, Daniel. *Conservative Parties and the Birth of Democracy*. New York: Cambridge University Press, 2017.

5 The economics of "autophagy"

Implications of the economy as "machine"

Introduction

In the transition from feudalism to capitalism, and the shift from hereditary monarchy to the liberal state, there was a great opening of debate regarding the proper sources of authority. Systematic attention was paid to natural science from gentlemen tinkerers to the state-supported Royal Society and to "reason of state" (Poovey 1998a), which later became political economy. The Enlightenment is a term generally used to refer to these massive innovations in the nature of legitimate authority. The sources of wealth were shifting, from trade to production, and there were explicit new designs for systems of employment, aside from traditional forms like guilds and household production. The moral dimensions of new practices such as "usury" and "slavery" were debated, along with emerging forms such as indentured servants and wage laborers. Extending an appeal to religion and building on the new status of natural science, the natural law "origin stories" of the pre-political individual forming a "social contract" still pervade our political and economic theory, with the associated commercial overtones about the inherent nature of society. The goal of political economy has become and remains the "wealth of nations."

The separation of certain spheres from others, such as the public/private divide, and the reification of production using humans as instruments, was one type of accommodation to these moral issues. The abstract notion of "the economy" is then driven by different principles, such as efficiency, regardless of the impact on those whose working lives are structured by this imperative (Davis 2015b). The effort is justified by the claim that "more is better," and humans as consumers are happier as a result of these efforts to maximize production, given resource and income constraints.

This chapter will proceed by reviewing the methods of organization of modern state and industrial production and the ways in which they were rationalized. We will analyze the ways in which this organization can be characterized as "autophagy," or feeding on itself, along with the moral, social, and political implications.

The modern liberal state

In the shift from hereditary monarchy to liberal state, certain functions were internalized, such as finance, military, and welfare (Davis 2015a; Dincecco and Onorato 2018). From tax farms to tax bureaucracies, finance became more reliable and predictable, allowing for the establishment of public credit. Mercenaries who were paid with bullion were replaced by standing armies. Instead of nobles obliged to serve their lord, or instead of citizen militias, citizens became taxpayers to support the professional military. Instead of parish Poor Laws, there were national programs to support deserving veterans, disabled workers, and widows with children. This professionalization of the state resulted in bureaucratization and impersonal relations among citizens instead of direct relations among neighbors (Calhoun 2007, 70–72). The associated formalization of rules had the potential of becoming an "iron cage" (Weber 1930) or the "road to serfdom" (Hayek 1945). Affective relations were confined to the family, relatively invisible in the context of the pursuit of the "wealth of nations" (Davis 2017a). That is, "human" relations became feminized and assigned to the private sphere.

As states became more complex, there was a formalization of rules and the rule of law in order to establish and maintain regular procedures, such as taxation and the administration of justice. Rationalized legal and administrative expertise became more important to replace manorial courts and arbitrary royal decrees. With economic modernization, the definition of property was subject to flux, from land and livestock to financial assets and information like patents (Davis 2015a). Yet the term, "property," could have the same connotation with the associated material foundation because of the extension of meaning of the same term. In this way, social institutions, like finance and patents, which are entirely human creations, can appear to have the same solidity as land, a form of reification, as discussed in Chapter 2. These institutions become "social facts" (Searle 2010) and have the same apparent immutability to the individual. Reification can be functional, appearing to be beyond the influence of the individual, while actually relying on the compliance of all individuals. In this way, "the economy," which is a hybrid of human and material elements (Latour 1993), can appear to be an object, like a machine (Mirowski 2002), to Nietzsche and his nineteenth-century peers (Safranski 2002, 122–123), for example.

Definition of capitalism

The state is integrally involved in the operation of capitalism (Pistor 2019). In this book, extending the discussion in Chapter 4, capitalism is understood to be a historically specific set of institutions which co-evolved with the nation-state (Davis 2015a). Hodgson (2015) has offered a list of key characteristics of capitalism. I would place particular emphasis on the motive of accumulation (Davis 2017c, 111–112). One important aspect of capitalism is the financial circuit, $M - C - M'$, the purpose of which is to use money to produce more money. This circuit includes an initial amount of money, either a previous surplus accumulation or credit, as well as a means of production and access to a wage labor force and a well-developed market which enables the realization of profit by sales revenue. As stressed by Marx (1967), these conditions were historically emergent, not universal.

Another important aspect is the production and transmission of value during the completion of the financial circuit, M – M'. Value is mobile throughout the process but stored or symbolized by the commodities themselves, a sum of money, as well as a means of production and the available wage labor force. A holistic view of capitalism would include all of these components, as well as the experienced population which is familiar with all of these aspects and recognizes their significance.

The "storage" of value in real objects, symbols of value like gold, or financial assets in the authorized language of commitment is understood by market participants. The value of the physical and financial assets of a company is reflected in its balance sheet, as a guide to its future profit expectations. The value of these assets can also change, given prospects of profitability, and can be "written down" if those prospects begin to look dim. This "language" of value is understood by all those who are preparing for a life in business or in the labor force and who may gain access to the means of life in this method.

Yet symbols of value are considered "fictitious" by Smith, Marx, and Polanyi, as if this genre is misleading and deceptive, not only variable. This sense of incredulity is based on the process of symbolization and constant motion of "value" and the tendency to always question its stability given the flux of the market. Such instability and insecurity have had an impact on personality, with the first widespread use of financial markets (Pocock 1975).

Given the bureaucratization of state finance and the corporate labor force, the use of "categories" of persons is also significant. It is on the basis of certain categories of eligibility that persons are given access to employment and credit by these perhaps arbitrary, if not impossible, judgments of future performance. Such performance depends on the incumbent and her characteristics, as well as the unknown conditions of future markets.

Although the financial circuit operates with words and symbols, it also mobilizes real things, such as raw materials and commodity production. The financial circuit is a "hybrid" (Latour 1993) consisting of symbols, human actions, and concrete materials.

In the left circle, A, are life processes such as species reproduction and global biogeochemical cycles which maintain nutrient flows. In the right circle, B, are financial flows, with the circular flow of production and consumption. The interface between the two processes consists of human labor and raw materials extraction from A to B, and the deposition of waste from B to A. The financial circuit in A operates as if there were no connection of the economy to the natural cycles, an assumption which is increasingly in error as global population and economic production expands.

Capitalism appears to exist on two levels, exchange value vs. use value, in Marxian terms, or market price vs. utility in mainstream economic terms. These

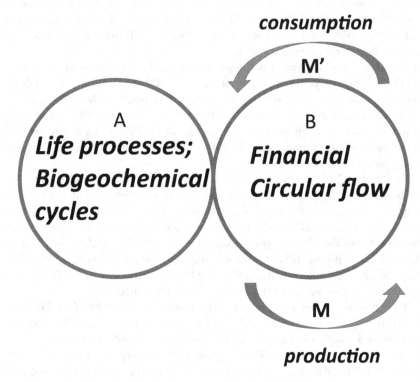

Figure 5.1 Double Circuits: Ecological and Financial

two levels are both within the economic sphere, B, with humankind as its instrument and its focus. On the other hand, in A there are the biogeochemical and life processes in the sphere of life, which participate in global energy and material transformations on a different time and geographic scale.

There is a form of double vision as a result. For day-to-day existence, one could presume that the economic sphere, B, is most important to obtain the necessities. On the other hand, one could hardly argue that human life could proceed without moderate temperatures suited to the limits of the human body, or adequate oxygen, clean water, and nutrition on a daily basis. Yet somehow the ecological sphere, A, seems less important and urgent, given the imperatives of financial flows.

In the right circle, B, money appears to grow by itself, M – M', while actually the "resources" for that growth are drawn from the living systems in A. This expansion of money, M – M', is necessary for the integrity of the financial system, for the repayment of debt with interest. The "dependence" of the financial system on the living systems is invisible and allows a form of autophagy. That is, for money to "grow," resources are drawn from the living systems and may not be replaced. The assumption of wages that cover the costs of reproduction is found in Marx as well as Gauthier (1982, 51) but depends on the bargaining power of labor and the "historical and moral element" (Marx 1967, Vol. I, Chapter 6, 170–171). The necessary investments in public goods like transportation, communication, waste disposal, environmental restoration, and human education are the responsibility of the state and are considered a burden on the taxpayer and a drain on profits rather than essential for the reproduction of the system as a whole. There is no explicit, consensus accounting system for "natural" or "human" capital (Stiglitz, Sen, and Fitoussi 2010) and no comprehensive mechanism for identifying externalities. Methods of calculating present discounted value tend to discount the future and to underestimate the value of environmental investments (Nordhaus 2013; Stern 2015).

In spite of the appearance of two worlds, financial and real, there is only one earth. For one to grow automatically, the other must shrink. With financial systems capable of compound growth (Harvey 2014, 222–245), the offsetting depletion would also be exponential. Financial incentives are said to improve innovation and productivity but may also deplete environmental resources and distort social systems.

Production with human instruments

Adam Smith's famous text begins with the division of labor as a technique for increasing productivity. This pursuit of increasing output per unit of time has led to a "treadmill" by which companies compete to reduce the working time necessary per unit of commodity production (Postone 1996). Commentators from Karl Marx (1967), the revolutionary thinker, to Alfred Chandler (1977), the prominent business historian, then examined the techniques for increasing productivity. Mechanization, automation, the application of science, and the professionalization of management were all techniques employed in this drive for productivity improvements (Poovey 1998b). From the use of codes to program textile machines, by Babbage, to modern computers and software, there was an attempt to extract knowledge from the skilled worker into management and into the machine itself. Perfection of production techniques led to the discipline of scientific management in the nineteenth century and cybernetics in the twentieth. From merely reducing labor time to eliminating the worker altogether, the human increasingly became an appendage to the machine. Information systems increasingly integrate global production and distribution processes, centralizing management functions in evermore sophisticated software like enterprise resource planning (ERP) (Haigh 2001). Big Data is the new thing in management, and the cloud computer providers are already a tight oligopoly (Amazon, Google, IBM, Microsoft). Artificial intelligence (AI) in current stages of development promises to integrate machine systems over the internet in global production and supply chains (Davis 2018a) to replace the driver in the family sedan, as well as the consumer's own intelligence in the home with automated voices impersonating a friendly assistant.

As is well known, for Smith, the division of labor was the primary principle of market economies, addressed in the opening chapter in the *Wealth of Nations*, as a means of increasing productivity. Smith also viewed "stock" or capital as an instrument of production for reducing labor, increasing productivity, and lowering the price of the commodity. In Book II, in the Introduction and Chapter 1, Smith discusses the types of "stock," including useful machinery (Smith 1994, 299–309).

> In all countries where there is tolerable security, every man of common understanding will endeavor to employ whatever stock he can command, in procuring either present enjoyment or future profit. . . . A man must be perfectly crazy who, where there is tolerable security, does not employ all the stock which he commands.
>
> (Smith 1994, Book II, Chapter 1, 309)

In Book II, Chapter 2, Smith discusses the purpose of machinery or "fixed capital" to increase productivity.

> The intention of fixed capital is to increase the productive powers of labour, or to enable the same number of labourers to perform a much greater quantity of work. . . . The expence which is properly laid out upon a fixed capital of any kind, is always repaid with greater profit, and increases the annual produce by a much greater value than that of the support which such improvements require.
>
> (Smith 1994, Book II, Chapter 2, 311–312)

Marx also discusses the role of productivity in increasing relative surplus value by decreasing the value of necessities, even with the same working day. (Marx 1967, Vol. I, Chapter 12).

> Hence there is immanent in capital an inclination and constant tendency, to heighten the productiveness of labour, in order to cheapen commodities, and by such cheapening to cheapen the labourer himself.
>
> (Marx 1967, Vol. I, Chapter 12, 319)

Mental/manual hierarchy

Western values have consistently ranked mental activity over manual and creative over necessary labor (Brown 2019, 46–50). Ancient Greek philosophers decried the realm of necessity in the *oikos*, inhabited by women, slaves, and children, and preferred the realm of freedom in the polis. Modern neuroscience has identified the mind/body split between higher cognition in the neocortex from instinctual or autonomic responses in the amygdala, a contrast between "thinking fast and slow" (Kahneman 2011).

The relationship of "self-ownership" typical of capitalism, discussed in Chapter 2, can be naturalized by the experience of the mind/body problem, with the conscious mind in control, mastering the instincts and drives of the body. Yet other relationships have been present in other cultures, such as Nietzsche's Apollonian/Dionysian split (Safranski 2002) and Foucault's study of the "care of the self" in ancient Greece. Christian asceticism can be contrasted with early eighteenth-century licentiousness, such as the writings of de Sade and Diderot, again compared with Victorian norms of gender and sexuality.

The separation of mental and manual labor, and relative valuation of mental over manual, was characteristic of workplace organization. What is widely known as "Fordism" is the use of the assembly line and standardized work protocols to reduce the skill levels of the workers and to make them more interchangeable and easier to replace, with lower wages. Famously, Fred Taylor, the developer of "scientific management," used the stop-watch and close observation to find the "one best way" for a given task to be performed. Fine divisions of labor encouraged workers to aspire to the next level in the hierarchy instead of to form solidarity among peers (Gordon, Edwards, and Reich 1982).

As production systems developed, standardized metrics and protocols were necessary to have systems of interchangeable parts (Noble 1977). As management observed and extracted knowledge from the skilled workers, the managers themselves became more professionalized (Chandler 1977). Some of the most notable experiments in regimentation of production were for the military, such as the Harpers Ferry Armory (Smith 1977) and computers in the modern era (Edwards 1996).

Abstraction

The organization of commodity production, based on the metric of productivity, led to the development of categories relevant to increasing output per unit of standard time. Productivity itself, still a ubiquitous indicator, generalizes all output, Q, relative to labor inputs, L, with labor considered as a "homogeneous" factor of production, used by economists as diverse as Marx and Keynes (Slobodian 2018, 107–108). Further, the production of surplus, savings, or profit, depends on reducing the time necessary for the production of wage goods relative to total production time (Davis 2017c). Whether the metric is Marx's relative surplus value or mainstream economics notion of shutdown point (based on maximum average labor productivity or minimum average variable cost), the goal is to increase production beyond consumption to allow for "savings" and investment.

Once increasing productivity can be generated, based on mechanization, automation, improvement of management, or globalization, the increased rate of return can be measured as a return on investment.

Formation of "fictitious" commodities

Both Marx and Polanyi are critical of the use of land, labor, and money as commodities in the capitalist system, yet both see these "fictional" roles as crucial to the operation of the system. These are "reifying abstractions" (Poovey 2002) but real in their effects in the construction and operation of the institutions of capitalism.

While Polanyi traces the institutional changes which support the market (Polanyi 1944; Block and Somers 2014), Marx traces these "moments" when labor and money become commodities. These changes refer to the ways in which money and labor are treated within economic processes, as well as the consciousness of the person, the worker himself.

Labor

In Chapter 6, Marx defines the "capitalist epoch . . . [as] characterized by this, that labour power takes in the eyes of the labourer himself the form of a commodity which is his property; his labour consequently becomes wage-labour. On the other hand, it is only from this moment that the produce of labour universally becomes a commodity" (Marx 1967, Vol. I, Chapter 6, p. 170, fn 2.).

That is, the consciousness of the worker of himself as a commodity is the transition point for the formation of commodities. A change in the self-conception of the worker changes the social understanding of his product as a commodity with "value."

At the end of the discussion of "fetishism of commodities" (Vol. I, Chapter 1, Section 4), Marx notes that exchange value is realized only in exchange, which is a "social process." In contrast to mainstream economics, where it is precisely the act of exchange that is considered to be a "market," a different kind of entity, Marx declares that the process of exchange is social. A difference in perception of the market, as an object rather than a social process, serves to mystify the nature of value.

Marx stresses the legal equality of the buyer and seller of labor power (Vol. I, Chapter 6, p. 168), while also ridiculing the sphere of circulation as the "Eden of the innate rights of man" (Vol. I, Chapter 6, p. 176), compared with the sphere of production. Here in the factory, the owner has the right to organize production and to command labor power which he has purchased as a commodity, with rights to "consume" it productively. As owner of the factory and purchaser of the commodity labor power, the "capitalist" has legal rights to the revenue from the sale of his "own" product.

Even the worker sees the value of this commodity as unrelated to his own effort at the workplace but containing "value" in itself. That is, laws matter and affect the consciousness of the worker.

Money

According to Marx, money is a symbol of the exchange value of commodities (Marx 1967, Vol. I, Chapter 1).

The realisation of a commodity's price, or of its ideal value-form, is therefore at the same time the realisation of the ideal use-value of money; the
conversion of a commodity into money, is the simultaneous conversion
of money into a commodity. The apparently single process is in reality a
double one.

(Marx 1967, Vol. I, Chapter 1, section 2.a, p. 108)

Once money is widely circulated, the person who accumulates money can
assume a new role as "capitalist" once he also finds the commodity labor power
for sale.

In order to be able to extract value from the consumption of a commodity, our friend, Moneybags, must be so lucky as to find, within the sphere
of circulation, in the market, a commodity whose use-value possesses the
peculiar property of being a source of value, whose actual consumption,
therefore, is itself an embodiment of labour, and, consequently, a creation
of value. The possessor of money does find on the market such a special
commodity in capacity for labour, or labour-power.

(Marx 1967, Vol. I, Chapter 6, p. 167)

Leaving the sphere of circulation, "we think we can perceive a change in the
physiognomy of our dramatis personae. He, who before was the money-owner,
now strides in front as capitalist . . . with an air of importance, smirking, intent
on business. (Marx 1967, Vol. I, Chapter 6, 176).

As Wolff (1988) points out, the use of rhetoric here reinforces Marx's point
regarding the critique of the role of the capitalist, here with irony. The role of
capital and labor, usually abstract in the analysis of capital, now take on a personification to emphasize the ways in which human conduct can be influenced
by prescribed roles in various legal and institutional contexts.

Hybrid commodities

The three commodities, land, labor, and money, which are considered "inputs"
into the production process, are "hybrids" (Latour 1993) consisting of both
human and natural resources.

That is, these "commodities" are abstractions consisting of both human and
material elements. Each one of them symbolizes the abstract "value" in motion in
the financial circuits while also having concrete material aspects. The complexity
of these "double" roles has been noted in Marx and Polanyi. Marx considers the
contradiction between use value and exchange value (Marx 1967, Vol. I, Chapter 1, section 3.b., 138), while Polanyi considers the economy as "disembedded"
from and "embedded" in society at once, compared with other types of economic
formation (Block and Somers 2014; Cangiani 2011). The purpose of the exchange
of these commodities is to expand "value," an abstract concept, represented by
money and other "financial assets" which in fact have fluctuating value.

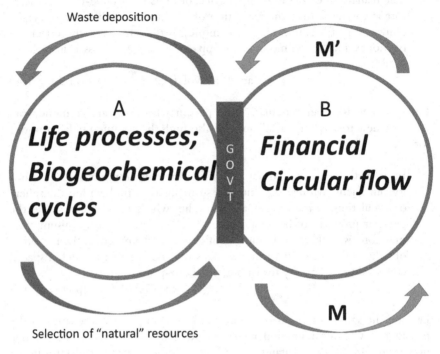

Waste deposition

A

Life processes; Biogeochemical cycles

GOVT

M'

B

Financial Circular flow

M

Selection of "natural" resources

Figure 5.2 The Role of Government

The peculiarity of considering labor power as a commodity is that it is both true and not true. The person himself sees himself as having "value" according to the expected wage or salary and competing to gain recognition from a higher salary (Frank and Cook 1995). The objective expression of that personal value is maintained by image (fashion) and consumer durables like jewelry and homes which are purposely made visible to the "gaze" of the "other" (Goffman 1959). Smith's "impartial spectator" gives some insight into the view of the person of himself, which is validated by "conspicuous consumption" (Veblen 1934; Galbraith 1958; Howell 2010; McKendrick, Brewer, and Plumb 1982). That is, consumerism is how the person knows and expresses his own "value." The typical member of the bourgeoisie plans for a lifetime to improve employment prospects, investing in "human capital" (Becker 1981; Bourdieu 1984). Yet whatever success there is seems ephemeral, always at risk, given the inevitability of fluctuating values in a complex market economy.

This is one of the paradoxes of capitalism, where "value" is represented in material form which has other uses, but the value of which can also fluctuate. The attempt to "fix" value in material objects can never succeed as a permanent store of value, since capitalism by nature is subject to flux and change. Both Marx and Smith consider "fictitious credit" as promising value in the future, which cannot be known with certainty in the present. In a sense, this notion of "fiction" can apply to all symbolic representations of value, in language or objects. Value is the outcome of exchange along financial circuits, which is subject to the operation of the entire social system, which is always changing.

These commodities, land, labor, and money, have "value" based on the human projection of use value and exchange value. Use value depends on the physical characteristics of the object, and exchange value depends on the market value in exchange at a given moment. The presence of two types of value at once introduces a duality, always in potential conflict. The human subject at the center of these projections of value becomes lost in the omnipresence of the market as the apparent source of "objective" value. The subject is invisible in the apparent universal objectivity of the "real" world. As in Marx's ironic discussion of the "fetishism of commodities," it is as though the commodities whisper to each other about their relative values, all the while not revealing the secret "social" substance that they all have in common, being the product of living labor (Marx 1967, Vol. I, Chapter 1 section 4).

The role of the household

If the role of living labor in the production of value is invisible, then even more so is the origin of that living labor in the household. Rather than reveal the dependence of the capitalist system on living labor for the production of value and surplus value, the production of living labor is rendered "dependent" on the wage laborer and his "family wage" and the market.

Marx places great emphasis on the concept of "self-ownership" of the commodity labor power, in which the worker offers himself for sale in return for a wage. Marx also mentions the household, where labor is reproduced on a daily and generational basis. Part of the "responsibility" of self-ownership is provision for one's own reproduction. In contrast to slavery, the cost of reproduction is the worker's own responsibility, not the owner of the factory, and not the employer of labor power.

As Marx elaborates in Chapter 6, Vol. I,

> The owner of labour-power is mortal . . . the seller of labour-power must perpetuate himself . . . by procreation. . . . Hence the sum of the means of subsistence necessary for the production of labour-power must include the means necessary for the labourer's substitutes (i.e. his children).
>
> (Marx 1967, Vol. I, Chapter 6, 171–172)

The extent to which reproduction of the worker is aided by the state is a result of political alliances, not the exchange of equivalents which is characteristic of capitalism (Davis 2004).

The category of "gender" is relevant to the issue of reproduction of the labor force. In the historical evolution of capitalism, the differentiation of gender roles becomes more polarized, as production is removed from the household and centralized in factories. There is a large literature documenting the evolution of gender norms, associated with female bodies, coincident with the expansion of the wage labor market (see, for example, Scott 1986; Davis 2017a). To briefly summarize a long and complex history, in peasant household reproduction, women and men were both involved in cooperative production of necessities for use. With the emergence of wage labor, gender roles became more specific, assigning women to the household and men to the labor force. While this pattern is also affected by class, norms for women's proper role become more explicit, with women assigned to the "private sphere," with norms considered "feminine." Historically, women were the first wage laborers in factories, replaced by men and immigrants in the early nineteenth century. As women's labor force participation continued to expand in the twentieth century, especially after World War II (Goldin 2006), these gender norms were increasingly challenged, with the second wave of the women's movement, for example, and the domestic labor debate. To the extent that women identify with "feminine" gender roles, nonetheless, the provision of reproductive services is free, or certainly less costly, accomplished by the production of use values in the private sphere.

Historically, women were agents in defining, performing, as well as challenging their proper roles. These articulations were important in influencing organizational forms and political impact. For example, Mary Wollstonecraft claimed the rights of women as "equal" in the early years of the French Revolution. Women were active advocates for equality in the abolition movement in the nineteenth century and the civil rights movement in the twentieth century. In the women's suffrage movement, women often claimed special knowledge as mothers (Koven and Michel 1993). In twentieth-century movements, women have claimed ownership of their own bodies to establish reproductive rights, as expressed in Roe v. Wade. In the domestic labor debate, women have claimed the importance of their indirect contributions to profit, which are not fully accounted for in either Marx or mainstream economic methodology. In the contemporary period, women challenge the linguistic referents, such as marital status (from the title "Mrs." to "Ms.") and the gender pronouns, help to rewrite marriage laws, confront compulsive heteronormativity, and resist sexual coercion in the #MeToo movement. On the other hand, women also form oppositional groups which represent "family values" and the "right to life."

Finance and automatic rate of return

Money became reified as a symbol representing the worker, the debtor, and the taxpayer, all important roles in modern economies. The use of money advanced to purchase materials and labor, to organize production, and to collect revenue from the sale of the product can be conceptualized as a financial circuit. From Aristotle and Marx, the circuit, $M - C - M'$, represented the possibility of making more money, M', from borrowed money, M, directed towards trade and production of the commodity, C. That is, the worker as a commodity labor power can be purchased for an amount of money, the wage, less than the value he creates during the working day, M'. The commodity labor power produces more value than he consumes. This is expressed by price mark-up over unit labor costs, at the micro level, and labor share at the macro level (Davis 2017d). Wages can be above or below subsistence, depending on the location in the labor hierarchy and degree of competition for employment.

Money lending then became profitable, and a separate financial sector became differentiated from production. The Bank of England, founded in 1694 as a merchant monopoly corporation, acquired public functions by the mid-nineteenth century. Given the time-based system, there was an imperative to make ever greater financial returns from any given project per unit of time, resulting in competition among the lenders and borrowers, extending credit, and an increasing rate of financial turnover. The expansion of finance has resulted in a global system, integrating producers, consumers, and nation-states. Lenders require a given rate of return from borrowers, and in this way money seems to expand by itself automatically. These financial relationships, based on human producers and consumers, appear automatic (Davis 2017d).

Because the financial circuit can provide necessities and luxuries, and appears to grow by itself, it seems to be a self-contained alternate reality. What we know as the circular flow economy is essentially exchange between the household and the firm, after splitting production from consumption, the worker from her product. This exchange is based on legally defined individual private property

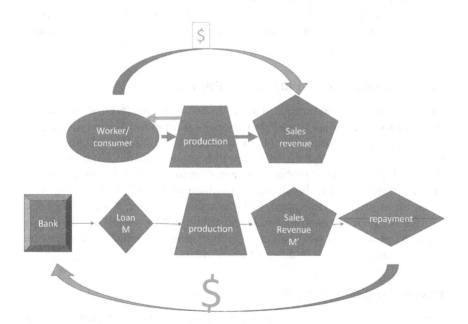

Figure 5.3 Financial Circuits

(Davis 2015a), defined in terms of parcelization of the earth, excluding the so-called externalities of human and ecological reproduction. Within its own terms, nonetheless, the financial system is vulnerable to over extension of credit and self-fulfilling bubbles, requiring periodic public backstop. For Polanyi (1944), the role of the central bank belies the myth of the "self-regulating" market. Further, economic financial models assume infinite time, and the models of calculating present discounted value tend to over-value the present and to "discount" the future. The circular financial flow of the economy abstracts from material and life-generating processes, which are presumably embedded in the abstract equations modeled on physics that connote absolute precision. Economic models are linear instead of truly "circular" including waste (McDonough and Braungart 2013), with no account of the costs of disposal. That is, there is a "circular flow" of the financial economy but not of physical or biological processes. Yet these self-referential global financial models would presume to encompass the earth. Ultimately the financial system based merely on quantitative expansion of M − M' is relatively meaningless, and the concentration of finance leads to excessive political power (Lessig 2018).

The operational requirement of the automatic expansion of money has led to financialization (Davis 2017d) in place of real investment. With increasing concentration of markets and income, there is an increasing ossification of the economy, with less resilience and more governmental support of "too big to fail" companies and banks. Instead of real productive investment, there is "accumulation by dispossession," by such means as privatization of existing assets (Harvey 2010). The financial system is focused on the production of "safe assets" instead of distributing the risk of innovation, much like a rentier economy (Davis 2018b). One outcome is the increasing number and size of financial crises.

Mass consumption and identity politics

Faced with impersonal bureaucracies of the state and the corporation, there is an effort to differentiate oneself in personal consumption, the presumed private sphere. With a cornucopia of consumer choices available, individuals tend to choose consumer styles to identify with some preferred group or image (Davis 2011), while the number of potential personae tends to multiply. Measures of health and well-being are diminishing in the US, nonetheless, with a culture of instant gratification, hedonism, and addiction. Rather than see a conflict between "recognition" and "redistribution" (Fraser 2013, 175–186), it is possible that neither work nor consumption offers meaningful rewards, while incomes stagnate for the middle and lower classes.

Reversal of life and death

There is a value system inherent in capitalism, identified in Smith as well as Marx, which values death over life. This leads to a relatively low valuation and investment in human reproduction and a tendency to deplete the human and ecological resources on which the system depends, or "autophagy."

Smith's "invisible hand"

With the goal of productivity among firms and the formalization of the state, many institutional settings in modern industrial economies are characterized by bureaucracy. As individuals are inducted to specific institutional roles, they are prescribed to perform certain actions, like the precision of double-entry book-keeping (Poovey 1998a, 33–65). The system as a whole enforces certain outcomes beyond the individual's control (Searle 2010). Sometimes celebrated as "market forces," the "invisible hand" can also be likened to a shroud (Rothschild 2001; Baucom 2005; Vogl 2015; Wennerlind 2011; perhaps "value" is Marx's version of the ghostly "invisible hand" capable of autonomous movement).

The economy can be imagined as a "machine" (Wilson 1998, 42) because individuals have relinquished their agency to become "objects for sale." Money enables the individual to express the most refined and distinctive preferences as a consumer, while objectifying others into prescribed roles as producers and then empowering each individual to reverse these roles. The worker is paid a money wage instead of control over his product, with which he can purchase any other commodities but in limited quantity. The mortal individual can "spend" her life working and saving with the promise of "perpetual" assets produced by the financial system and the state.

Marx

Marx makes much of the reversal of living and dead in *Capital*. Value is produced only by living labor, and machines only transmit value when used in production (like depreciation) (Marx 1967, Vol. I, Chapter 7, Section 1, 183; Section 2, 195; Chapter 11, 310). This value is only realized when sold to (living) consumers.

But there is a reversal with commodity fetishism (Davis 2017d). Workers believe that the commodities are valuable in themselves, not due to their own involvement in the production process. The population considers money as valuable in itself and able to grow automatically over time.

Machines certainly contribute to enhanced productivity, as noted by both Smith and Marx. But as mechanization develops, the worker is more like an appendage to the machine. The machine keeps the pace of the production process, as with the assembly line. In the factory, the machine is the most obvious presence, filling the entire space, increasingly as production is automated. Knowledge of the production process is no longer on the shop floor, with skilled workers, but embedded in the software of the machine. Ultimately machines can be produced by machines in the capital goods sector manifesting the peripheral role of living labor. Increasingly even intelligence can be automated, with the development of "artificial intelligence," or AI.

The living worker is dominated by "dead" labor, embedded in the machine and the knowledge extracted from the production process, or separately organized research and development by the corporation. The most highly remunerated occupational categories are management, engineering, and finance rather than human reproduction or agricultural production or conservation. There is a clear color-coded hierarchy of pay, with white collars receiving more than blue or pink. The household does not produce value at all, according to both mainstream and heterodox accounting systems (Davis 2017a).

The so-called "monopoly" of the ownership of the means of production is the institutional leverage over the labor force by employers, who can treat the employment of workers as contingent on profitability, an abstract category with no apparent connection to their own contribution to the production process.

The workers are treated as objects, and the commodities and money are treated as valuable, manifesting a complete reversal of the human, with the priority of the "dead" over the "living." At the end of the long chapter on machinery in Volume One of *Capital*, Marx notes that mechanization can increase the production of relative surplus value, but the ultimate source of wealth is humans and the soil.

> Capitalist production, therefore, develops technology, and the combining together of various processes into a social whole, only by sapping the original sources of all wealth – the soil and the labourer.
>
> (Marx, *Capital*. 1967, Vol. I, Chapter 15
> "Machinery and Modern Industry," Section 10, p. 507)

That is, the system which appears automatic, to grow by itself, actually depletes its true sources of wealth, the population and nature (Moore 2015; Slobodian 2018, 16). This can be called a form of "autophagy," or feeding on itself.

Repeal of the "right to live"

Wage labor is assumed to be voluntary and efficient in mainstream economics. Yet historic evidence is documented by Marx (1967, Vol. I, Ch. 6, 167–176) and Polanyi (1944) regarding the repeal of the "right to live," with the end of the parish welfare system in early modern England and the Poor Law Reform of 1834. With wage labor as the primary means of earning access to subsistence, labor force participation can be viewed as "coerced," as a form of discipline (Davis 2015b). In this way, the true motor of the abstract market system is the human desire for life, made contingent by the separation of the worker from his product and means of subsistence. The "invisible hand" is the human survival instinct, channeled into repetitive institutional processes like a machine. Instead of "invisible," perhaps this normalized routine threat to human existence is unspeakable. With a rhetorical flourish, Polanyi's "prod of hunger" becomes market "incentives."

"Biopolitics"

Foucault also discusses the role of life and death in modern economies, with a more productive focus on life. Rather than legal or juristic views, he emphasizes the incitement of sexuality as a relation of power. This applies to the individual body and to the population as a whole, with such techniques as "confession" to the church and to the couch, as well as the channeling of desire by such structural features as the incest taboo. The focus on education and health in modern economies is one version of enhancing the quality of life as an incentive, as a means to improve "governmentality" (Foucault 1978, 1991).

Energy

Economics does not address the need for energy in order to achieve continuous production (West 2017). With increasing productivity, there is an increasing accumulation of physical output, which continually degrades into waste. Contrary to the assumptions of mainstream economics, there is a cost to waste disposal.

Initially powered by living labor (animal and human) and hydro power, there was an increasing use of preserved energy is the extensive use of fossil fuels in industrialization, first coal and then petroleum. These fuels enabled the continuous flow of production, with liquid chemical processes and then with flows of electrons, or electricity; that is, the material characteristics of some substances actually improved on the smooth flow of labor time. These innovations made production more susceptible to control. For example, striking coal miners were replaced with automated oil pipelines, and the governance of entire countries was affected to maintain a stable oil supply (Citino 2010). Flows of global credit were assured by collateral based on oil production and reserves, supported by arms sales to stabilize allied governments (Mitchell 2009). When evidence mounted regarding the impact of CO_2 emissions on global warming, these scientific results were denied (Oreskes and Conway 2010, 295–307), and the fossil fuel industry initiated a concerted campaign to alter the operation of US democratic processes (Mayer 2016). The improved technology of renewable energy, especially solar, threatens the leverage of the oligopolistic energy corporations and states, as these resources are in fact already widely distributed globally, as the sun rises and sets.

Recovery of agency with the public/private divide

Citizenship represents the individual in the state, who may otherwise relinquish agency as a worker.

To allow for agency, there is a separation of state from market, a public/private divide, as discussed in Chapter 3, and a presumed system of checks and balances. An expanded view of the "social contract" of market economies is to submit to market discipline in return for the availability of cheaper commodities

and a quest for upward mobility. While the individual is subsumed in performing according to market requirements, each citizen is presumably represented
in the state apparatus, where agency is recovered. But separation of powers in
the structure of the state reduces the direct impact of the voter (Polanyi 1944,
225–226), even without voter suppression and electoral fraud.

The post-human future

In popular science fiction, as well as academic analysis, it is increasingly possible
to imagine a production process entirely without humans. That future process
could be performed by a combined integration of computer and person (Brynjolfsson and McAfee 2014) or a new form of machine/person like "cyborgs"
(Haraway 1991). Because of the capitalist economic imperative for productivity
improvements, in the workplace and in the military, there is a long-term bias
towards labor-saving technological change; that is, towards increasing automation. As a result, there is a direction to invention that may not benefit humankind more generally, but instead will focus on productivity and profitability.
Such objectives as public health and education, and assurance of minimal standards of nutrition, are feasible (Jasanoff 2016) but have a low priority.

Nietzsche's notion of the "last man" was based on presumed mediocrity
(Fukuyama 1992), but the relative disappearance of humans from production
persists in a culture that claims individual freedom. In contrast to this inexorable
replacement of the human in the operation and conception of the economy,
alternatively there could be a shift in economics, philosophy, and social science away from the productivity imperative and the purported anthropocen-
tric goals of material wealth and consumer satisfaction. The natural law origin
stories assumed that the earth was created for human and for human preservation rather than respect for its life processes. Rather than the objectifying
stance of modern science and social science (Nelson 1996), we could develop a
common perspective of life on earth, such as shared metabolic processes across
species, which are remarkably sensitive to temperature (West 2017, 174–177,
236–245). Rather than forms of "consumption" which actually degrade life on
earth, there could be an appreciation of the true sources of wealth (Schor 2010)
with new forms of community and sustainability (Davis 2017b).

Conclusion

The value system inherent in capitalism, to prioritize "dead" capital over living
labor, is ultimately self-defeating. The human will for survival is the ultimate
motor of the economy, made contingent by "economic incentives." This prod
behind the "invisible hand" is unspoken in an economy which celebrates trans-
parency, rationality, and publicity, perhaps unspeakable. The term "autophagy," or
self-consumption, could be used to describe this phenomenon. Capitalism consumes its workers in the process of production but does not adequately provide
for or reward the re-production of the labor force or sustainable investments in

ecology. Rather, the need for labor discipline requires the impoverishment of humans in terms of health and education and other improvements in human capabilities, a neglect which can contribute to political instability.

In the capitalist system, money "grows" by hijacking the methods of reproduction of plants, animals, and humans, the regeneration of all living things which is redirected to the financial circuits of capital. The technology for such transposition, such as domestication, breeding, and genetic modification, is becoming more sophisticated. The replacement of living animal and human labor by fossil fuel accelerates this process, such that the living conditions for species on earth are subverted. Ironically, climate change, from the replacement of living labor with fossil fuels, threatens the stability and permanence of the original meaning of "property" in land. Such a system is only sustainable with globalization in a labor surplus economy, always seeking new frontiers, leaving behind despoiled wastelands in its wake.

Bibliography

Baucom, Ian. *Specters of the Atlantic: Finance Capital, Slavery, and the Philosophy of History*. Durham, NC: Duke University Press, 2005.

Becker, Gary S. *A Treatise on the Family*. Cambridge, MA: Harvard University Press, 1981.

Block, Fred L. and Margaret R. Somers. *The Power of Market Fundamentalism: Karl Polanyi's Critique*. Cambridge, MA: Harvard University Press, 2014.

Bourdieu, Pierre. *Distinction: A Social Critique of the Judgement of Taste*. Cambridge, MA: Harvard University Press, 1984.

Brown, Wendy. *In the Ruins of Neoliberalism: The Rise of Antidemocratic Politics in the West*. New York: Columbia University Press, 2019.

Brynjolfsson, Erik and Andrew McAfee. *The Second Machine Age: Work, Progress, and Prosperity in an Age of Brilliant Machines*. New York: W.W. Norton & Company, 2014.

Calhoun, Craig J. *Nations Matter: Culture, History, and the Cosmopolitan Dream*. New York: Routledge, 2007.

Cangiani, Michele. "Karl Polanyi's Institutional Theory: Market Society and Its 'Disembedded' Economy." *Journal of Economic Issues*, Vol. 45, No. 1, March 2011, 177–197.

Chandler, Alfred D. Jr. *The Visible Hand: The Managerial Revolution in American Business*. Cambridge, MA: Harvard University Press, 1977.

Citino, Nathan J. "Internationalist Oilmen, the Middle East, and the Remaking of American Liberalism, 1945–1953," *The Business History Review*, Vol. 84, No. 2, Summer 2010, 227–251.

Cook, Eli. *The Pricing of Progress: Economic Indicators and the Capitalization of American Life*. Cambridge, MA: Harvard University Press, 2017.

Davis, Ann E. "(De)Constructing Dependency: Institutional, Historical Perspectives of Welfare," *Review of Radical Political Economics*, Vol. 36, No. 1, Winter 2004, 37–51.

Davis, Ann E. "The New 'Voodoo Economics': Fetishism and the Public/Private Divide," *Review of Radical Political Economics*, Vol. 45, No. 1, March 2013, 42–58.

Davis, Ann E. *The Evolution of the Property Relation: Understanding Paradigms, Debates, Prospects*. New York: Palgrave MacMillan, 2015a.

Davis, Ann E. "The Process of Provisioning: The Halter for the Workhorse," *Journal of Economic Issues*, Vol. XLIX, No. 2, June 2015b, 449–457.

Davis, Ann E. "Paradoxical Positions: The Methodological Contributions of Feminist Scholarship," *Cambridge Journal of Economics*, Vol. 41, No. 1, 2017a, 181–201.

Davis, Ann E. "The Practical Utopia of Ecological Community," in Richard Westra, Robert Albritton, and Seongjin Jeong (eds.), *Varieties of Alternative Economic Systems: Practical Utopias for an Age of Global Crisis and Austerity*. New York: Routledge, 2017b, 52–70.

Davis, Ann E. *Money as a Social Institution: The Institutional Development of Capitalism*. New York: Routledge, 2017c.

Davis, Ann E. "Fetishism and Financialization," *Review of Radical Political Economics*, Vol. 49, No. 4, December 2017d, 551–558.

Davis, Ann E. "Global Production Networks and the Private Organization of World Trade," *Journal of Economic Issues*, Vol. 52, No. 2, June 2018a, 358–367.

Davis, Ann E. "The New Triffin Dilemma," *Review of Radical Political Economics*, Vol. 50, No. 4, December 2018b, 691–698.

Davis, John B. *Individuals and Identity in Economics*. New York: Cambridge University Press, 2011.

Dincecco, Mark and Massimiliano G. Onorato. *From Warfare to Wealth: The Military Origins of Urban Prosperity in Europe*. New York: Cambridge University Press, 2018.

Edwards, Paul N. *The Closed World: Computers and the Politics of Discourse in Cold War America*. Cambridge, MA: MIT Press, 1996.

Ferber, Marianne A. and Julie A. Nelson (eds.). *Beyond Economic Man: Feminist theory and Economics*. Chicago: University of Chicago Press, 1993.

Foucault, Michel. *History of Sexuality. Volume I: An Introduction*. New York: Pantheon Books, 1978.

Foucault, Michel. "Governmentality," in Graham Burchell, Colin Gordon, and Peter Miller (eds.), *The Foucault Effect: Studies in Governmentality*. Chicago: University of Chicago Press, 1991, 87–104.

Frank, Robert H. and Philip J. Cook. *The Winner-Take-All Society*. New York: Free Press, 1995.

Fraser, Nancy. *Fortunes of Feminism: From State-Managed Capitalism to Neoliberal Crisis*. New York: Verso, 2013.

Fukuyama, Francis. *The End of History and the Last Man*. New York: The Free Press, 1992.

Galbraith, John Kenneth. *The Affluent Society*. Boston: Houghton Mifflin, 1958.

Gauthier, David. "No Need for Morality: The Case of the Competitive Market," *Philosophic Exchange*, Vol. 13, No. 1, Summer 1982, article 2, 41–54.

Goffman, Erving. *Presentation of Self in Everyday Life*. Garden City, NY: Double Day, 1959.

Goldin, Claudia. "The Quiet Revolution That Transformed Women's Employment, Education, and Family," *American Economic Review*, Vol. 96, No. 2, 2006, 1–21.

Gordon, David M., Richard Edwards, and Michael Reich. *Segmented Work, Divided Workers: The Historical Transformation of Labor in the United States*. New York: Cambridge University Press, 1982.

Haigh, Thomas. "Inventing Information Systems: The Systems Men and the Computer, 1950–1968," *The Business History Review*, Vol. 75, No. 1, 2001, 15–61.

Haraway, Donna J. *Simians, Cyborgs, and Women: The Reinvention of Nature*. New York: Routledge, 1991.

Harvey, David. *The Enigma of Capital and the Crises of Capitalism*. New York: Oxford University Press, 2010.

Harvey, David. *Seventeen Contradictions and the End of Capitalism*. New York: Oxford University Press, 2014.

Hayek, Friedrich A. von. *The Road to Serfdom*. Chicago: University of Chicago Press, 1945.

Hodgson, Geoffrey M. *Conceptualizing Capitalism: Institutions, Evolution, Future.* Chicago: University of Chicago Press, 2015.

Howell, Martha C. *Commerce Before Capitalism in Europe 1300–1600.* New York: Cambridge University Press, 2010.

Jasanoff, Sheila. *The Ethics of Invention: Technology and the Human Future.* New York: W.W. Norton & Company, 2016.

Kahneman, Daniel. *Thinking, Fast and Slow.* New York: Farrar, Straus, and Giroux, 2011.

Koven, Seth and Sonya Michel (eds.). *Mothers of a New World: Maternalist Politics and the Origins of Welfare States.* New York: Routledge, 1993.

Latour, Bruno. *We Have Never Been Modern.* Cambridge, MA: Harvard University Press, 1993.

Lessig, Lawrence. *America, Compromised.* Chicago: University of Chicago Press, 2018.

Marx, Karl. *Capital.* New York: International Publishers, 1967.

Mayer, Jane. *Dark Money: The Hidden History of the Billionaires Behind the Rise of the Radical Right.* New York: Doubleday, 2016.

McDonough, William and Michael Braungart. *The Upcycle: Beyond Sustainability – Designing for Abundance.* New York: North Point Press, 2013.

McKendrick, Neil, John Brewer, and J. H. Plumb. *The Birth of the Consumer Society: The Commercialization of Eighteenth Century England.* Bloomington: Indiana University Press, 1982.

Mirowski, Philip. *Machine Dreams: Economics Becomes a Cyborg Science.* New York: Cambridge University Press, 2002.

Mitchell, Timothy. "Carbon Democracy," *Economy and Society,* Vol. 38, No. 3, 2009, 399–432.

Mitchell, Timothy. "Economentality: How the Future Entered Government," *Critical Inquiry,* Vol. 40, Summer 2014, 479–507.

Moore, Jason W. *Capitalism in the Web of Life: Ecology and the Accumulation of Capital.* London: Verso, 2015.

Nelson, Julie A. *Feminism, Objectivity and Economics.* New York: Routledge, 1996.

Nelson, Julie A. *Economics for Humans.* Chicago: University of Chicago Press, 2006.

Noble, David F. *American By Design: Science, Technology and the Rise of Corporate Capitalism.* New York: Alfred A. Knopf, 1977.

Nordhaus, William D. *The Climate Casino: Risk, Uncertainty, and Economics for a Warming World.* New Haven: Yale University Press, 2013.

Oreskes, Naomi and Erik M. Conway. *Merchants of Doubt: How a Handful of Scientists Obscured the Truth on Issues from Tobacco Smoke to Global Warming.* New York: Bloomsbury Press, 2010.

Pistor, Katharina. *The Code of Capital: How the Law Creates Wealth and Inequality.* Princeton, NJ: Princeton University Press, 2019.

Pocock, J. G. A. *Machiavellian Moment: Florentine Political Thought and the Atlantic Republican Tradition.* Princeton, NJ: Princeton University Press, 1975.

Polanyi, Karl. *The Great Transformation.* Boston: Beacon Press, 1944.

Poovey, Mary. *A History of the Modern Fact: Problems of Knowledge in the Sciences of Wealth and Society.* Chicago: University of Chicago Press, 1998a.

Poovey, Mary. "The Production of Abstract Space," in Susan Hardy Aiken, Ann Brigham, Sallie A. Marston, and Penny Waterstone (eds.), *Making Worlds: Gender, Metaphor, Materiality.* Tucson: The University of Arizona Press, 1998b, 69–89.

Poovey, Mary. "The Liberal Civil Subject and the Social in Eighteenth-Century British Moral Philosophy," *Public Culture,* Vol. 14, No. 1, 2002, 125–145.

Poovey, Mary. *Genres of the Credit Economy: Mediating Value in Eighteenth-and Nineteenth-Century Britain.* Chicago: University of Chicago Press, 2008.

Postone, Moishe. *Time, Labor, and Social Domination: A Reinterpretation of Marx's Critical Theory.* New York: Cambridge University Press, 1996.

Rothschild, Emma. *Economic Sentiments: Adam Smith, Condorcet, and the Enlightenment.* Cambridge, MA: Harvard University Press, 2001.

Safranski, Rudiger. *Nietzsche: A Philosophical Biography.* New York: W.W. Norton & Company, 2002.

Schor, Juliet B. *Plenitude: The New Economics of True Wealth.* New York: Penguin Press, 2010.

Scott, Joan W. "Gender: A Useful Category of Historical Analysis," *American Historical Review,* Vol. 91, No. 5, December 1986, 1053–1075.

Searle, John R. *Making the Social World: The Structure of Human Civilization.* New York: Oxford University Press, 2010.

Slobodian, Quinn. *Globalists: The End of Empire and the Birth of Neoliberalism.* Cambridge, MA: Harvard University Press, 2018.

Smith, Adam. *An Inquiry into the Nature and Causes of the Wealth of Nations.* New York: Modern Library, 1994.

Smith, Merritt Roe. *Harpers Ferry Armory and the New Technology: The Challenge of Change.* Ithaca, NY: Cornell University Press, 1977.

Stern, Nicholas H. *Why Are We Waiting? The Logic, Urgency, and the Promise of Tackling Climate Change.* Cambridge, MA: MIT Press, 2015.

Stiglitz, Joseph E., Amartya Sen, and Jean-Paul Fitoussi. *Mismeasuring Our Lives: Why GDP Doesn't Add Up: The Report. Commission on the Measurement of Economic Performance and Social Progress.* New York: New Press, 2010.

Temin, Peter. "Finance in Economic Growth: Eating the Family Cow," INET Working Paper No. 86, December 17, 2018.

Veblen, Thorstein. *Theory of the Leisure Class. An Economic Study of Institutions.* New York: Modern Library, 1934.

Vogl, Joseph. *The Specter of Capital.* Stanford, CA: Stanford University Press, 2015.

Weber, Max. *The Protestant Ethic and the Spirit of Capitalism.* New York: Scribner, 1930.

Wennerlind, Carl. *Casualties of Credit: The English Financial Revolution, 1620–1720.* Cambridge, MA: Harvard University Press, 2011.

West, Geoffrey. *Scale: The Universal Laws of Life, Growth, and Death in Organisms, Cities, and Companies.* New York: Penguin, 2017.

Wilson, Edward O. *Consilience: The Unity of Knowledge.* New York: Alfred A. Knopf, 1998.

Wolff, Robert Paul. *Moneybags Must Be So Lucky: On the Literary Structure of Capital.* Amherst, MA: University of Massachusetts Press, 1988.

6   Methods of social science

Social science methods

It is possible that social science methodology reflects the major paradigms of a given period of history (Sewell 2008). If so, this relationship is important to take into account in such methodologies for a more comprehensive and critical perspective. This awareness of periodization may be termed a form of "reflexivity." Such reflexivity would involve understanding the particular period of history, the distinct methods of social science, and one's personal relationship to both, as illustrated by recent work (Eley 2005).

"Objectivity" in social science

One example of the rise of certain standards in knowledge production is the emergence of the criterion of "objectivity" is social science. The reification of key categories like "the individual" and "property," as discussed in earlier chapters, is pervasive in modern social science (Daston and Galison 2007; Davis 2019; Poovey 2002). The use of abstractions to refer to social institutions helps to reinforce the "solidity" and "permanence" of those social institutions and to make them appropriate, discreet objects of study (Sewell 1980, 143–144). In this guise, the social scientist is not also a part of the object of study, or "society." And yet the production of the social science model of society may influence the operation of that model by shaping expectations and behavior of those "individuals" whose actions constitute the model/society. The importance of "objectivity" in scientific methods also reinforces the scientific "voice," which is "a view from nowhere," (Nagel 1986; Bourdieu 2004, 115–116), disembodied, yet omniscient, to replace the dethroned deity of the pre-modern period. This may also be the merchant's view of the world, always scanning for objects, any object that can be sold for a higher price than it cost. Such a world view creates "property" as an object for sale by seeing all objects as potential commodities. This objective standpoint of the scientist and social scientist then naturalizes and legitimates the view of humans and nature as instruments for human utility and wealth.

This stance of objectivity removes the use of first-person plural, either the dyad (Taylor 1989, 2016) or the exhortation (Marx 1967), by the social scientist. The so-called dichotomy of agent/structure is a result of the choice of objective voice, which distances the social scientist from the population, as an object. Such abstraction and objectivity reinforce the status quo and discourage reflection outside the norms and habits of the present. These reified social objects of study then provide a means for managing time, by the assumption of stable, static social institutions, like "the market," over infinite time. That is, reification helps to remove the influence of time on social science categories, like the "perpetual" market of economists.

The standpoint of the social scientists treats "society" as an object. In turn, this is an internalization of the relationship of "property in the person," a characteristic of capitalism (Pateman 1988; MacPherson 1962). That is, the commodity "labor power" is a person, an abstract object which can be owned by himself and his employer. This scientific stance mirrors and legitimates the objectification of persons with the aura of "progress" and improvement. The social scientist's mission is to promote happiness, a common goal of economists' "utility." Sewell, like Taylor, understands that the economy operates "behind the backs" of economic agents (Sewell 2005, 353), which is endorsed if this market mechanism brings about progress (Searle 2010). Whether these market mechanisms can be known and consciously managed is a matter of debate between theorists, such as Lange vs. Hayek in the socialist calculation debate, for example (Davies 2015).

The formulation of "society" as an object constitutes the social scientist as "objective" observer, a modern standpoint which is outside that object. This contrasts with the "corporatist" standpoint in which the person is a member of a collective and conscious of that collective while also participating in it, with rights to make decisions and to be recognized as a member. This direct participation in a collective entity, like a guild or commune, is contrasted with indirect representation. One example is the formulation of suffrage rules in the constitutional provisions of the liberal nation-state by collective deliberation. These rules provide a transition from the corporate consciousness of the *ancien regime* to the new individual citizen represented in the liberal nation-state. These criteria for "citizenship" determine who counts in future deliberations and establish *categories* of eligibility. These categories are then applied objectively by bureaucratic procedures, a type of fairness and impersonality (North, Wallis, and Weingast 2009; Weber 1978). The objective standpoint of the modern social scientist then mirrors and legitimates the treatment of the other as a category, or object, which is pervasive in the wage labor relationship of modern capitalism. The ability to understand and analyze such "reifying abstractions" then becomes the "modern" world view and role for modern professionals, who stand outside any conflict in the society to play the role of analysts, problem solvers, and policy-makers.

Such a transition can be observed historically in mid- to late-nineteenth-century Germany (Beck 1995), when social science and its methods were being developed, a new nation-state was emerging, and the modern "welfare" state was being instituted amid the active suppression of socialism. The rise of objective professionals also served to resolve the widespread unrest in the late-nineteenth-century, and to undergird the role of the Progressive movement in the US (McGerr 1986, 2003).

Abstract, ahistorical social science enabled its practitioners to avoid moral questions like the "social problem." This explicit feature of methodology was debated by Schmoller, a member of the German Historical School, and Carl Menger, a founder of the Austrian School, in the latter half of the nineteenth century (Grimmer-Solem 2003, 248–260; Milonakis and Fine 2009, 101–115). Menger made "a sharp distinction between economic theory and history," positing that "the axioms of praxeology were a priori true and were not subject to refutation by empirical test" (Slobodian 2018, 5). At a time when the use of coercive power of the state and censorship was widespread, the use of abstract categories avoided any mention of the domination of labor as an inherent part of the nature of capitalism (Hodgson 2015; Pateman 1988). The firm could remain a "black box" and the market mechanism merely a "machine."

Openings

There is a recent debate regarding methodologies in the social sciences, which provides an opening to dialogue and consideration.

Debate on methodologies

The series of forums on methodology in the *American Historical Review* in special issues (Volume 113, No. 2, April 2008, 391–437 and Volume 117, No. 3, June 2012, 698–813) reflect the debate among professional historians with regard to method. The first forum discussed the "turn" from social history to "cultural" history, including the "linguistic turn." The second proceeded to discuss the phenomena of "turns" themselves, and potential new ones such as "material," "affective," and "environmental" turns. This process of reflection encourages debate on the profession of history itself, and its practices, and whether always for academic audiences or also influencing public discourse.

To me, this degree of reflexivity is instructive. The profession of history provides insights into the present and the possibility of critique from alternative perspectives. That is, rather than perpetual concepts, which are defended from change by reification, historical methods can serve to document changing meanings and institutions, as well as comparative analysis or periodization and "genealogy." Whether there is a direction to history, such as a teleology of "progress," and whether the present emerges from the past, as in "path dependence," the emergence and evolution of institutional forms are important considerations.

First-person plural

Academic discourse tends to be in third person, with an "objective" voice. A recent exception to this pattern is work by Judith Butler (2015).

> We can make this into a broad existential claim, namely, that everyone is precarious, and this follows from our social existence as bodily beings who depend upon one another for shelter and sustenance and who, therefore, are at risk of statelessness, homelessness, and destitution under unjust and unequal political conditions.
>
> (Butler 2015, 118)

In discussing public assembly, she notes that bodies are present in public space, in their concrete material form, communicating a message, whether spoken or silent. She stresses the materiality of the body and the infrastructures necessary for its persistence, its life. Environmental resources, such as air, water, and food, are often assumed rather than examined for their contingency. The social recognition of each body, as a distinctive human person, is also necessary for that person's capacity to speak, during one's early lifetime as well as at the moment of appearance in public. The contingency of recognition of each person is also social, with certain categories receiving more value than others, governed by certain norms of appearance. A single body would not convey the message as forcefully as a gathering of many such persons, which has the power to challenge existing political and economic structures.

Butler focuses on "precarity," not just of employment but also of the environmental and social infrastructures which empower a person to appear and be recognized in a public forum. By including citizens and noncitizens, as well as marginal and dominant populations, she is raising the question of who has a right to live. The allocation of social and environmental resources is a political process which determines who has the right to merely survive and who has the potential to flourish with a life worth living. By articulating the social and political natures of these decisions, as well as interdependency, she raises the issue of responsibility. To allow any population to die, whether intentionally or by neglect, is to permit genocide, with its moral implications. The combination of vulnerability and dependency can lead to solidarity of humankind in the face of shared mortal threats. Alternatively, Davies sees "exterminism" as the super-rich separating themselves from unfolding ecological disasters (Davies 2018, 27–28).

There is a long history of "assembly," revolts and revolutions, who may declare new nations and constitutions, claiming legitimacy of the sovereignty of the people. Butler tends to idealize the "public sphere," even while noting some of the issues with Arendt's formulation (Butler 2015, 44–46, 204–209; Eley 2011, 562–565), in contrast with the more unruly formulations of Hardt and Negri (2000, 2004, 2009, 2017). The definition of "the people" is now in question, with the rising influence of populist movements around the globe, threatening traditional "conservatism" (Economist cover story July 6–12, 2019,

16–18). The threat and the potential of public assembly includes changing the meaning of key terms, such as "property" (Blaufarb 2016), as well as establishing new institutions, such as the "Third Estate" in the French Revolution. The origin of modern social science may well have been to avoid such potential disruptions to the status quo to discipline the mob (Ross 1991; Baretz 1960).

Performativity

The concept of performativity can serve as a bridge between long-standing dichotomies such as social history, which draws upon a Marxist legacy, and cultural history and the "linguistic turn." The presumed divide was a social history which used "class" as a key category, with a definition based on the economic structure, compared with a cultural history which used discourse and symbols (Jameson 1998; Williams 1977; Hall 2016).

Drawing upon Searle, Austin, and Butler, the meaning of a linguistic term is based on norms, enforcement, and behavior, which reinforces that meaning in practice. According to Butler,

> There is an invariably performative dimension to the kinds of demand that are made [in recent assemblies ... whether those of the Occupy movements or los Indignados in Spain], where performativity functions as a chiastic relation between body and language.
>
> (Butler 2015, 137)

The methodology recommended in this book involves key terms and the related institutional practices, as interpreted and reinforced by experts. Behavior involves the material body as well as means of production, along with subjective intentions and psychic rewards. A social science or a history can incorporate both aspects, the material and the symbolic, in an analysis of social behavior and historical change (Jameson 2019, 210–214). To open the question of change may also challenge the professional and the academic, nonetheless, as to whether to engage with current issues, political, economic, and moral, or to maintain the "objective" stance of the professional. Politicization of the university in the 1960s in France and the US was contentious and continues to be debated.

Historical institutional methodology

The method of historical institutionalism, discussed in Davis (2015, 2017, 2019) and Chapter 3 consists of three aspects:

- Key terms, like property and "the individual."
- Historically specific institutions, like courts and markets.
- Knowledge and professional expertise, like economics, law, history, psychology, and political science.

Important features of this methodology are drawn from other work, such as historical institutionalists like Pistor (2019); Thelen (2014); Mahoney and Thelen (2015); Hall and Soskice (2001); Streeck (2005).

In this approach, the form of the state is endogenous with the evolution of the market (Davis 2015; Padgett and Powell 2012).

There is an influence of dominant institutions, like the state and the market, on forms of knowledge and subjectivity (Foucault 1994). These forms of knowledge in turn enhance the stability of the state and the market, as well as influence individual "identities."

This historical institutional methodology can incorporate additional elements, such as a) "reflexivity," b) the role of values, and c) language.

Reflexivity

Reflexivity can be seen in economics, with investors judging the expectations of other investors and also intentionally trying to influence their expectations (Davis 2015, 148–149). Paradigms can influence sensory perceptions as well as actions and consequently can affect the reproduction of those world views (Davis 2017, 25–27, 164–165). Ideally one becomes aware of cultural influences and how they affect oneself, as well as one's own ongoing behavior and how it contributes to the continuity of those cultural influences. Reflexivity in this broad definition is inherently social, perceiving the history as well as the values of one's own community in a critical way and ideally in discussion with that community about that reflection (Bourdieu 2004).

Values

According to Honneth (2011) and Boltanski and co-authors (1999, 2005, 2006), the role of values is more than simply legitimation. In one's daily activities and practices, there are actions, habits, and norms which reflect values endorsed by the person and the group. Without the salience of such values, behavior would be less predictable and institutions would be less stable. Achievement of recognition and personal satisfaction would be less routine. That is, values are functional for the stability of institutions but require reinforcement by habits and routines to reinforce those values in everyday language and experience.

Outrage and unrest are possible outcomes if expectations are not met and values are not enforced, especially around such central issues as work, citizenship, and property.

Language

The language in which norms and values are expressed is social, while at the same time providing an individual method of cognition and expression. Institutions are based in language, according to Searle (2010), and are performed based on common meanings and commitments.

Language can be viewed as a public good to which all have access and to which all contribute to its continuation. Official language can be the product of a nation-state, which seeks to standardize its practice by means of educational institutions, in the pursuit of an official bureaucracy (Bourdieu 1991). Language itself is often historically bounded in a nation or a population, with rules of grammar and definitions, shared in literature (Jameson 2019, 23, 197). Often that literature becomes a matter of national pride, and one's specific dialects become distinctive of one's region and class.

Biographies, institutions, and values

Padgett (2001, 2012a, 2012b) develops social science methodology by reaching across the impersonal institution and linking it to the personal histories of the incumbents in terms of individual careers and family histories. In this way, the perpetuity of the abstract institution is linked to the unique personal histories of members, and their individual choices, as well as the influence of those institutions on those individuals in a mutually interactive dialectic. Such interactions can lead to the emergence of new institutional forms over time, such as business partnerships in early modern Florence, embraced by the families and communities which sustain them.

Reflexivity would bring this analysis full circle, from the biographies and institutions to their effect on norms and values and the subsequent effect on biographies and institutions. Such reflexivity would involve a long-term historical perspective and attention to the cultural forms and genres.

The involvement of multiple levels of analysis, and long time periods, may lend itself to the form of allegory, like epic poetry and national imaginaries. One example is religious allegory. That is, a notable individual, like Jesus, has a unique life history, which is also associated with a larger community, in this case Christians (Jameson 2019, 18–22, 332–333). Here the individual and the social seem unrelated, but bringing into relationship the two levels by narrative makes both more meaningful.

Such a reflexivity would examine the historical chronology, as well as the cultural forms and key terms. The narratives would incorporate values shared by the community, as a way to articulate them in a form accessible to each member, as well as to model how such values would guide the life of the community towards its collective goals.

Money as a bridge between material and ideal

There are additional implications for methodology. In my view, the role of money as a distinct institution has been overlooked in modern social sciences (with the exception of economic sociologists such as Krippner 2011). Drawing from both the "linguistic" and the "material" turns, there is a method for incorporating money as a social institution (Davis 2017).

Performativity can help resolve the tension between "fiction" and "real" commodities since the actual behavior of market participants is the focus. For example, Polanyi (1944) designated three "fictional" commodities, land, labor, and money, and the "utopian" self-regulating market. Money is both an institution and an instrument, facilitating the reification of the other "fictional commodities" by means of exchange for a price. But the methods of production of money are different from the other two commodities. Money, markets, and the state are co-constituted. Money is a symbol designated by the state to acquire certain functions, means of payment, store of value, unit of account. Money also symbolizes the whole, all of the users who recognize a given sovereign currency and who exchange their labor for commodities and money. Without the entirety of the user community, money would have no value and the detailed division of labor would not be possible. Financial circuits are managed by the state so that borrowers are capable of expanding its value and returning interest to lenders and taxes to the state. The liberal state is based on money and guarantees that money and credit. The means of life are made contingent on the acquisition of money, which is the foundation of "market incentives" and the origin of the power of the currency. It is not possible to examine any institution in a capitalist state without reference to money. Money is a symbol which provides the structure for capitalist institutions. Its apparently voluntary use ties each person into an interlinked structure of discipline managed by the state. Money is both material and symbolic, which confounds the dichotomies which are related to the various "turns" of methodologies.

Given the discipline of the labor market, it has become normalized in market economies to assume that the conditions of life are properly contingent on the performance of work for a wage. To receive a "handout" is cause for guilt and condemnation, to be stigmatized as "dependent" (Fraser and Gordon 2013). Rather than question or resist the necessity to sell oneself as a commodity, the demand instead is for full employment. One's status is based on one's salary and conspicuous consumption.

Money represents all users, a form of collective, most often members of a national community (Davis 2015, 124–134) rather than specific persons. When the social is symbolized by the money commodity, there is no direct, face-to-face encounter with the other worker or consumer and no mutual recognition or responsibility. Social relationships become modeled on the prototype of contract by self-interested parties who are only interested in price, an abstract metric of social valuation. "The individual" is empowered by money and markets and need not have any concern for other individuals who are likewise assumed to be self-interested and competitive. Money is a tool of individuation, tracking each person's balance sheet of assets and liabilities and enabling "the individual" to survive alone (with the social institutions invisible). The morality of markets is based on reward commensurate with effort, not with social provisions for the unemployed.

In this way, the reification of money and property enables the individuation of human persons, the eschewing of responsibility for others, and the denial of "the social" entirely. Economics, as a social science, has no need to recognize this omission.

Without money, there would be no public/private divide, no separation of state or society from the market. Money is the medium and the marker of the economy. Without money, there would be no separate economy and no economists.

A linguistic turn in economics

The importance of "fictional commodities" and the "utopian" free market to Smith, Marx, and Polanyi points to the significance of language. Increasingly economists are also studying values and beliefs, as well as narratives and categories of identity. These recent works begin to bring economists beyond the insistence on the rational, self-interested individual with exogenous tastes to treat phenomena which are more inherently social.

Narrative economics

In Shiller's analysis of the financial crisis of 2008, he noticed the importance of narratives, such as "home prices never fall." Such a belief would encourage continued investment in the housing market, even as the rate of price increase exceeded determinants such as costs, population growth, and income. These beliefs become "contagious," once observers see the media promulgation of them and also observe the rising trend in home prices. Shiller develops concepts like "information cascade," where individuals change their beliefs in observing the spread of ideas among others, even if not personally convinced of the accuracy of these beliefs (Shiller 2008, 47). Fascinated by the quantitative patterns of the spread of ideas, he pursued the metaphor of "contagion" and applied epidemiology in subsequent work, using Google Ngrams (Shiller 2017).

In later work, Shiller seems convinced that humans are inherently social.

> In a psychologically healthy environment, narratives establish honored membership in community. Everyone wants to be loved. Everyone feels a deep need to be part of a community that at the very least respects one's contribution.
>
> (Shiller 2019a, 4)

At the same time, relative status is important.

> Narratives can trigger deep feelings based on the instinct for hierarchy. The pecking order matters to humans just as to chickens.
>
> (Shiller 2019a, 16)

Shiller's analysis of the concept of the narrative is an important contribution which could be extended further. Shiller applied the concept of narratives to explore the personal meaning of work and the threat of technological unemployment (Shiller 2019a), quoting the Bible but not Marx or Keynes. He misses the origin of the word "robot" in eighteenth-century serf contracts in Eastern Europe. He does not explore the origin of these narratives, nor the implicit values expressed. In recommending policies, he prefers the model of "insurance" to "tax" as being more compatible with existing value systems, which remain unexplored. He does not consider the possibility that economic models and policies can change values and so does not consider reflexivity. Although Shiller uses the term "narrative," which suggests a linguistic focus, he does not examine the "fictional commodities" of land, labor, and money, or corporations as "legal fictions" (Pistor 2019, 48, 52). An extension of the methodology of historical institutionalism as explored here would trace the origin of the narratives and the cultural and economic influences. This exploration would include nationalism, and "imaginary communities," as discussed by Anderson and Taylor, as well as religions, social science, and scientific world views. Shiller's initiative, nonetheless, raises important questions for economists to consider.

Identity economics

An approach entitled "identity economics" takes into consideration the effects that individuals may have on each other in terms of associating with groups with certain characteristics and levels of social esteem (Akerlof and Kranton 2010). These identity categories are then determinants in individual utility functions and can change economic behavior.

> Identity is associated with different social categories and how people in these categories should behave.
>
> (Akerlof and Kranton 2000, 715)

There are norms of behavior which are shared by members of a distinct identity group. There is a new type of "externality": one person's actions may have meanings for others in terms of willingness to affiliate. Identity and norms are "fractal," where there are multiple levels of interaction and influence in a variety of institutional settings (Kranton 2016, 405). This literature is explicitly interdisciplinary, drawing upon sociology and psychology, as well as anthropology and history, and views humans as social and cooperative (Kranton 2019). The framework is still the individual decision-maker, nonetheless, choosing among options with a budget constraint. There is no larger historical or institutional inquiry regarding the origin of these institutions and norms.

Performative finance

A growing literature raises the question regarding whether financial models are performative (Callon 2007). That is, once a model has been developed and prices can be estimated, does the model then facilitate trades on financial markets that would not otherwise have been possible? Brine and Poovey trace the evolution of the field of finance and its differentiation from economics. One key distinction between economics and finance is that economics produces policies and finance produces financial products. Without the increasingly sophisticated financial models, along with information technology and global deregulation of capital, the dramatic expansion of the scale of financial markets since 1980 would not have occurred (Brine and Poovey 2017, 294–295, 307, 314–325, 339). Financial markets assume an infinite time horizon, which is feasible with "perpetual" nation-states and corporations, which create and trade financial products to produce "convertibility" (Pistor 2019, 13–18, 77–79) and liquidity (Davis 2017). The assumptions of the models, nonetheless, are only an approximation of reality, which can then lead to unforeseen financial crises, such as the market crash of 1987.

History of capitalism

There is an emerging interdisciplinary school called "History of Capitalism," based in Harvard, Columbia, and Cornell Universities, including work by Sven Beckert and Christine DeSan, associated with the Weatherhead Initiative on Global History (https://wigh.wcfia.harvard.edu/). This work is extending earlier world systems approaches like Foner, Hobsbawm, Wallerstein, Arrighi, and Braudel and assuming historically evolving systemic interconnections. Recent work by Frances Fukuyama and Douglass C. North also consider the history of social systems from a long-term institutional perspective.

Categories of exclusion: the literature of post-colonial, feminist, stratification economics

There has been a recent expansion of attention to multiple categories of disadvantaged populations compared with adult white males from hegemonic countries. Drawing upon Bourdieu, there is an analysis of the emergence of these categories from the "bureaucratic field," by which the state manages marginal populations with both symbolic and coercive methods. That is, the marginalization of these categories of persons occurs by the operation of the market economy and then managed by the state (Wacquant 2009). That is, these so-called "identity" categories are developed by the bureaucratic processes of the large corporation and the state for differential treatment rather than only by voluntary association by individuals seeking affiliation, as discussed in "identity" economics.

Using the approach by Wacquant, which draws upon both symbolic and material resources, we can see that the category is 1) linguistic, a symbol which is invested with meaning by the operation of bureaucratic procedures and rules. But also 2) material; that is, the category also applies to a marked body, a specific type of person, whether differentiated by race, gender, ethnicity, country of birth, sexual preference, or class. Once the category is in widespread use with normative associations, it carries its own meaning, both to the bureaucrat and to the population (Alexander 2010, 26–30). Based on physical or social characteristics of distinct populations, the treatment of that category of persons becomes naturalized, as if an inherent feature of that population. That is, the understanding of each category becomes stereotyped, affecting the behavior of the persons and those with whom they interact, reinforcing the distinctive behavior. Such characterizations can be resisted, such as the movement Black Lives Matter (Kruse and Zelizer 2019, 325–329), the success of which depends on the resources for political mobilization and the capacity for cultural reinterpretation.

It is almost as if each person has dual identities, one unique biological body and the other the image. The body needs nutrition and social interaction. The image is represented by documents, credentials, and rankings. Image can even be separated from the body on social media, the "virtual" world where self-promotion is feasible to raise status and career options, as well as opportunities for social relationships. It is even possible to manage one's image and to be victimized by "identity theft."

Interdisciplinary/natural science

Recent new directions in economics include complexity, behavioral, and ecological economics. All three engage with natural science (like the earlier models influenced by physics (Mirowski 2002)). These innovations are still in the mode of "objective" science focused on "the individual" but are more inclusive in terms of disciplinary categories and greater capacity to consider more complex motives and interactions among individuals (Costanza et al. 2015). Agents react to the state of economy, which is composed of the actions of these agents, to which these agents again react, a form of "reflexivity" (Arthur 2015, 5). These complex adaptive systems include heterogeneous agents, with path dependence, endogenous network structures, and emergent properties, approaching a new paradigm, compared with the stable equilibria and optimal outcomes of neoclassical economics (Elsner 2017; Foxon et al. 2013). While promising, these models do not yet address the central role of human labor in the economy and the role of the person as a "double agent," both worker and consumer, as well as citizen. They do not address the role of language as a medium of communication and coordination, as well as a source of meaning and identity.

The "view from nowhere": objective ranking in a society of "equals"

As Bourdieu points out in his discussion of reflexivity, there is a need to provide an objective view of the subject of science, that is, "objectivating the subject of objectivation" or viewing the professional scientist, economist, or sociologist as if from outside or "nowhere" (Bourdieu 2004, 88–94). While it is hard to match Bourdieu's clever turn of phrase, I think there is a more direct method for understanding the process of "objectivation" which takes place in capitalist societies.

Given the dominance of the market and the importance of ranking or valuation which drives the system, I contend that the method of "objectivation" is the ranking of individuals by means of bureaucratic categories and by market position, such as occupation and salary. These markers, the categories and the wage payments, place each person in a hierarchy which determines access to means of life and social status. Yet both methods, markets and bureaucracies (Williamson 1975, 1985), are presumed neutral and objective, providing consistent incentives for the activities and goals of each person and fitting rewards for effort. In the context of the liberal foundation of "equal individuals," providing a method of consistent ranking is significant and supports trust and belief in the fairness of the system.

The importance and pervasiveness of these ranking systems are invisible to social scientists, who are divided by "field" and rarely view the operation of the system as a whole. This disciplinary division then obstructs public awareness of the operation of the whole, even with those "objective" methods that would appear to assure such neutrality. That is, the structure of social science disciplines has a social effect which is beyond the awareness of the practitioners of those disciplines, which they then fail to take into account. In particular, for the most part, social scientists leave the study of money to economists and so do not take it into account as a social institution (Davis 2017).

The modern individual

Certainly not every human person on the planet is a modern individual. For such an identity, there is a necessary "background" (Searle 2010), a type of *savoir faire* necessary for participation in modern institutions, as well as adequate resources.

Such an "individual" would have the following skills and capacities:

- A capacity for self-presentation, even "branding" (Goffman 1959; Hochschild 2013, 3, 101–110).
- A capacity to view oneself as others view her (Smith's "impartial spectator").
- A capacity to calculate the advantage for each allocation of time (Franklin's "time is money").
- A capacity to plan one's life to maximize income and status, including the choice of mate (Weber 1978; Veblen 1934).
- A capacity to narrate one's own story in a manner to gain the empathy of others (Gazzaniga 2018).
- A capacity to compete with other individuals for a position in the state and the market, which recognize and selectively reward them.
- And the ability to use money at face value without reflection.

Throughout one's life, one would reflect on one's own personal progress in achieving these capacities, which cannot be assumed at the outset but is rather the outcome of intensive socialization and striving. This world view is the ultimate product of Enlightenment rationality and seems obvious, self-evident, and purposeful.

That is, the "individual" is the outcome of modern institutions, and such a self-understanding then reinforces those modern institutions. This interactive complex of ideas and institutions is self-fulfilling and so becomes more stable. This distinctly modern "identity" may even escape the critical awareness of those who enact this role. It becomes "habit" (Bourdieu 1977), merely taken for granted for those who are immersed in this world view. Our self-concept as modern individuals fits the image of social science and the structure of modern institutions and facilitates our personal effectiveness in this milieu; hence, it is rewarded and rewarding.

Not every contemporary human person is a modern "individual" (Chatterjee 2010) in terms of self-concept, infrastructure (Joyce 2002; Cronon 1991) or institutional scaffolding like money and markets.

In development theory and some institutional history, there is a prevalence of "stages" theory, with a notion of progress embedded in the categories of analysis. That is, in Smith, Hegel, and Marx, as well as Adam Ferguson, some forms of property are considered more advanced than others (Davis 2015, 59). Is this notion implicit in the concept of "modernity" and Enlightenment "progress"? Is "the individual" one of those categories with an implicit teleology, a status which some will never achieve?

Disciplinary limitations

The argument in this book is that the focus of the economics profession on the individual, whether with exogenous or endogenous preferences, limits its ability to address contemporary issues, such as the following:

a)   Financial crises and contagion.
b)   Group behavior and needs for association and esteem.
c)   Changes in norms and values from collective behavior.
d)   Changes in culture from the influence of media (print, broadcast, and social media) and genres (fact or fiction, science or art).

Methodological individualism explicitly eliminates the social and other influences beyond the individual, such as language, norms, and culture. While certain recent methodological innovations seek to go beyond these constraints, the basic unit of analysis is still the individual, limiting the effect.

New subjectivity

The modern subjectivity of the "individual" is based on "ownership" of individual private property, as discussed in the previous chapters, at least self-ownership. This is a type of freedom of "equal" owners, while not considering the experience of being owned, or "subject" in a double sense. That is, this form of subjectivity based on property ownership hides a form of domination, when the labor market is the dominant form of work (Harvey 2014). Relationships are based on the subject/object dichotomy, with continual striving to reach the subject position, with agency, in competition with all others. This competitive striving drives the system, with the unacknowledged instrumental use of humans.

It is possible to consider an alternative subjectivity of mutuality and cooperation (Harvey 2014), based on the standpoint of a resident of the earth, the only living planet in the universe. It is possible to consider the common experience of "a woman born," with vulnerable bodies outside a small range of temperature, who live in groups who produce and share their own food. It is possible to consider one's culture in the context of a division of labor and long years of socialization and schooling, and the specific forms of schooling in post-industrial America. It is possible to draw upon the long legacy of concern with education, beginning with Locke and Rousseau, as well as American innovators (Dewey 1916, 1930; Goldin and Katz 2008; Katz 1968; Goodman 1960, 1964; Neill 1960). It is possible to be an informed citizen of modern science, complete with insight into climate change and the impact of modern agricultural techniques and industrial production. It is possible to wish to provide for one's heirs a living climate, fertile with many species and with sustainable biogeochemical processes intact.

Rather than the subjectivity of the property owner, either the peasant plot owned and managed by the household, or the real estate investment managed for sale for profit, the human population would have usufruct rights to the planet earth, collaboratively managed in regional ecologies for the purpose of the overall sustainability of the earth. See further discussion of these alternatives in Chapter 11.

Conclusion

The irony of "the individual" may be that the assumption, the social acceptance of its existence, may make it true by its influence on behavior. That is, the individual is a "reifying abstraction" with real effects (Poovey 2002).

> The characteristic *sacredness* with which the human being is now invested ... is not inherent. . . . Man has no innate right to this aura that surrounds and protects him against *sacrilegious trespass*. . . . Thus very far from there being the *antagonism* between the individual and society which is often claimed, moral individualism, the *cult* of the individual, is in fact the product of society itself. It is society that instituted it and made of man the *god* whose servant it is.
>
> (Durkheim quoted in Cladis 1992, 115; italics in original)

In other words, there is a parallel between ideas and institutions. Ideas that are part of conventional beliefs can affect behavior, which can make those beliefs "true" in a self-fulfilling dynamic. These beliefs are rationalized and legitimated by experts and help shape existing institutions, which can delay and modify impulses and challenges for change.

Consequently, there is considerable importance of education and socialization in such institutions as schools, universities, churches, and families, as stressed by Locke and Rousseau, as well as Dewey, along with modern observers like Goldin and Katz. Hence it is possible to consider a "social construction of reality," as in Berger and Luckmann's title (1966), as discussed further in Chapter 7.

As Hayek says, social science differs from natural science, or Latour's "modern constitution." In economics, unlike natural science, "a body of suitably chosen experts may [not] be in the best position to command all the best knowledge available" since only individuals know their own circumstances (Hayek 1945, 521–522). But, following Hayek, the experts have designed institutions, such as the market, which are given "autonomy" in operation.

On the other hand, in the twenty-first century, behavioral economics and cognitive science may seek to breech the divide between natural and social science, with AI and Big Data (Zuboff 2019), to make social science and society itself predictable and perfectible by social/science techniques, if not also perfectly controlled.

The alternative is to reintegrate economics and political economy (Milonakis and Fine 2009) and to view the market, the state, and the "individual" as the result of long-term institutional co-evolution (Padgett 2012a, 2012b; Davis 2015). While these forms are long-standing, it is important to recognize their continuing evolution, with the possible emergence of new institutional forms and values, and new forms of expertise. The methodological individualism of mainstream economics assumes a given human nature, based on assumptions of what people most want, rather than view human subjectivity itself as endogenous, as a product of the period and culture as well as its agent. To understand institutional change, a *long duree* period of analysis is important, allowing such changes to become manifest. And the salience of "the individual" may itself be a characteristic of a distinctive period in history, which the performance of the economics discipline may serve to extend.

Bibliography

Akerlof, George A. "'We Thinking' and Its Consequences," *American Economic Review*, Vol. 106, No. 5, 2016, 415–419.

Akerlof, George A. and Rachel E. Kranton. "Economics and Identity," *Quarterly Journal of Economics*, Vol. 115, No. 3, August 2000, 715–753.

Akerlof, George A. and Rachel E. Kranton. *Identity Economics: How Our Identities Shape our Work, Wages, and Well-Being*. Princeton, NJ: Princeton University Press, 2010.

Alexander, Michelle. *The New Jim Crow: Mass Incarceration in the Age of Colorblindness*. New York: The New Press, 2010.

Ardalan, Kavous. *Paradigms in Political Economy*. New York: Routledge, 2016.

Arthur, W. Brian. *Complexity and the Economy*. Oxford, UK: Oxford University Press, 2015.

Baretz, Loren. *Servants of Power: A History of the Use of Social Science in American Industry*. Middletown, CT: Wesleyan University Press, 1960.

Beck, Hermann. *The Origins of the Authoritarian Welfare State in Prussia: Conservatives, Bureaucracy, and the Social Question, 1815–70.* Ann Arbor: University of Michigan Press, 1995.

Beckert, Jens. *Imagined Futures: Fictional Expectations and Capitalist Dynamics.* Cambridge, MA: Harvard University Press, 2016.

Berger, Peter L. and Thomas Luckmann. *The Social Construction of Reality: A Treatise in the Sociology of Knowledge.* New York: Doubleday & Company, 1966.

Bevir, Mark and Frank Trentmann (eds.). *Markets in Historical Contexts: Ideas and Politics in the Modern World.* New York: Cambridge University Press, 2004.

Blaufarb, Rafe. *The Great Demarcation: The French Revolution and the Invention of Modern Property.* New York: Oxford University Press, 2016.

Boltanski, Luc and Eve Chiapello. *The New Spirit of Capitalism.* London: Verso, 2005.

Boltanski, Luc and Laurent Thevenot. "The Sociology of Critical Capacity," *European Journal of Social Theory,* Vol. 2, No. 3, 1999, 359–377.

Boltanski, Luc and Laurent Thevenot. *On Justification: Economies of Worth.* Princeton, NJ: Princeton University Press, 2006.

Bourdieu, Pierre. *Outline of a Theory of Practice.* New York: Cambridge University Press, 1977.

Bourdieu, Pierre. *Language and Symbolic Power.* Cambridge, MA: Harvard University Press, 1991.

Bourdieu, Pierre. *Acts of Resistance: Against the Tyranny of the Market.* New York: The Free Press, 1998.

Bourdieu, Pierre. *Science of Science and Reflexivity.* Chicago: University of Chicago Press, 2004.

Brine, Kevin R. and Mary Poovey. *Finance in America: An Unfinished Story.* Chicago: University of Chicago Press, 2017.

Butler, Judith. *Notes Toward a Performative Theory of Assembly.* Cambridge, MA: Harvard University Press, 2015.

Callon, Michel. "What Does It Mean to Say that Economics is Performative?" in Donald A. Mackenzie, Fabian Muniesa and Lucia Siu (eds.), *Do Economists Make Markets? On the Performativity of Economics.* Princeton, NJ: Princeton University Press, 2007, 311–357.

Charusheela, S. *Structuralism and Individualism in Economic Analysis: The "Contractionary Devaluation Debate" in Development Economics.* New York: Routledge, 2005.

Chatterjee, Partha. *Empire and Nation: Selected Essays.* New York: Columbia Press, 2010.

Cladis, Mark S. *A Communitarian Defense of Liberalism: Emile Durkheim and Contemporary Social Theory.* Stanford, CA: Stanford University Press, 1992.

Costanza, Robert, John H. Cumberland, Herman Daly, Robert Goodland, Richard B. Norgaard, Ida Kubiszewski, and Carol Franco. *An Introduction to Ecological Economics.* 2nd ed. New York: CRC Press, 2015.

Cronon, William. *Nature's Metropolis: Chicago and the Great West.* New York: W.W. Norton & Company, 1991.

Daston, Lorraine and Peter Galison. *Objectivity.* New York: Zone Books, 2007.

Davies, William. "The Return of Social Government: From 'Socialist Calculation' to 'Social Analytics'," *European Journal of Social Theory,* Vol. 18, No. 4, 2015, 431–450.

Davies, William (ed.). *Economic Science Fictions.* London: Goldsmiths Press, 2018.

Davis, Ann E. *The Evolution of the Property Relation: Understanding Paradigms, Debates, Prospects.* New York: Palgrave MacMillan, 2015.

Davis, Ann E. *Money as a Social Institution: The Institutional Development of Capitalism.* New York: Routledge, 2017.

Davis, Ann E. "Is There a History of Property? Periodization of Property Regimes and Paradigms," in Staci M. Zavatarro, Gregory Peterson, and Ann E. Davis (eds.), *Exploring Property Rights in Contemporary Governance.* Albany: SUNY Press, 2019, 5–24.

Dewey, John. *Democracy and Education: An Introduction to the Philosophy of Education.* New York: MacMillan, 1916.

Dewey, John. *Individualism, Old and New.* New York: Minton, Balch and Company, 1930.

Eley, Geoff. *A Crooked Line: From Cultural History to the History of Society.* Ann Arbor: University of Michigan Press, 2005.

Eley, Geoff. "The Past Under Erasure? History, Memory, and the Contemporary," *Journal of Contemporary History,* Vol. 46, No. 3, 2011, 555–573.

Elsner, Wolfram. "Complexity Economics as Heterodoxy: Theory and Policy," *Journal of Economic Issues,* Vol. 51, No. 4, 2017, 939–978.

Foucault, Michel. *The Order of Things: An Archaeology of the Human Sciences.* New York: Vintage, 1994.

Foxon, Timothy J., Jonathan Kohler, Jonathan Michie, and Christine Oughton. "Towards a New Complexity Economics for Sustainability," *Cambridge Journal of Economics,* Vol. 37, 2013, 187–208.

Fraser, Nancy and Linda Gordon. "A Genealogy of 'Dependency': Tracing a Keyword of the US Welfare State," in Nancy Fraser (ed.), *Fortunes of Feminism: From State-Managed Capitalism to Neoliberal Crisis.* New York: Verso, 2013, 83–110.

Gazzaniga, Michael S. *The Consciousness Instinct: Unraveling the Mystery of How the Brain Makes the Mind.* New York: Farrar, Straus and Giroux, 2018.

Goffman, Erving. *Presentation of Self in Everyday Life.* Garden City, NY: Double Day, 1959.

Goldin, Claudia Dale and Lawrence F. Katz. *The Race Between Education and Technology.* Cambridge, MA: Harvard University Press, 2008.

Goodman, Paul. *Growing Up Absurd: Problems of Youth in the Organized System.* New York: Random House, 1960.

Goodman, Paul. *Compulsory Mid-Education and the Community of Scholars.* New York: Vintage, 1964.

Grimmer-Solem, Erik. *The Rise of Historical Economics and Social Reform in Germany 1864– 1894.* Oxford: Clarendon Press, 2003.

Hall, Peter A. and David Soskice (eds.). *Varieties of Capitalism: The Institutional Foundations of Comparative Advantage.* New York: Oxford University Press, 2001.

Hall, Stuart. *Cultural Studies 1983. A Theoretical History.* Durham, NC: Duke University Press, 2016.

Hardt, Michael and Antonio Negri. *Empire.* Cambridge, MA: Harvard University Press, 2000.

Hardt, Michael and Antonio Negri. *Multitude: War and Democracy in the Age of Empire.* New York: Penguin, 2004.

Hardt, Michael and Antonio Negri. *Commonwealth.* Cambridge, MA: Harvard University Press, 2009.

Hardt, Michael and Antonio Negri. *Assembly.* New York: Oxford University Press, 2017.

Harvey, David. *Seventeen Contradictions and the End of Capitalism.* New York: Oxford University Press, 2014.

Hayek, Friedrich A. von. "The Use of Knowledge in Society," *American Economic Review,* Vol. 35, No. 4, September 1945, 519–530.

Hochschild, Arlie Russell. *So How's the Family? And Other Essays.* Berkeley: University of California Press, 2013.

Hodgson, Geoffrey M. *Conceptualizing Capitalism: Institutions, Evolution, Future.* Chicago: University of Chicago Press, 2015.

Honig, Bonnie. *Public Things: Democracy in Disrepair.* New York: Fordham University Press, 2017.

Honneth, Axel. *Freedom's Right: The Social Foundations of Democratic Life.* New York: Columbia University Press, 2011.

Jameson, Fredric. *The Cultural Turn: Selected Writings on the Postmodern, 1983–1998.* New York: Verso, 1998.

Jameson, Fredric. *Allegory and Ideology.* London: Verso, 2019.

Joyce, Patrick. *The Social in Question: New Bearings in History and Social Science.* New York: Routledge, 2002.

Katz, Michael B. *The Irony of Early School Reform: Educational Innovation in Mid-Nineteenth Century Massachusetts.* Cambridge, MA: Harvard University Press, 1968.

Konings, Martihn. *Capital and Time: For a New Critique of Neoliberal Reason.* Stanford, CA: Stanford University Press, 2018.

Kranton, Rachel E. "Identity Economics 2016: Where Do Social Distinctions and Norms Come From?" *American Economic Review,* Vol. 106, No. 5, 2016, 405–409.

Kranton, Rachel E. "The Devil is in the Details: Implications of Samuel Bowles's *The Moral Economy* for Economics and Policy Research," *Journal of Economic Literature,* 57(1), 2019, 147–160.

Krippner, Greta R. *Capitalizing on Crisis: The Political Origins of the Rise of Finance.* Cambridge, MA: Harvard University Press, 2011.

Kruse, Kevin M. and Julian E. Zelizer. *Fault Lines: A History of the United States Since 1974.* New York: W.W. Norton & Company, 2019.

Latour, Bruno. *We Have Never Been Modern.* Cambridge, MA: Harvard University Press, 1993.

MacPherson, C. B. *The Political Theory of Possessive Individualism: Hobbes to Locke.* Oxford: Clarendon Press, 1962.

Mahoney, James and Kathleen Thelen. *Advances in Comparative Historical Analysis.* New York: Cambridge University Press, 2015.

Maier, Charles. *Leviathan 2.0: Inventing Modern Statehood.* Cambridge, MA: Harvard University Press, 2012.

Marx, Karl. *Capital.* New York: International Publishers, 1967.

Marx, Karl and Frederick Engels. *The German Ideology.* New York: International Publishers, 1947.

McGerr, Michael E. *The Decline of Popular Politics: The American North, 1865–1928.* New York: Oxford University Press, 1986.

McGerr, Michael E. *A Fierce Discontent: The Rise and Fall of the Progressive Movement in America, 1870–1920.* New York: Free Press, 2003.

McLean, Paul. *Culture in Networks.* Cambridge, UK: Polity Press, 2017.

Mehta, Uday Singh. *Liberalism and Empire: A Study in Nineteenth-Century British Liberal Thought.* Chicago: University of Chicago Press, 1999.

Menand, Louis. *The Metaphysical Club: A Story of Ideas in America.* New York: Farrar, Straus, and Giroux, 2001.

Milonakis, Dimitris and Ben Fine. *From Political Economy to Economics: Method, The Social and the Historical in the Evolution of Economic Theory.* New York: Routledge, 2009.

Mirowski, Philip. *Machine Dreams: Economics becomes a Cyborg Science.* New York: Cambridge University Press, 2002.

Nagel, Thomas. *The View from Nowhere.* New York: Oxford University Press, 1986.

Neill, A. S. *Summerhill: A Radical Approach to Child Rearing.* New York: Hart Publishers, 1960.

North, Douglass Cecil, John Joseph Wallis, and Barry R. Weingast. *Violence and Social Orders: A Conceptual Framework for Interpreting Recorded Human History.* New York: Cambridge University Press, 2009.

Padgett, John F. "Organizational Genesis, Identity, and Control: The Transformation of Banking in Renaissance Florence," in James E. Rauch and Alessandra Casella (eds.), *Networks and Markets*. New York: Sage Foundation, 2001, 211–257.

Padgett, John F. "The Emergence of Corporate Merchant-Banks in Dugento Tuscany," in John F. Padgett and Walter W. Powell (eds.), *The Emergence of Organizations and Markets*. Princeton, NJ: Princeton University Press, 2012a, 121–167.

Padgett, John F. "Transposition and Refunctionality: The Birth of the Partnership System in Renaissance Florence," in John F. Padgett and Walter W. Powell (eds.), *The Emergence of Organizations and Markets*. Princeton, NJ: Princeton University Press, 2012b, 168–207.

Padgett, John F. and Walter W. Powell (eds.). *The Emergence of Organizations and Markets*. Princeton, NJ: Princeton University Press, 2012.

Pateman, Carole. *The Sexual Contract*. Stanford, CA: Stanford University Press, 1988.

Pistor, Katharina. *The Code of Capital: How the Law Creates Wealth and Inequality*. Princeton, NJ: Princeton University Press, 2019.

Polanyi, Karl. *The Great Transformation*. Boston: Beacon Press, 1944.

Poovey, Mary. "The Liberal Civil Subject and the Social in Eighteenth-Century British Moral Philosophy," *Public Culture*, Vol. 14, No. 1, 2002, 125–145.

Rosenboim, Or. *The Emergence of Globalism: Visions of World Order in Britain and the United States, 1939–1950*. Princeton, NJ: Princeton University Press, 2017. (with discussion of Mannheim and Raymond Aron).

Ross, Dorothy. *Origins of American Social Science*. New York: Cambridge University Press, 1991.

Searle, John R. *Making the Social World: The Structure of Human Civilization*. New York: Oxford University Press, 2010.

Sewell, William H. Jr. *Work and Revolution in France: The Language of Labor from the Old Regime to 1848*. New York: Cambridge University Press, 1980.

Sewell, William H. Jr. *Logics of History: Social Theory and Social Transformation*. Chicago: University of Chicago Press, 2005.

Sewell, William H. Jr. "Crooked Lines," *American Historical Review*, Vol. 113, No. 2, April 2008, 393–405.

Shiller, Robert J. *Subprime Solution: How Today's Global Financial Crisis Happened and What to Do About It*. Princeton, NJ: Princeton University Press, 2008.

Shiller, Robert J. "Narrative Economics," *American Economic Review*, Vol. 107, No. 4, April 2017, 967–1004.

Shiller, Robert J. "Narratives About Technology-Induced Job Degradations Then and Now," NBER Working Paper 25536, February 2019a.

Shiller, Robert J. *Narrative Economics: How Stories Go Viral and Drive Major Economic Events*. Princeton, NJ: Princeton University Press, 2019b.

Slobodian, Quinn. "Perfect Capitalism, Imperfect Humans: Race, Migration and the Limits of Ludwig von Mises's Globalism," *Contemporary European History*, Vol. 28, No. 2, May 2019, 143–155.

Stanfield, J. Ron. *The Economic Thought of Karl Polanyi*. New York: St. Martin's Press, 1986.

Strathern, Marilyn. *The Gender and the Gift: Problems with Women and Problems with Society in Melanesia*. Berkeley: University of California Press, 1988.

Streeck, Wolfgang. *Beyond Continuity: Institutional Change in Advanced Political Economies*. New York: Oxford University Press, 2005.

Taylor, Charles. *Sources of the Self: The Making of Modern Identity*. New York: Cambridge University Press, 1989.

Taylor, Charles. *The Language Animal: The Full Shape of the Human Linguistic Capacity*. Cambridge, MA: Harvard University Press, 2016.

Thelen, Kathleen. *Varieties of Liberalization and the New Politics of Social Solidarity*. New York: Cambridge University Press, 2014.

Veblen, Thorstein. *The Theory of the Leisure Class: An Economic Study of Institutions*. New York: Modern Library, 1934.

Wacquant, Loic. *Punishing the Poor: The Neoliberal Government of Social Insecurity*. Durham, NC: Duke University Press, 2009.

Weber, Max. *Economy and Society: An Outline of Interpretive Sociology*. Berkeley: University of California Press, 1978.

Webster, Charles. *The Great Instauration: Science, Medicine, and Reform 1626–1660*. New York: Holmes and Meier Publishers, 1975.

Williams, Raymond. *Marxism and Literature*. New York: Oxford University Press, 1977.

Williamson, Oliver E. *Markets and Hierarchies: Analysis and Antitrust Implications*. New York: MacMillan, 1975.

Williamson, Oliver E. *The Economic institutions of Capitalism. Firms, Markets, Relational Contracting*. New York: MacMillan, 1985.

Yuran, Noam. *What Money Wants: An Economy of Desire*. Stanford, CA: Stanford California Press, 2014.

Zein-Elabdin, Eiman O. "Economics, Postcolonial Theory and the Problem of Culture: Institutional Analysis and Hybridity," *Cambridge Journal of Economics*, Vol. 33, 2009, 1153–1167.

Zein-Elabdin, Eiman O. *Economics, Culture and Development*. New York: outledge, 2016.

Zuboff, Shoshana. *The Age of Surveillance Capitalism: The Fight for a Human Future at the New Frontier of Power*. New York: Public Affairs, 2019.

7 "Unique individuals"

Introduction

The liberal state can avoid addressing "society" by the formation of a set of "unique individuals," like private business corporations which are in fact collective entities. These so-called individuals are constructed with language statements, circumscribed by law, and differentiated from other entities by legal borders and boundaries. The overall integration is provided by financial flows and budgets, which provide the discipline of the "bottom line" as a survival constraint, ultimately managed by the state. Yet language, money, and finance are not typically considered "social," and so reality seems to consist only of these unique "individuals."

This chapter will proceed by examining the language statements with which each "individual" is constructed, and then to a consideration of each one, such as the modern business corporation and the family. The particular "language game" of modern capitalism may be a frequent reversal of reification/personification, which is typical of the ambiguous relationship of persons and property, as discussed in Chapter 2.

Borders and boundaries

The discreet entity of "the individual" and "property" is bounded by physical constraints and by legal limits delineated in language. The notion of independent private property has boundaries for the object which is owned, which enables the exclusion of non-owners, as a basic principle of property. The owner is likewise an "individual" with boundaries of the "self" (Mill 2003) within the private sphere (Berlin 1969). The liberal nation has "hard" borders, separating this competing nation from others. Boundaries and borders are key concepts in the liberal era (Brown 2010; Maier 2016) at the different scales of the person, the object, and the governing entity.

The interpenetrating "flows" of capital and labor, and likewise the ecology, are exceptional and frozen in time by reification and double-entry bookkeeping, if "counted" at all. Economics "flows" are documented in a series of snapshots per period, with "income" statements, with an aggregation at a longer time interval, considered "stocks" or balance sheets.

The global space of the earth and the continuous time are divided and segmented for management. The individual self is divided from others and "accountable" as a responsible individual, contrary to the "mob" of inebriated celebrants, armies of the unemployed, or vengeful pogroms.

Definition of property

The definition of property in language statements can be demonstrated in a logical series. For example, the property relation is a status function declaration, as defined by Searle (2010, 96–122), such as (1) below.

(1) X counts as Y in C.

where

X is any tangible object or relationship, such as a tool, a promise to pay, a corporation, or a patent, with potential use or exchange value.

Y is the concept of property with a list of rights (Alexander and Penalver 2012; MacPherson 1978; Ostrom 2010, 651; Ryan 1987; Banner 2011) such as exclusive use rights, alienation, returns, extraction, and transformation.

C is a court of law.

Searle's formula is general and can apply to other functions and objects. Property as defined this way is a type or relationship expressed in language, interpreted and enforced by the authorities of the state, conventionally recognized and legitimated. The set of objects in X can vary and historically has had wide application (Banner 2011). The notion of property is so useful because it is general, a relationship expressed in language, and the foundation for institutions such as the market.

These institutions exist because they are represented as existing, even if "people do not typically understand what is going on." That is, these language statements can create an institutional reality which can appear natural, or even Divine (Searle 2010, 95–96, 107).

Ownership is a particular relation with respect to the object, S.

(2) O has Y rights over X, enforced by C.

Where O is the owner, recognized by C against all non-owners.

In the early twentieth century, the legal realist school considered property as a "bundle of sticks" which could be separated, a discreet set of rights. The continuity provided in the concept of property is the specification of the ownership rights associated with Y, which exclusively reside in a specific "owner," O.

The notion of the protection of "property rights" can be interpreted as recognition and enforcement of the relationship as articulated by the formal statement (1) as applied to a given X. Yet "property" itself has no rights, if property is the inanimate object, and the so-called "rights" belong to the humans in the relationship. This concept of "property rights" is a form of "personification"

(Jameson 2019, 346–347), the opposite of reification. That is, it is clear that the agency belongs to the owner, O, and the enforcer, C. Except for land and human relationships, "property" is an object with no agency of its own.

When workers are separated from their own product and means of production, as well as means of subsistence, exchange becomes general, mediated by money, M.

(3) M can be exchanged for all X, among all O, according to rules of C.

When money can be exchanged for all commodities, including means of subsistence and means of production, the use value of the commodity labor power, as well as recognition, it becomes a generalized symbol of value. The money symbol represents value to humans but seems to represent value itself as an objective feature of the money symbol.

The person, the commodity labor power, becomes an "object," while the object "money" represents value to humankind. The money symbol represents value to humankind and becomes the most important means to survival and social esteem. This reversal is what Marx calls "commodity fetishism" and "money fetishism" (Davis 2017). The agency of the owners, O, becomes invisible relative to the flows of money, M, which seem to have autonomous movement, recorded in data with respect to "the economy," like the vapor trail of the jet airplane.

As the representation of generalized market exchange, the value of money is affected by the division of labor, cooperation, and technological innovation, as well as human striving and desire for survival and recognition. In such a case, there could be a love of money, like the fable of King Midas (Konings 2015). Ownership and exchange become the dominant social relationships, and money represents the power of that specific organization of the social whole. Money reflects the human condition but is ostensibly not about humans at all.

The relationship of "ownership"

The relationship of ownership conveys control and the right to appropriate, with no concern for the residue. Ownership can apply to land and to portions of labor time offered by an employee within the context of a labor contract.

According to Locke, this relationship of ownership is modeled on the Creator, which mankind can enact with respect to other persons and objects. The involvement of one's own labor is used to justify "ownership" of "property," but then the ownership quickly applies to one's own "servant" and his product. Then once owners have been created, their social contract to form the state protects this property, potentially against other workers. The formal "equality" in the state is among owners, who may or may not have created their "own" property by their "own" labor. The owners retain a right to revolution, should the operation of the state fail to protect their rights. The basis for freedom resides in the property owner, while government and taxation of property are the only forms of coercion, in this view.

This relationship contains a view of the world, including land and other humans, based on an implicit hierarchy. Once the commons are privatized, based on the rationale of increased productivity, access to the means of survival is only acquired by wage labor. The property-creating capacity of labor provides the rationale for ownership of the commons but then quickly disappears in the operation of money and division of labor in markets. Owners can command the labor of their employees, or "servants."

Yet the relationship of command is fully justified and pervasive throughout relations in liberal society, based on this initial contribution of one's own labor. What is at first an equalizer becomes a rationale for domination. That is, property ownership empowers "the individual" but only by entangling him in relationships of power. Market "incentives" operate by putting the conditions of life at risk for non-owners, a foundation of coercion which is invisible because of the transformation of the categories of the living person and the dead commodity, as discussed in Chapter 5. This inversion of living and dead is further revealed in the typical discussion of "human rights," which can only be "negative," protecting property, rather than "positive," assuring the conditions of life (Searle 2010, 184–194).

Literature on freedom

The canonical view of the liberal state is the foundation on freedoms of the individual and property (Persky 2016). Free, voluntary, rational exchange is fundamental to property and financial markets.

The liberal and libertarian view emphasizes the rational voluntary nature of these exchanges. This is a key difference from the institutionalist and critical views, which regard markets as based on coercion (Fried 1998; Judson 1996; MacPherson 1962; Pateman 1988). Accordingly, the same institutions can be viewed as forms of domination, as shown in Figures 7.1 and 7.2.

What is viewed as voluntary by market fundamentalists is based on the focus of individual choices of particular products and employers. The nature of these choices in a market economy with detailed division of labor is determined at a macro level, or the "social" dimension, integrated at the national level among competing nation-states in the global economy. The growth imperative for each state and the division of labor at the global level then shapes the options and constraints at the individual level.

The overarching norms and incentives are to maximize the monetary value of property by investment, production, and exchange. The individual decision-makers operate within this context, according to these norms. This macro-economic/social context of individual decisions renders the notion of the self-organizing market as possibly oversimplified; while Hayek was skeptical of socialists' ability to conduct rational economic planning (Konings 2018,

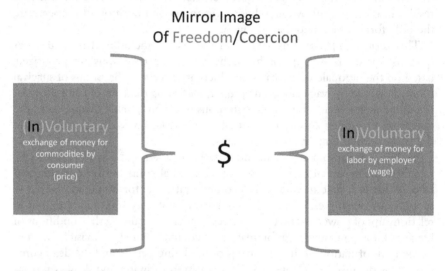

Figure 7.1 The Exchange Relation

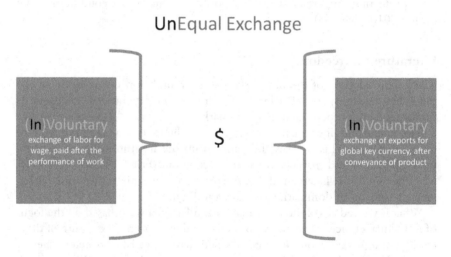

Figure 7.2 Market Coercion

100–106), it may also be naïve to underestimate the power of the imperatives of capital accumulation as an organizing template.

Money as a symbol of value

Given the definition of key terms and the associated institutional context described earlier, money can serve as a symbol of value.

Value is a human projection onto an object, based on its use value, including status with respect to non-owners.

If a word can refer to a thing or object, then a symbol, such as money, can refer to many objects.

In a market economy, money can be exchanged for any commodity, as defined by law (Sandel 2012; Pistor 2019) and enforced by courts. As a result, the symbol of money can signify this general capacity to acquire any object in exchange.

The market system involves human labor as a commodity in production and humans as consumers of commodities. The entire market system is human-relative, although it is perceived as being entirely about objects.

The "value" of the commodities reflects the human production time necessary and the various uses in human consumption.

The utility of the commodity is based on the assumed valuation by the **homo economicus**, a human person who perceives himself as a self-interested "individual," maximizing utility within a budget constraint. This role model is selected and enforced by the "market mentality" (Polanyi 1944; Stanfield 1986) which becomes pervasive in the market economy, and reflected in modern institutions.

(4) M can acquire any X, which counts as Y, according to C.

That is, money, or M, can be used in legal exchange to acquire any object, X, which is considered property, Y, according to the courts, C. Since X can be any means of subsistence or means of production, and which can only be acquired by M, and which access to M is restricted by financial systems, then M represents value in general in the human market system. Liquidity is ultimately enforced by the state for the specific object or symbol that is designated as legal tender (Pistor 2019), rather than "psychological preferences," which determine the composition among assets of different risk/return profiles in a given portfolio (Keynes 1964, 165–172).

Reification as a language game

Searle notes that the social contract theorists ignore the role of language. That is, the social contract is an abstract concept expressed in language, signifying the association of a set of people by formal agreement (Searle 2010, 62, 165).

> Once you have a shared language you already have a social contract; indeed you already have society. If by 'state of nature' is meant a state in which there are no human institutions, *then for language-speaking animals, there is no such thing as a state of nature.*
>
> (Searle 2010, 62; italics in original)

As Searle mentions, the corporation is an example of an institution with no necessary material foundation. The corporation can be created by authoritative statements, assigning functions to persons, which are enforced by the courts (Searle 2010, 20, 97, 100, 115, 119–120; Davis 2019).

> Limited liability corporations do not have any physical existence (this is why they are called "fictitious persons").
>
> (Searle 2010, 115)

Pistor reinforces the same point with the notion of "legal code," which can create "capital." In her analysis, the necessary characteristics which can transform a financial asset into "capital" are durability, transferability, and universality, which is based on the prototype of land (Pistor 2019, 5, 13, 19). That is, "legal fictions" are intangible assets that are "created in law," that are as durable as objects (Pistor 2019, 13). This modular use of "code," which can create new assets as valuable as if they were land, is a flexible and ubiquitous feature of capitalism. Treating a social institution as a physical object, or reification, was discussed in Chapter 2, naturalizes the relationship of ownership. When such a practice is widespread in a certain economic system, we may call this a "language game," drawing upon Wittgenstein (Sluga 2011, 62–64).

Because "property" is an organizing concept of capitalist society, there is a routine reversal of living and dead, as discussed in Chapter 5. Property, as a thing, a material object, cannot itself organize humans. Rather, the specific historical social relations of the property paradigm can be naturalized by referring to them as a thing, a natural object (Jameson 2019, 40–41, 98–99). We have also noted the reverse, that "property" is treated as an agent with rights, a form of personification. Arguably, capitalism systematically reverses the living and the dead as a way to naturalize the notion that money "grows," as if by its own power.

The importance of "fictitious commodities" in market economies has been noted by classical theorists such as Smith, Marx, and Polanyi, as well as contemporaries such as Jens Beckert. That is, regardless of the physical characteristics, a discreet object or function can become "property" by the rules with respect to its use. This potential disjuncture between the physical characteristics and the social/legal role can lead to a "problematic of representation" (Poovey 1998, 2008). For example, the commodity "labor power" can be seen as a form of freedom, as self-employment, by libertarians, or can be seen as a form of self-alienation, as discussed in Chapter 2. Well-accepted norms are for each person to be employed, to "work for a living," without which a person is not deserving of social support, or "handouts." When there is widespread unemployment, nonetheless, there is a crisis of meaning, which can lead to political unrest. That is, rather than single persons waiting patiently in the labor market queue for the next available position, there may be a collective response, which can challenge the meaning of the political norms.

Modern financial systems

Since "alienation" for sale is commonly one of the rights associated with property, there is implicitly a market and a modern financial system (Dincecco and Onorato 2018) to maintain a robust institution of individual private property. The integration of fiscal and military functions within the modern state evolved from trade and military competition in the fifteenth through the nineteenth centuries in the "fiscal military state" (Davis 2015). Credit skills capable of financing the military were directed to commodity production and innovation in the nineteenth and twentieth centuries. But the institutions of finance depend on the existence of the corporation and the state, as perpetual institutions capable of performing the requisite trades over an infinite time period.

Important for modernization and for the operation of financial markets was the assumption of abstract homogeneous time (Postone 1996; Thompson 1964; Ogle 2015; Galison 2003). The exact measurement of time, at specific locations, and the delineation of uniform time zones across the globe, was an important material manifestation of this new assumption. Along with these measurements and assumptions of productivity growth over time, the financial markets made time tradable.

That is, the trading of financial assets in capital markets is only possible because of the set of related assumptions and institutions illustrated in Figures 7.3 and 7.4.

The nation-state was able to assume perpetual life and so was able to issue perpetual debt. This future-oriented finance then enabled military finance, which then assured the continued existence of the state. Financial markets can function to provide credit, develop innovations, and to absorb uncertainty, as well as to intensify it in periodic self-fulfilling financial crises (Brine and Poovey 2017; Konings 2018, 3–4, 14–18; Davis 2018, 18–19).

> Governments typically hold out the promise of future growth to back the money they (or their central banks) issue or the debt they use instead to fill their state coffers. States at least have the power to impose obligations on their citizens to make good on these promises; even if this means that they have to impose draconian austerity measures on them.
>
> (Pistor 2019, 102)

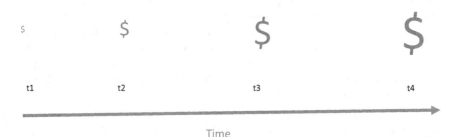

Figure 7.3 Capital Markets in Infinite Time

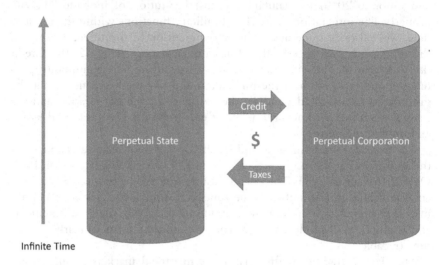

Figure 7.4 Perpetual Financial Markets

Unique institutions

By considering these "unique institutions" as a complete set, we can see how they are all constructed in language, in different categories of legal regimes. Rather than "the social," the liberal state only sees of a set of individuals, a set of unique, discreet institutions which are composed of human collectives. Each institution is a corporate form to discipline individual members with respect to a specific function with separate boundaries. The interface among these separate institutions is money, according to well-defined financial circuits.

Security comes from the collective, allowing for pooling of risks, but individuals must be disciplined. So the collective is denied, while "risk" is conceptualized abstractly and priced, using the market to manage and offset unforeseen outcomes or "systemic fallouts" (Searle 2010, 22, 116–119, 120–121; Beck 1992).

In the modern liberal state, there are unique institutions which are collective but are considered "individual," to be consistent with the liberal model. These unique "individuals" contain agency and subjectivity in distinct functional units or containers, within which relationships are substantive, personal, emotional, and embodied. There are separate domains of juridico-bureaucratic operation (example of the Austrian state; Judson 2016; Deak 2015) to manage the body and the population in temporal/geographic flows. Each of these unique "individuals" evolves historically and typically becomes more individuated over time, from original corporate form.

Corporations

The corporate form has a long history, even beginning with the medieval commune (Davis 2015, 2019). The corporation is a group of human persons who form a collective unit by oath, considered as one, with rotating membership, collective decision-making processes, and a common mission.

The modern private business corporation evolved from the guild and the monopoly merchant corporation of the early modern period. The key distinction was the permanent membership of skilled labor in the guild, once proceeding through apprenticeship and performance criteria, compared with the contingent employment of skilled and unskilled labor in the modern private business corporation.

The evolution of the corporate "legal person" has continued, influenced by law, technology, and the competitive environment (Pistor 2019, 47–76). The control of the corporation has shifted from the founding entrepreneur to management to the shareholder (Fligstein 1990). The internal organization of the corporation has shifted from a singled vertically integrated production flow, or "Fordist" model of sourcing, production of components, and final assembly in a single location. There was a lifetime employment model and internal labor market, which enabled a person to have an entire career in a single firm.

Large firms became multinationals in the early twentieth century (Wilkins 1970, 1974) and changed internal organization under the influence of global investment opportunities and information technology. The development of a "New Economy Business Model" shifted from secure employment to remuneration with stock options, so that mobility was enabled and potential rewarded (Lazonick 2009). Rather than internally generated innovation, there was acquisition of small start-ups to maintain the flow of new technologies and products. High-tech firms became noted for stock buy-backs, to maintain share prices, rather than for risky investments.

With deregulation of global finance in the 1980s, firms shifted again to "global supply chains," which integrated the production process across contract manufacturers and across countries (Milberg and Winkler 2013; Baldwin 2016). The strategy for development for emerging countries shifted from import substitution to export orientation. Participation in and "moving up" the global supply chains was the goal for the country, influenced by the sourcing decisions of the brand name lead manufacturing company (Davis 2018). The ability to shift supply chains from country to country, based on incentives and resource pricing, generated another level of insecurity for employees, companies, and emerging countries.

While incomes have increased in emerging countries, the loss of core employment has led to backlash in the heartland (Rajan 2019, 175–211). The entire global economy is subject to the financial decisions by major corporations.

Labor market institutions

Labor market institutions were in turn shaped by the evolving corporation. From sworn, fully enfranchised members of the guild to contingent employees of the modern business corporation, the status of labor was affected by corporate policies and management approaches, such as "scientific management," as well as the legal institutions in each country. The "varieties of capitalism" can be differentiated by the treatment of labor in terms of employment security, benefits, and rights to organize (Thelen 2014; Hall and Soskice 2001).

Family

The biological family is the oldest form of collective organization, from tribes and clans in prehistoric periods. The legal organization of the family is, nonetheless, important in the modern period. Modern states "identify" each individual by parents, name, date and location of birth, as part of a modern census of population.

The biological kinship group is often formally recognized by the legal relation of marriage. The family is often considered a collective entity, with responsibility assigned to the "head of household," or primary earners. Income is pooled among members for the purposes of personal development, socialization, and maturation of the next generation. Economic theory has assigned altruism to the family, in contrast to the usual assumption of self-interest (Folbre 1994). The rational gender division of labor is assumed to be based on gains from specialization and comparative skills (Becker 1981).

Long-term changes have included the traditional consideration of marriage as an indissoluble bond and the expectation of female chastity to the modern view of no-fault divorce. Women have been considered the husband's property, under the doctrine of coverture (Staves 1990; Basch 1982). Legal movements to allow for married women's property gained credence in the nineteenth century, while the Equal Rights Amendment failed (Kruse and Zelizer 2019, 66–80) in the twentieth century. As women's labor force participation increased after World War II, claims to equality were more successful, but women are still considered under the rubric of the family and reproduction.

Demographic trends result from a complex set of institutions and practices such as contraception, fertility options, adoption, custody, foster care, and age limits on marriage. Religious institutions typically provide the norms for sexuality. Access to any income outside of the labor market has been controversial and considered a cause for weaker work incentives for labor market participation and higher incidence of births outside of marriage. Stricter gender norms are emphasized by conservatives, who otherwise typically support privacy and autonomy of the private sphere (Latour 2018), in order to consolidate "unpaid" reproduction in the family without needing the support of the state (Cooper 2017).

Social reproduction theory has considered the conditions under which the labor force is replaced. For example, there are four stages in forms of the family (Fraser and Jaeggi 2018, 31–35, 82–88), evolving along with systems of commodity production. In the evolution from the mercantile to the industrial period,

> Social reproduction [was detached from] broader forms of community life, [and] recast as the province of women within the private family ... the

liberal regime invented a new bourgeois imaginary centered on intensified gender difference and the new ideal of 'separate spheres.'

(Fraser and Jaeggi 2018, 83)

Norms of monogamy, chastity, and inheritance have been methods for conveying property across generations (Glendon 1987; Basch 1982; Cott 2000; Hartog 2000; Davidoff and Hall 1987; Cooper 2017).

Treatment of the biological family as a cohesive unit has varied historically. For example, slave families were not recognized as collective entities (Stanley 1998), and, more recently, Hispanic immigrant families have been separated at the border by the Trump administration.

Once the legally defined nuclear family was considered the "container" responsible for social reproduction, any dysfunction can be blamed on the welfare state, or on feminist organizing, by critics from the right. As a result, political positions of women have been divided. Women have mobilized politically for equal rights and equal pay, while women have also supported political organizations which stress the importance of the family and the male family wage. Family stability and human development indicators also vary by class (Carlson and England 2011), allowing critics on the left to attribute any family "crisis" to inequality and instability of economic conditions.

Gender norms have become less restrictive to qualify for the marriage contract. While the Equal Marriage Act was recognized by the Supreme Court on June 26, 2015, allowing same-sex marriage in all 50 states, further changes in this long-standing institution are expected.

Church

The US Constitution protects the practice of religion from state interference, documenting the shift from state religion and mediation by priest to the individual private relation to the deity, with multiple Protestant sects and formal religious tolerance. Although religious institutions are formally separate from the state, there is increasing political mobilization based on religious affiliation.

Others

It is beyond the scope of this chapter to review all other "unique individuals" who are a formal legal part of the liberal state, and manage important functions. Such others include educational institutions, public and private, as well as local municipalities, which are often incorporated and chartered. There are not-for-profit corporations which perform public roles, as well as political parties.

Nation

The modern nation-state is an entity competing with others in a global international system, for territory and trade. The nation-state manages domestic production within its own borders while also managing flows of capital and labor across borders to maximize profit and growth. As Smith articulates, the goal is the "wealth of nations," based on a system of relationships, with factor mobility and profit incentive.

Summary

For each of these separate unique "individuals," there are participants recruited from the population, according to certain rules, regulations, and laws, which allow each to persist over time. Each of these unique "individuals" must also have a location for its operations, at a given space. That is, each of these "individuals" interacts with the markets for land and labor, in a cross-cutting competition, and also with overlapping membership. Corporations and families rent or buy land and construct and occupy buildings which provide permanent shelter. Each of these unique "individuals" are prescribed by laws, rules, and norms but also involve physical bodies and material spaces. There are also interactions among them; for example, members of the family may participate in the labor market, employed by a corporation, the survival of which affects the stability of the family (Cooper 2017). Such interactions are rarely considered when studying each separate "individual."

Modern culture

While each of the aforementioned "unique individuals" contains personal, emotional, and embodied relationships within a legal boundary, expression of emotion in public is often by means of "culture." That is, public emotional expressions are mediated by a public culture, consisting of print culture, novels, movies, mass media, sports competitions, and recently, social media. As a result, public performers are typically highly remunerated, with mass followings for acclaimed actors, musicians, sports stars, and authors.

In commercial venues, emotions are rendered objective and observable, such as movies or TV, from a distance, rather than expressed in immediate personal physical contact. In this sense, emotions are also objectified, produced, and exchanged via cultural objects, as commodities.

There are only "individuals"

As Thatcher has declared, "there is no such thing as society." In this chapter we have explained the logic of this position: there are only "individuals," which can include collective entities composed of overlapping generations of individual persons who coordinate functions in well-defined roles.

According to the analysis of reification in Chapter 2, money represents the whole, although not recognized as a representation of society. Money is treated merely as a convenience, a form of individual private property. The collective nature of money is not acknowledged by users or economic theorists, although it would have no meaning if not recognized by other users and reinforced by the state.

As a result, the management of money devolved to professional "money managers" (Brine and Poovey 2017; Tymoigne and Wray 2016) and holders of significant wealth who are also courted by the state as investors in public debt. The safety of money is based on the pooling and diversification of risk within a larger collective, a matter which is considered only abstractly as managing and pricing "risk" (Beck 1992; Beckert 2016; Rajan 2005). The social nature of "risk management" is not considered relevant by professionals, only the assessment of probabilities and placement of wagers. The other side of the wager, the counter party, is not explicitly theorized and can lead to the emergence of "systemic risk" quite unexpectedly, as in AIG in 2008. The goals of money managers then become the preservation of wealth rather than productive investment, enriching money holders even further by means of public backstop. The public capacity becomes focused on wealth management and the production of "safe assets" (Davis 2017) rather than public goods and private growth. Income inequality and financial instability are the outcome.

Conclusion

Each of the earlier-mentioned "unique individuals" is assumed to have perpetual life, but in fact there is considerable flux in definition and relative power. Because these "unique individuals" are typically considered separately, the impact of one on the other is rarely studied. For example, the decline of secure employment in corporations affects families and communities, as well as finance and culture (Cooper 2017). Because money is the link among these "unique individuals," and money is not understood as social, the social disappears.

Division is a strategy for governance, even if borders and boundaries are arbitrary. These institutional divisions are established in law, managed by bureaucracy, and embedded in the identities of discreet "individual" participants. As a result, conflict is contained within each "unique individual," such as conflict between employers and workers within the corporation, or conflict regarding gender roles as managed within the family. "Moral panics" can occur when the conflict is no longer contained but spills over across the jurisdictional boundaries of each "unique individual." For example, the women's movement spilled out of the family into the political sphere in pursuit of women's suffrage, and later equal rights and equal pay, and with protests against sexual harassment at work, or quantitative indicators of "crisis" such as too many unwed women or too many births out of wedlock. The "social" is a symptom of the dysfunction of "unique individuals" rather than a critique of individuation itself.

Whenever these spillovers occur, there are "social problems." That is, the concept of the "social" is an expression of a problem which is not adequately managed by the responsible "unique individual." In the context of the liberal state, the problem cannot be attributed to the strategy of individuation itself but always to the poor performance of a particular one of them. There is an interface by money and financial flows. Because money is the only means of managing the whole, contradictions are expressed by financial crises.

"The individual" and "the social" are logically complementary, although reified abstractions presume to treat each concept separately. The denial of this integral connection is part of the paradigm of individual private property and its paradox. Such conceptual inadequacy leaves the state and the economy vulnerable to political and financial instability.

Bibliography

Alexander, Gregory S. and Eduardo M. Penalver (eds.). *An Introduction to Property Theory.* New York: Cambridge University Press, 2012.

Baldwin, Richard. *The Great Convergence: Information Technology and the New Globalization.* Cambridge, MA: Harvard University Press, 2016.

Banner, Stuart. *American Property: A History of How, Why, and What We Own.* Cambridge, MA: Harvard University Press, 2011.

Basch, Norma. *In the Eyes of the Law: Women, Marriage, and Property in Nineteenth Century New York.* Ithaca, NY: Cornell University Press, 1982.

Bauman, Zygmunt and Thomas Leoncini. *Born Liquid: Transformations in the Third Millennium.* Cambridge, UK: Polity Press, 2019.

Beck, Ulrich. *Risk Society: Towards a New Modernity.* London: Sage, 1992.

Becker, Gary S. *A Treatise on the Family.* Cambridge, MA: Harvard University Press, 1981.

Beckert, Jens. *Imagined Futures: Fictional Expectations and Capitalist Dynamics.* Cambridge, MA: Harvard University Press, 2016.

Bell, Daniel. *The Cultural Contradictions of Capitalism.* New York: Basic Books, 1978.

Berlin, Isaiah. *Four Essays on Liberty.* New York: Oxford University Press, 1969.

Brine, Kevin R. and Mary Poovey. *Finance in America: An Unfinished Story.* Chicago: University of Chicago Press, 2017.

Brown, Wendy. *Walled States, Waning Sovereignty.* New York: Zone Books, 2010.

Carlson, Marcia J. and Paula England (eds.). *Social Class and Changing Families in an Unequal America.* Stanford, CA: Stanford University Press, 2011.

Champlin, Dell P. and Janet T. Knoedler (eds.). *The Institutionalist Tradition in Labor Economics.* Armonk, NY: M.E. Sharpe, 2004.

Cooper, Melinda. *Family Values: Between Neoliberalism and the New Social Conservatism.* New York: Zone Books, 2017.

Cott, Nancy F. *Public Vows: A History of Marriage and the Nation.* Cambridge, MA: Harvard University Press, 2000.

Cutler, A. Claire. *Private Power and Global Authority.* New York: Cambridge University Press, 2003.

Davidoff, Leonore and Catherine Hall. *Family Fortunes: Men and Women of the English Middle Class, 1780–1850.* Chicago: University of Chicago Press, 1987.

Davis, Ann E. *The Evolution of the Property Relation: Understanding Paradigms, Debates, Prospects.* New York: Palgrave MacMillan, 2015.

Davis, Ann E. "Fetishism and Financialization," *Review of Radical Political Economics,* Vol. 49, No. 4, December 2017, 551–558.

Davis, Ann E. "Global Production Networks and the Private Organization of World Trade," *Journal of Economic Issues,* Vol. 52, No. 2, June 2018, 358–367.

Davis, Ann E. "Is There a History of Property? Periodization of Property Regimes and Paradigms," in Staci Zavattaro, Gregory R. Peterson, and Ann E. Davis (eds.), *Property Rights in Contemporary Governance.* Albany: State University Press of New York, 2019, 5–24.

Deak, John. *Forging a Multinational State: State Making in Imperial Austria from the Enlightenment to the First World War*. Stanford, CA: Stanford University Press, 2015.

Dincecco, Mark and Massimiliano Gaetano Onorato. *From Warfare to Wealth: The Military Origins of Urban Prosperity in Europe*. Cambridge, UK: Cambridge University Press, 2018.

Fligstein, Neil. *The Transformation of Corporate Control*. Cambridge, MA: Harvard University Press, 1990.

Folbre, Nancy. *Who Pays for the Kids? Gender and the Structures of Constraint*. New York: Routledge, 1994.

Fraser, Nancy, and Rahel Jaeggi. *Capitalism: A Conversation in Critical Theory*. Edited by Brian Milstein. Cambridge, UK: Polity Press, 2018.

Fried, Barbara. *The Progressive Assault on Laissez Faire: Robert Hale and the First Law and Economics Movement*. Cambridge, MA: Harvard University Press, 1998.

Galison, Peter. *Einstein's Clocks, Poincare's Maps: Empires of Time*. New York: W.W. Norton & Company, 2003.

Glendon, Mary Ann. *Abortion and Divorce in Western Law*. Cambridge, MA: Harvard University Press, 1987.

Goldin, Claudia. "The Quiet Revolution that Transformed Women's Employment, Education, and Family," *American Economic Review*, Vol. 96, No. 2, May 2006, 1–21.

Hall, Peter A. and David Soskice (eds.). *Varieties of Capitalism: The Institutional Foundations of Comparative Advantage*. New York: Oxford University Press, 2001.

Hartog, Hendrik. *Man and Wife in America: A History*. Cambridge, MA: Harvard University Press, 2000.

Hochschild, Arlie Russell. *The Outsourced Self: Intimate Life in Market Times*. New York: Henry Holt and Company, 2012.

Hochschild, Arlie Russell. *So How's The Family? And Other Essays*. Berkeley: University of California Press, 2013.

Jameson, Fredric. *Allegory and Ideology*. London: Verso, 2019.

Judson, Pieter M. *Exclusive Revolutionaries: Liberal Politics, Social Experience, and National Identity in the Austrian Empire, 1848–1914*. Ann Arbor: The University of Michigan Press, 1996.

Judson, Pieter M. *The Habsburg Empire: A New History*. Cambridge, MA: Harvard University Press, 2016.

Keynes, John Maynard. *The General Theory of Employment, Interest, and Money*. New York: Harcourt, Brace & World, 1964.

Konings, Martijn. *The Emotional Logic of Capitalism: What Progressives Have Missed*. Stanford, CA: Stanford University Press, 2015.

Konings, Martijn. *Capital and Time: For a New Critique of Neoliberal Reason*. Stanford, CA: Stanford University Press, 2018.

Kruse, Kevin M. and Julian E. Zelizer. *Fault Lines: A History of the United States Since 1974*. New York: W.W. Norton & Company, 2019.

Latour, Bruno. *Down to Earth: Politics in the New Climatic Regime*. New York: Polity Press, 2018.

Lazonick, William. *Sustainable Prosperity in the New Economy? Business Organization and High-Tech Employment in the United States*. Kalamazoo, MI: W.E. Upjohn Institute for Employment Research, 2009.

MacPherson, C. B. *The Political Theory of Possessive Individualism: Hobbes to Locke*. Oxford: Clarendon Press, 1962.

MacPherson, C. B. *Property, Mainstream and Critical Positions*. Toronto: University of Toronto Press, 1978.

Maier, Charles S. *Leviathan 2.0: Inventing Modern Statehood*. Cambridge, MA: Harvard University Press, 2012.

Maier, Charles S. *Once Beyond Borders. Territories of Power, Wealth, and Belonging Since 1500.* Cambridge, MA: Harvard University Press, 2016.

Milberg, William and Deborah Winkler. *Outsourcing Economics: Global Value Chains in Capitalist Development.* New York: Cambridge University Press, 2013.

Mill, John Stuart. *On Liberty.* New Haven: Yale University Press, 2003.

Ogle, Vanessa. *The Global Transformation of Time: 1870–1950.* Cambridge, MA: Harvard University Press, 2015.

Ostrom, Elinor. "Beyond Markets and States: Polycentric Governance of Complex Economic Systems," *American Economic Review,* Vol. 100, No. 3, June 2010, 641–672.

Pateman, Carole. *The Sexual Contract.* Stanford, CA: Stanford University Press, 1988.

Persky, Joseph. *The Political Economy of Progress: John Stuart Mill and Modern Radicalism.* New York: Oxford University Pres, 2016.

Pistor, Katharina. *The Code of Capital: How the Law Creates Wealth and Inequality.* Princeton, NJ: Princeton University Press, 2019.

Polanyi, Karl. *The Great Transformation.* Boston: Beacon Press, 1944.

Poovey, Mary. *A History of the Modern Fact: Problems of Knowledge in the Sciences of Wealth and Society.* Chicago: University of Chicago Press, 1998.

Poovey, Mary. *Genres of the Credit Economy: Mediating Value in the Eighteenth-and Nineteenth-Century Britain.* Chicago: University Press, 2008.

Postone, Moishe. *Time, Labor, and Social Domination: A Reinterpretation of Marx's Critical Theory.* New York: Cambridge University Press, 1996.

Rajan, Raghuram G. "Has Financial Development Made the World Riskier?" Cambridge, MA: National Bureau of Economic Research #11728, November 2005.

Rajan, Raghuram G. *The Third Pillar: How Markets and the State Leave the Community Behind.* New York: Penguin, 2019.

Rudolph, Julia (ed.). *History and the Nation.* Lewisburg: Bucknell University Press, 2006.

Ryan, Alan. *Property.* Minneapolis: University of Minnesota Press, 1987.

Sandel, Michael J. *What Money Can't Buy: The Moral Limits of Markets.* New York: Farrar, Straus, and Giroux, 2012.

Searle, John R. *Making the Social World: The Structure of Human Civilization.* New York: Oxford University Press, 2010.

Sluga, Hans. *Wittgenstein.* Oxford, UK: Wiley-Blackwell, 2011.

Stanfield, J. Ron. *The Economic Thought of Karl Polanyi: Lives and Livelihood.* New York: St. Martin's Press, 1986.

Stanley, Amy Dru. *From Bondage to Contract: Wage Labor, Marriage, and the Market in the Age of Slave Emancipation.* New York: Cambridge University Press, 1998.

Staves, Susan. *Married Women's Separate Property in England, 1660–1833.* Cambridge, MA: Harvard University Press, 1990.

Thelen, Kathleen. *Varieties of Liberalization and the New Politics of Social Solidarity.* New York: Cambridge University Press, 2014.

Thompson, E. P. *The Making of the English Working Class.* New York: Pantheon, 1964.

Tymoigne, Eric and L. Randall Wray. *The Rise and Fall of Money Manager Capitalism: Minsky's Half Century from World War Two to the Great Recession.* New York: Routledge, 2016.

Wilkins, Myra. *The Emergence of the Multinational Enterprise: American Business Abroad from the Colonial Era to 1914.* Cambridge, MA: Harvard University Press, 1970.

Wilkins, Myra. *The Maturing of the Multinational Enterprise: American Business Abroad from 1914 to 1970.* Cambridge, MA: Harvard University Press, 1974.

8 The property paradigm

Property paradigm as a world view

Consolidating the discussion in earlier chapters, it is important to emphasize how property as a paradigm pervades the world view of modernity (Davis 2015, 9–17, 32–42). The individual, private property, and the state form a trinity of this world view (Davis 2015, 11–13), which sees the earth as formed by God for human sustenance and flourishing, providing the materials for potential commodities for production and sale. This is an instrumental view of life on earth, providing for the "wealth of nations." The term "property" is like a metaphor (Haraway 2004) for a subsistence farm, a parcel of land allocated to an individual which allows autonomy and self-sufficiency outside of the state. This image carries the feasibility of an isolated life being viable and allows the elision of the norms and institutions by which modern individuals actually exist. This reification of the term property, by which social institutions appear to be a simple object, removes awareness of the world view of modern market economies and renders this individual in a Lockean state of nature.

If the term "property" is a metaphor for ownership of means to independent subsistence, then "self-ownership" can be understood as a form of freedom, by analogy. Certain libertarians do make this association (Cohen 1995), although it can also be considered a form of self-alienation and splitting.

In the name of property, one can control others for the purposes of expanding value and wealth. Discussing the Enlightenment, Horkheimer and Adorno write:

> What men want to learn from nature is how to use it in order wholly to dominate it and other men. That is the only aim. Ruthlessly, in despite of itself, the Enlightenment has extinguished any trace of its own self-consciousness.
>
> (Horkheimer and Adorno 1972, 4)

Referring to the power of chief executives of business corporations, Baritz termed this the "divine right of property (Baritz 1960, 4).

This world view could be called the "merchant's view." Foucault (1994) developed the concept of *epistemes*, or ways of viewing knowledge in distinct historical periods. Historians of science have noted the development of the "objective" gaze, adopted by the scientists to assure colleagues of reliability and replicability of experiments (Daston and Galison 2010; Poovey 1998). Latour observes the same approach to methodology in economics, which has become a valueless science of values (Latour 2013, 447–450). Like Smith's "impartial spectator" (Kuiper 2003; Poovey 1995, 32–33), the scientific self was split into an "active experimenter and passive observer," which was inherently unstable (Daston and Galison 2010, 250–251). Warner mentions the "self-abstraction" of the mass subject (Warner 1992).

This objective "view from nowhere" (Poovey 2002; Taylor 2007; Nelson 2016; Nagel 1986; Bourdieu 2004, 115–116) can be attributed to the merchant's gaze, in my view[1]. An early seventeenth-century Italian monetary theorist, Bernardo Davanzati, describes the merchant's view of the world (Foucault 1970, 168–174; Maifreda 2012, 94).

> To be always acquainted with the Rule and Arithmetical proportion which things bear among themselves and with Gold, it were [sic] necessary to looke down from Heaven, or some exalted Prospect upon all the things that exist, or are done upon the Earth; or rather to count their Images reflected in the Heavens as in a true Mirror. Then we might cast up the Sum and say, There is on Earth just so much Gold, so many Things, so many men, so many Desires: As many of those Desires as any thing can satisfy, so much it is worth of another thing, so much Gold it is worth.
>
> (quoted in Vilar 1976, 190–191)

Nagel explores the notion of the "objective self" which is capable of viewing itself from outside and seeing its own subjective self as one among many others (Nagel 1986, 54–66). Rather than see this notion as related to the emergence of the market and modernity, he sees the existence of dual perspectives, subjective and objective, as "a problem that faces every creature with the impulse and the capacity to transcend its particular point of view and to conceive of the world as a whole" (Nagel 1986, 3). This description implies a positive value to objectivity, while he also identifies certain difficulties, such as a tendency to nihilism (Nagel 1986, 209, 219–220). This "objective self" is very abstract and detached and has no particular allegiance to the family and personal relationships by which it may have been formed (Nagel 1986, 165, 175–180). One outcome of achieving such objectivity is an ethics from a universal standpoint, but it is only one of five possibilities (Nagel 1986, 193–200). This divided self, between subjective and objective, can be integrated with religion, commitment to certain missions beyond oneself (what he calls "conversion"), and to politics (Nagel 1986, 206–207, 210). Although Nagel seeks to find a way to integrate these two world views, he ultimately concedes that the achievement of the "objective self" is an unstable position.

I argue that this world view is associated with modernity and the emergence of the market, but Nagel sees it as "natural," with only one brief reference to "bourgeois morality" (Nagel 1986, 166). To me, the instability of this construct, the "objective self," reveals the contradictions of modernity and the impulse to personal attachment and to differentiation that is often observed to escape these dilemmas.

This shift in perspective was also evident in Renaissance art and cartography (Harvey 1990, 245–253). The notion of paradigm, or "background" (Searle 2010) or "social imaginary" (Taylor 2002, 2007) is often used to convey this notion of conventional wisdom which is necessary to navigate contemporary institutions with "savoir faire."

> Our social imaginary . . . incorporates a sense of the normal expectations that we have of one another, the kind of common understanding which enables us to carry out the collective practices that make up our social life. This incorporates some sense of how we all fit together . . . [and] is both factual and 'normative.'
>
> (Taylor 2002, 106)

The merchant's knowledge was all-encompassing, as anything on earth could become a commodity. The merchant's special expertise was knowing what commodities could be produced in what location, for what each commodity could be sold in another location, and when. Initially dealing with bullion, the merchant's skills at developing credit instruments proved essential to emerging nation-states constantly at war. As Italian city-states developed skills in public finance, the merchants became more powerful in organs of government.

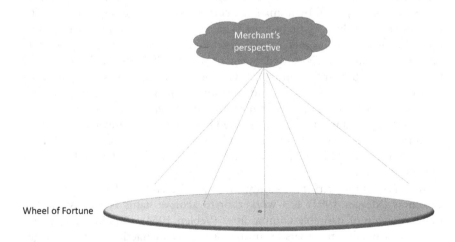

Figure 8.1 The Merchant's Gaze

Such a "totalizing" world view could also represent the role of capital as an active agent (Postone 1993, 78–80, 349–352) in organizing financial flows throughout the ever-extending geography of world trade. According to Marx, the emerging class would claim its power by "universalizing" its particular perspective (Tucker 1978, 173–188). The ability of modern science to observe a phenomenon, analyze its discrete components, and recombine into new materials was brought in aid to capital in the process of commodity production and automation (Marx 1967, Vol. I, Ch. 15, 386–387, 486).

This merchant's view of the world would encompass all human bodies as potential commodities, as well as natural objects and potential scientific transformations. The "value" would appear as imminent in the objects themselves, in the price they could garner in a particular market place in a discrete time. This "sciences of man" (Foucault 1970, 344–348) places humans at the center while also displacing any particular person into the abstracting financial flows of the capitalist circuits. That is, humans are at the center of the universe, but only as "abstract Man," in the general role of production and consumption to expand value. The source of value seems to be money itself, which has no necessary "body" at all, and yet can represent all bodies.

That is, the merchant's view, or "the economy" as an abstraction, contains a perspective on the human and natural world, which assesses the value of each as potential commodities. This is a way of knowing the world, a paradigm. Humans are viewed as objects of potential value, a perspective that they understand and seek to enhance. That is, there is a particular subject/object perspective embedded within capitalism.

The embedded individual, institutions, and world view

The individual must participate in the market to gain access to the means of subsistence and to gain social recognition. The market is a method of objectifying the value placed by humans on certain commodities, which appear to have intrinsic "value" in themselves. The market is an "autonomous agent," operating as a "steering mechanism" for humans, who respond to price signals. Such actions are rewarded by increasing wealth, even if by means of treating other humans as instruments. The market operates entirely with respect to humans as producers and consumers but appears entirely objective. Like Wittgenstein's conditions of meaning for language, "the economy" is a series of terms and institutions, elaborated by experts, interpreted and enacted by humans, without which it would not operate (Nagel 1986, 105–109). That is, the economy seems to be an autonomous machine but is only by and for humans.

To survive in a market economy, one must be able to demonstrate value to others (Meister 1991) as a worker, or to achieve status as a consumer by the ownership of desirable commodities (Veblen 1934). One becomes aware of one's own value to others by means of market interactions, which trigger efforts to enhance that value. The agency of "the individual" is constrained within certain roles, norms, and channels established by the financial circuits,

Figure 8.2 Circulating "Bodies" of "Equal Individuals" Organized by Financial Flows of Wheel of Fortune

the imperative of which is to expand. Self-objectification is a form of self-awareness which is well suited to such participation in market processes.

Each individual is aware of competition with many others and so seeks advantage and differentiation, or alliances and associations, to enhance personal competitiveness. Such efforts by individuals serve to drive the market as a whole.

The irony of money is that it represents and expresses the value of commodities to humans but seems to be entirely objective. Prices are the means of calculation for "rational" investments to expand value and wealth (Cook 2017). Yet prices also reflect social valuation of commodities and persons, as CEO pay reflects the status and performance of that particular manager. As visible indicators of value, both personal and impersonal, the total compensation of the CEO becomes a matter of competition to expand the range of applicants (Frank and Cook 1995). Like "conspicuous consumption" of luxury goods, the value of the commodity is reflected in its price (Veblen 1934).

Money is both an indicator of status and an instrument for acquiring means of subsistence. In this sense the debate between "recognition" and "distribution" (Fraser 2013; Butler 2008) does not fully acknowledge the social role of money, as well as its economic role. Money as an incentive competes with intrinsic motives (Bowles 2016) but can also be understood as reflecting social metrics of common desirability.

Money as an objective metric of social subjective value is another peculiar inversion of subject and object in capitalism. A person pursuing wealth can be understood as serving society, as well as pursuing self-interest, according to Smith and Mandeville, in the common defense of the market. Yet that person seems to be an autonomous "individual," with no social connections at all. That is, the only "social" connection is money, which is understood to be individual and private, the very opposite of social.

Each individual user of money offers herself as an object for sale and also expresses her personal preferences and achieves her symbolic status by her purchases. Both aspects are intensely social, even as one dimension is objective and the other subjective. The individual is split into two aspects, which Nagel is trying to integrate (Nagel 1986), while apparently not recognizing the inherent splitting of the human agent in capitalism. That is, social recognition for individuals is mediated abstractly by means of money in a market economy.

As market society develops, each person internalizes the "merchant's view" of herself as she seeks to find positions in the market economy, in employment and in social networks. The subjective/objective dimensions are manifested separately in each person's self-awareness, as well as in socio-economic processes. That is, the "individual," or Nagel's "objective self," is vulnerable and fragile (Riesman 1950; Lasch 1977).

Money is the mirror for the "looking-glass self"

Hegel discusses the market from the point of view of the subject and object, which are integrated by participation in the market (Meister 1991, 32–43). A market participant becomes effective the more she can discern the values and needs of others and can develop the capacity to meet those needs. That is, we develop an awareness of the standpoint of the other and use that awareness to develop ourselves.

> Markets would not exist if we did not need material objects in order to survive. Yet possessions have value in the marketplace only insofar as they are socially recognized as valuable by others. In a system of exchange, ownership is a form of social power allowing us to fulfill our needs by satisfying the needs of others. . . . In an important sense, our only real economic need is a need to be needed.
>
> (Meister 1991, 33)

As early modern consumers became accustomed to express status and individuality through dress and fashion (Howell 2010; McKendrick, Brewer, and Plumb 1982), after the repeal of sumptuary legislation, so do individuals in the modern period express themselves through stylized objects. The more expensive the commodity, the higher the status in terms of "conspicuous consumption" (Veblen 1934). Further, money itself has become a status good. For example, CEO pay is reported and ranked among leading corporations, indicating which person has achieved the enviable status of the richest. The pay competition has become a "winner-take-all" game to increase incentives and expand the number of applicants and aspirants (Frank and Cook 1995).

In fact, money itself expresses social value by means of the market. While extolling the perfectly competitive market as no longer requiring morality, Gauthier uses Marx to express the role of the price.

> Although prices are determined, given the technology of production, purely by the subjective value – the preferences – of the individuals interacting in the market, yet they present themselves to each as an objective datum, an objective value to which s/he must conform in his/her activities. Marxist analysis provides us with a useful term for this appearance of objectivity – it is a form of fetishism.
>
> (Gauthier 1982, 44)

The market orients each individual to seek the activities and capacities that are most valued by others. Such individuals are rewarded by developing a capacity to see themselves from the market's point of view. Such a split between subject and object is resolved by receiving the compensation which is the market's judgment and reward. One becomes whole again having won this form of pecuniary recognition from a generalized "other." But this satisfaction lasts only until the next paycheck and the next job. One must repeat the personal financial circuit – work, pay, consumption, display – to achieve personal integration on an ongoing basis. Money is as necessary to the post-modern personality as property was to Hegel's early modern personality. In this context, there is no divide between recognition and distribution, in the debate between Fraser and Butler (Butler 2008; Fraser 2013, 175–186). Money provides the means for both recognition and distribution.

In this context, this modern subjectivity is amenable to Smith's extension of the market and later to further financialization of social relations.

According to Marshall McLuhan (1967), the medium is the message. In this example, we are our money. Our money is us.

Gender as a special category

In a society based on "self-ownership," women and slaves are not capable of owning themselves. This lack of ownership assigns women and slaves to a different social status. To Aristotle, women are "defective," and men regard women as the "Other," instead of the typical reciprocity of social relationships (Beauvoir 1952, xviii–xix; Strathern 2016). Women's labor is considered the "property of another" (Gilman 1899, 7). Her economic dependence prevents her full development and capacity for political solidarity. Women's loyalty can be divided based on relationships with their husbands, who support them, vs. solidarity with other women, whom they may employ as servants (Meister 1991, 331–334). If property is necessary for personality, according to Hegel, then women's status *as* property may inhibit their personal development.

Women's differential treatment as self-owners has been grounded on the transmission of property across generations. The requirement of chastity for women of the middle class has been primarily to assure the clear identification of heirs, the formation of kinship alliances, and assurance of ethnic purity (Davidoff and Hall 1987; Foucault 1978). Marriage is presumed to be a voluntary legal contract between consenting adults (Pateman 1988; Basch 1982; Hartog 2000; Cott 2000; Staves 1990). The traditional definition of "femininity" has included being sexually attractive to men, to make herself both "object and prey" (Scott 1996, 170). When marriage was the only route to economic sufficiency for women, this behavioral norm of desirability was a matter of survival.

A series of reforms has improved the status of women, from coverture to the married women's property acts, women's suffrage, active participation in the wage labor force, and equal pay amendments. Yet differential treatment of women provides a template for "natural" inequality. Such differentiation, in the context of de jure equality, underscores the possibility of subordination, a potential risk for every so-called "individual."

As women's education has improved, and their labor force participation has increased, they have claims to self-ownership as their capacities increase. The treatment of capacity for reproduction as owned by women has been recognized in the US Supreme Court case, Roe v. Wade. In this context, however, self-ownership has been contradictory. While it gives women greater control over their own bodies, birth and human reproduction are unavoidably collective. The claim to an individual woman's exclusive right to decide regarding her "own" fertility opens conflicts regarding an issue of greater than personal significance, the rate of growth of the population as a whole. Women's individual claims in this regard then conflict with economic interests and with religious world views, setting up an ongoing contentious political debate. Some women defend the family and male authority, in the hope of protection for their children, while others defend women's rights to equal employment and equal wages, in the hopes of equality and independence.

As historian Joan Scott has said, feminism is the result of liberal individualism and is one of its contradictions (Scott 1996, 18, 168). Women claim to be self-owners, like all other "individuals," which then provokes the unavoidable schisms which are "central to the ideological organization" of the state (Scott 1996, 175).

Formation of the subject in discourse

According to Scott, "discursive processes – the epistemologies, institutions, and practices ... produce political subjects ... [and] many factors constitute [a woman's] agency" (Scott 1996, 16). I propose that the paradigm of property produces subjects, authorizing and privileging actors who own and who protect property. This paradigm can help to explain the anomalies of "the individual," who is often conceived as a self-owner. All are "equal" owners and so are recognized before the law. But property ownership can include ownership of other people, whose owners are then doubly empowered. Then the categories of people who have been owned historically still retain that mark of lack of self-ownership like a stigma, like gender in the case of women and skin color in the case of former slaves and immigrants. Even workers have been owned, at least for part of the working day, and their equality has been subject to repeated threat, such as fluctuating rights at the workplace and rights to organize. Full suffrage was only gradually granted to all males, which included workers, and citizenship remains a contingent and contested category. Human rights for all humans are officially recognized by international institutions but are differentially enforced when citizenship is not also available in a nation-state which recognizes human rights for all individuals (Searle 2010, 174–198; Meister 2011).

As a result of these contingencies and exceptions, it is the adult white males who are citizens of hegemonic countries who remain the paragon of "the individual."

The white male property owner can claim his "entitlements" to the returns from his own "property" as a matter of well-established legal rights. With reification of property and money, there is a legitimation of his authority and privileges which appears undeniable and unassailable. He claims independence and autonomy while all others are "dependent" on his generosity and creation of wealth. In fact, the owner is dependent on the social institutions which inscribe and reiterate his individual private property "rights" through an invisible process of reification.

As we assert our respective "individualities" by means of consumer styles and occupational choices, we assume that we are the only ones feeling secretly insecure and vulnerable. So we proceed to compete with each other evermore assiduously and desperately.

Collective agency is embedded in money and markets, along which each "individual" is carried over waves of speculation and cycles of asset prices. There is no possible "strike" in financial markets without endangering everyone at once. So systematically important financial institutions, or SIFIs, are too big to fail, or TBTF and the central bank acts as market maker of last resort (Mehrling 2011; Tooze 2018, 13, 311–313, 402). The purpose of government is to protect the currency and the financial markets (Polanyi 1944), a replay of the 1930s at a larger scale.

The other

The "other" has had a complex relationship to the unity of the nation since the rise of nationalism in the early nineteenth century. For Jameson, the collective, such as a nation, cannot be conceptualized satisfactorily and so is personified (Jameson 2019, 194–201, 346–347), the opposite of the reification of the group. In this way, whole countries and populations are given the characteristics of a human person, with the possibility of stereotype.

The Jew

The Jew has a contradictory relationship with the Christian West, given the usury prohibition of the Catholic Church. Jews were valued for their skills with finance but also resented and abhorred for their complicity with capitalist social relations.

According to Horkheimer and Adorno (1972, 170–176), the hostility of their reception was due to the disappointment with the actualization of equality in liberal societies and with their service to the monarchs on behalf of market relations. Further,

> Bourgeois anti-Semitism has a specific economic reason: the concealment of domination in production.
>
> (Horkheimer and Adorno 1972, 173)

According to Postone (1986, 306), the abstract domination of capitalism was personified with the figure of the Jew (Postone and Santner 2003; Trivellato 2019).

The black youth

Because of their distinctive histories, the black and immigrant populations are often subject to differential treatment in the industrialized countries where they settle. Often they reside in separate quarters and have differential access to health and education. These factors can be perpetuated by discrimination in access to occupations and income, and by cyclical hiring and firing, resulting in a differential consciousness and image in the predominant society. These differences can be exaggerated in the news media and can lead to targeted treatment by the courts and the police. These differentiated populations can be a focus of public anxieties and insecurities, such as "moral panics," related to perceived threats from social deviance and resistance (Hall et al. 1978; Alexander 2010; Wilson 1987). The differential and often harsh treatment of these minority populations is a reflection of the "violence" of the state (Hall et al. 1978, 257–258).

Recognition

There is literature on interpersonal "recognition" as a basic human need, particularly for personality formation. That is, the individual identity is the outcome of the internalization of intersubjective experiences from childhood, which requires constant reinforcement (Honneth 2012b). These works draw upon philosophers such as Hegel (Honneth 1996, 2012a; Benjamin 1988, 1998) as well as psychologists (Chodorow 1978; Winnicott 1987; Klein 1984). That is, the basic contours of one's "self" are internalized by early formative relationships. Others mention dialogue and reciprocal awareness as the expression of one's personality, and the means of solidifying relationships and continuing personal development (Buber 1970; Taylor 2016; Wolff 1968). Meaningful recognition is unique to each person and to each relationship, in contrast to the abstract "individual," and a means of encouraging and supporting continuing individuation and maturation. Such recognition need not be a "struggle," as in Hegel's master/slave dialectic, but could be cooperative and developmental, as in the examples of teacher/student, sexual partners, and in mother/child relations.

In tracing the dialectic of recognition in Hegel's *Phenomenology of Spirit*, Honneth (2012a) reviews the stages of developing self-consciousness. There is desire, a sense of physical bodily needs which are at first merely material, such as mother's milk. The child may then become aware that the mother persists, in spite of the infant feeding on her, consuming her. The nursing couple may become aware of each other, the infant gaining nutrition and physical comfort, with the mother receiving recognition in the child's gaze and smiles. The mutual bonding is enhanced by oxytocin in the breast milk, which induces joy in both members of the nursing couple. The child becomes gradually aware that the mother is reliably attentive, placing the infant's needs above her own, at least for discreet intervals. The growth of self-consciousness, in this context, is the mutual recognition that each is aware and attuned to the other, which is also a source of pleasure and reinforcement for both. Based on such early bonding experiences, the child becomes more capable of independence, also relying on a carefully sequenced series of education and training, growing autonomy with ongoing support.

If the mother/child dyad is at least one form of intersubjective recognition (Honig 2017, 16–17), this interaction clearly changes both participants. The child moves from the womb to the external world, even if at first into her mother's enfolding arms. The person becomes a parent, surely a significant change in most cultures. The dependence of all institutions ultimately on human reproduction is not reliably expressed in a valuation of this relationship but varies considerably by class, period in history, and by culture. For example, the Madonna and Child is a ubiquitous icon in Christianity but does not guarantee that all mothers have adequate conditions for child care, but such treatment varies by legal status of the parents (whether slave or free), by marital status, and by race. Differential treatment of families is one method of reproducing class and status hierarchies. This differential in turn provides "incentives" for women in choosing their partners and occupations, to the extent that choice is permitted. Rules of marriage and kinship are one foundation of social structure across periods of history and geography (Foucault 1978, 106–114).

In the context of formative dyads, frequent communication would be a form of self-expression and mutual reinforcement, rather than wasteful. Such opportunities would be available for adults in the public sphere, as well as at work and in the family. In the divided institutions of modern society, nonetheless, there are few occasions for holistic awareness and self-expression. There are separate identities at home, at work, in volunteer associations, and as a citizen.

If such recognition were a basic need, it would help explain the vulnerability of the modern "individual" to surplus extraction by the "Big Other," where online social media behavior is codified to extract information to target advertising more effectively. Such targeted ad placement can also begin to influence behavior more effectively than advertising in mass media (Zuboff 2019). Major platform companies offer "free" services in return for access to detailed comprehensive consumer behavior. Recognition from social media "friends" can then substitute for other types of recognition such as civil society and the public sphere.

New media and the public sphere

In Habermas's discussion of the public sphere, there was the assumption of rational debate among informed citizens (and bourgeois) regarding the actions of the state. This informed electorate provided a critical guidance mechanism to maintain the engagement of the public and to maintain effectiveness of the government. The media provided accurate information, which was further discussed and disseminated in new institutions like cafes and by print. The state was the clear authority, in the person of the monarch, or the official representative institutions such as Parliament or Congress.

The role of the public sphere is newly important in capitalism, for several reasons:

1) The "social imaginary" is the foundation for national identity and loyalty and must be periodically reinforced in public rituals and celebrations (Davis 2015, 124–125).
2) Confidence in the currency is the foundation for public credit, and benefits from expressions of civic pride and national cohesion.
3) Conspicuous consumption relies upon a *visible* public sphere, to be effective, such as suburban homes facing the street, with picture windows.
4) International prestige rests on the quality of the public debate, its rationality, reliability, and values.

Standards for professional journalism have upheld the role of the "Fourth Estate," and stable, large-circulation newspapers provide in-depth coverage of local and national issues. Independent journalists, such as "muckrakers" like Ida Tarbell and Upton Sinclair, revealed unsafe working conditions and business corruption, which later become relevant to corrective national legislation.

The transformation of the public sphere was due to the influence of commerce, on the one hand, and the change in technology, on the other. The Republic of Letters was conducted with personal, hand-written letters in the eighteenth century. In the nineteenth century, the media shifted from single-page print broadside to large-circulation newspapers and continued with the transformation to radio and TV forms of broadcast from one to many in the twentieth century. With electronic social media in the twenty-first century, the business model continues to rely on advertising, with much more effective targeted ad placement. With mobile phones, the data available on users has rapidly expanded, providing social media platform companies with a rich resource for developing new products. Advertising techniques have become increasingly sophisticated, capable of subliminal influences and emotional triggers (Wu 2016).

There is widespread discussion in the first quarter of the twenty-first century that there is another "transformation" of the public sphere in process. Among these trends include increasing concentration of media corporations (McChesney 2013), less support for investigative journalism, the development of cable news channels which are targeted to political niches (Peck 2019; McKnight 2013), and the dissemination of news on social media like Facebook with little professional control of the accuracy of content.

If the public sphere provided a forum for recognition for citizens, and information for political choices, this transformation and potential content distortion is problematic. If representative democracy depends on accurate information received by aware voters, this degradation of accuracy leads to ineffective public institutions (Muirhead and Rosenblum 2019). With misleading and inaccurate information disseminated at warp speeds on social media like Facebook or Twitter, the potential for "information cascades" increases (Shiller 2008).

With the many-to-many communication capabilities of social media, new groups can form easily and new norms can be developed, as well as new discourses. The somber objectivity of the post-war broadcast network news commentators is replaced by the provocative, aggressive interview style of the cable channels. Rather than social media applied to developing a new capacity for direct democracy, there is greater invasion of personal relationships with commercial messages couched in the most addictive forms.

Learning from tabloid news and talk radio, there is a focus on sensationalism to increase profits, which can affect the world views of heavy TV viewers (Jamieson and Romer 2017). With the lower cost of cable and the internet, it is feasible to serve smaller, narrower audiences. The tendency to choose channels which support one's existing views leads to fragmentation and polarization, and more extreme political views (Winneg et al. 2017; Bergstrom and Bak-Coleman 2019; Stewart et al. 2019). That is, the medium, along with commercial motives, can influence culture and political beliefs.

Representation of the public to itself, a function of democratic government, is now implemented by social media. The platform companies, Facebook, Google, Amazon, Apple, Netflix, and Microsoft, accumulate more knowledge of the population than the government and routinely reflect each user to her own audience of influential peers, members of her reference group. These public functions are conducted with techniques of advertising, rather than rational public debate among informed voters. The sudden awareness of the collapse of the distinction of the public/private divide occurred with the realization that "Big Data" from mobile phones was used to target advertising for *electoral* campaigns in the 2016 US election, with the help of Cambridge Analytica, using Facebook data, not just *marketing* campaigns (Confessiore 2018). In summary, one's sense of self (Langlois and Elmer 2019), political views, and culture are increasingly mediated by for-profit platform companies.

Neoliberalism and the public/private divide

Once again there is a "doubling" (see Chapter 2). The population is important to the economy as producers and consumers. The population is important to be represented, as a result, as the source of sovereignty in explicit organs of government. Yet the population is mediated by the economy and "objectified" as "individuals," represented by money. So the population must be both unified, as the ultimate source of public credit, and divided, represented separately, as persons and as objects. In this way, the modern liberal state is paradoxical, reflecting the paradoxes of property. Marx was aware of the ambiguous distinction of the public and private spheres (Meister 1991, 147). The liberal state was always a compromise between the protection of property and democratization through a separation of powers and checks and balances.

With neoliberalism, the state was made to resemble the market through privatization for the aim of efficiency. Income distribution was allowed to become increasingly unequal through deregulation and tax cuts, and more restrictive welfare (Dean 2019; Davies 2017). With Congress subject to lobbying and campaign finance, the motives of public welfare become merged with economic gain. With political campaigns run like market operations, there is only appeal to the passions rather than policy commitments. The entrepreneurial individual seeks status through cultivated image, salary, and luxury consumption. The "wealth of nations" becomes the only goal. To the extent that the public and private spheres were ever separate, such distinctions have become moot. The discipline which was always present in the labor market becomes more explicit and punitive in periods of economic crisis (Blyth 2013), and the "authoritarian" tendencies become more explicit (Hall 1980). The rise of populism is "a symptom of the deadlock produced by the contradictions and antagonisms that constitute present-day instituted post-democracy in its articulation with a deepening process of neoliberalization" (Swyngedouw 2019, 268).

Money has always been the contradiction of the public/private divide, requiring a unified state but establishing the explicit demarcation of market from society at the same time. The paradox is fundamental, based on the defining characteristics of money. First, money is the product of the state and relies on the entire national GDP to support credit (Davis 2017). Second, money is considered individual private property by the holder of cash. There are additional aspects of its dual role:

a)   Money is an instrument of discipline and coercion, by its capacity to hire labor power, a form of public power for private purposes, while also empowering the individual.
b)   Money is a symbol of value, which shapes a person's self-concept, influence, and capacities.
c)   Money is a unit of account, which expresses the relative value of people by their salaries, and of commodities.
d)   Money is a store of value, taking and supplementing the role of material property as a temporal fix, as permanent.
e)   Money reflects the power of the state, and by its ubiquitous presence as markets expand, becomes more powerful while simultaneously expanding the capacity of the state.

When computers and information technology combine with financial circuits, the concept of the public becomes subsumed into money. The purpose of the state becomes supporting the financial sector for the purposes of wealth, security, and global power.

In this way, money and markets occupy the public sphere, displacing any concern with citizenship and political deliberation. The dominant form of representation, for the person and the state alike, is money. Money is both personal and political, representing both the concrete human body and the abstract human collective, also called a "body politic."

Next stage of capitalism?

Zuboff articulates some of the same insights. Her concept of the "Big Other" has some resemblance to the merchant's gaze discussed earlier (Zuboff 2019, 376–382, 445). She also discusses self- and social-objectification (Zuboff 2019, 399–415, 448, 464). One wonders if these terms represent a common condition of capitalist social relations and capitalist social sciences.

Western civilization celebrates the public sphere, with self-governance and rational deliberation and debate. Yet modern capitalism capitulates control to the automatic market as a "steering mechanism." Money includes public power, which presumably is simply in everyone's interest, to designate what can be considered property, conditions of its sale, how ownership is defined, and who has access to credit. Yet these institutions are best left unexamined (Searle 2010, 106–107, 140), influenced by corporate lobbyists who have "free speech" (Mayer 2016; Winkler 2018).

When work disappears, and automation and artificial intelligence become the dominant methods of production, income distribution will no longer be justified based upon marginal contribution to output, so-called "incentives." Facebook ads and "likes" will influence consumer choice, purchased with Facebook cryptocurrency, so this social media site with others will acquire the information regarding financial flows now accessed only by the government. Basic income guarantees of various sorts will be the prime source of living expenses.

The leader for our time

Trump is the supposed apotheosis of the "self-made" businessman, whose self-promotion schemes are understood to be fake, like all marketing. He abrogates any divisions between self-aggrandizement and the public interest, seeing his businesses and his family as the model for the nation and its highest expression. Wealth, fame, and beauty are the ultimate goals, and all else is mere envy, to be ridiculed if there is a pretense of a higher motive and public duty. He is capable of cruelty to the vulnerable and pandering to power. He is the voracious consumer of all things, with no respect for limits, with self-proclaimed entitlement to the best. With the market as the ultimate arbiter of value, vanity is the dominant passion, however fragile and unstable.

Note

1 Taylor's view of modernity is related to providence through his discussion of Locke. The contract theory of society is based on the assumption of equal rational individuals created by God who operate for mutual benefit. As the contract view of society extends to various spheres, the economic purpose becomes the most important and operates by impersonal rules "behind the backs" of the individuals. Such a view of modernity is "bi-focal,"

partly intentional and partly the outcome of the "invisible hand" (Taylor 2007, 159–207). According to Taylor, "[the market] is not an order of collective action; for the 'market' is the negation of collective action" (Taylor 2007, 183).

Bibliography

Alexander, Michelle. *The New Jim Crow: Mass Incarceration in the Age of Colorblindness*. New York: Perseus, 2010.

Baritz, Loren. *The Servants of Power: A History of the Use of Social Science in American Industry*. Middletown, CT: Wesleyan University Press, 1960.

Basch, Norma. *In the Eyes of the Law: Women, Marriage, and Property in Nineteenth Century New York*. Ithaca, NY: Cornell University Press, 1982.

Beauvoir, Simone de. *The Second Sex*. New York: Random House, 1952.

Benjamin, Jessica. *The Bonds of Love: Psychoanalysis, Feminism, and the Problem of Domination*. New York: Pantheon, 1988.

Benjamin, Jessica. *The Shadow of the Other: Intersubjectivity and Gender in Psychoanalysis*. New York: Routledge, 1998.

Bergstrom, Carl T. and Joseph B. Bak-Coleman. "Gerrymandering in Social Networks," *Nature,* Vol. 573, September 5, 2019, 40–41.

Blyth, Mark. *Austerity: The History of a Dangerous Idea*. New York: Oxford University Press, 2013.

Bourdieu, Pierre. *Science of Science and Reflexivity*. Chicago: University of Chicago Press, 2004.

Bowles, Samuel. *The Moral Economy: Why Good Incentives are No Substitute for Good Citizens*. New Haven: Yale University Press, 2016.

Brine, Kevin R. and Mary Poovey. *Finance in America: An Unfinished Story*. Chicago: University of Chicago Press, 2017.

Buber, Martin. *I and Thou*. New York: Scribner, 1970.

Butler, Judith. "Merely Cultural," in Kevin Olson (ed.), *Adding Insult to Injury: Nancy Fraser Debates Her Critics*. New York: Verso, 2008, 42–56.

Chodorow, Nancy. *Reproduction of Mothering: Psychoanalysis and the Sociology of Gender*. Berkeley: University of California Press, 1978.

Cohen, G.A. *Self-Ownership, Freedom, and Equality*. New York: Cambridge University Press, 1995.

Cohen, Lizabeth. *A Consumers' Republic: The Politics of Mass Consumption in Postwar America*. New York: Random House, 2003.

Confessiore, Nicholas. "Cambridge Analytica and Facebook: The Scandal and the Fallout So Far," *The New York Times,* April 4, 2018.

Cook, Eli. *The Pricing of Progress: Economic Indicators and the Capitalization of American Life*. Cambridge, MA: Harvard University Press, 2017.

Cott, Nancy F. *Public Vows: A History of Marriage and the Nation*. Cambridge, MA: Harvard University Press, 2000.

D'Arista, Jane. *All Fall Down: Debt, Deregulation and Financial Crises*. Cheltenham, UK: Edward Elgar, 2018.

Daston, Lorraine and Peter Galison. *Objectivity*. New York: Zone Books, 2010.

Davidoff, Leonore and Catherine Hall. *Family Fortunes: Men and Women of the English Middle Class, 1780–1850*. Chicago: University of Chicago Press, 1987.

Davies, William. *The Limits of Neoliberalism: Authority, Sovereignty, and the Logic of Competition*. London: Sage, 2017.

Davis, Ann E. *The Evolution of the Property Relation: Understanding Paradigms, Debates, and Prospects*. New York: Palgrave MacMillan, 2015.

Davis, Ann E. *Money as a Social Institution: The Institutional Development of Capitalism*. New York: Routledge, 2017.

Dean, Mitchell. "Rogue Neoliberalism, Liturgical Power, and the Search for a Left Governmentality," *South Atlantic Quarterly*, Vol. 118, No. 2, April 2019, 325–342.

Eichengreen, Barry. *Global Imbalances and the Lessons of Bretton Woods*. Cambridge, MA: MIT Press, 2007.

Eichengreen, Barry. *Exorbitant Privilege: The Rise and Fall of the Dollar and the Future of the International Monetary System*. New York: Oxford University Press, 2011.

Epstein, Gerald A. *Financialization and the World Economy*. Cheltenham, UK: Edward Elgar, 2005.

Foroohar, Rana. *Makers and Takers: The Rise of Finance and the Fall of American Business*. New York: Crown, 2016.

Foucault, Michel. *The Order of Things: An Archaeology of the Human Sciences*. New York: Pantheon, 1970.

Foucault, Michel. *The History of Sexuality. Vol. I: An Introduction*. New York: Random House, 1978.

Foucault, Michel. *The Order of Things: An Archaeology of the Human Sciences*. New York: Vintage Books, 1994.

Frank, Robert H. and Philip J. Cook. *The Winner-Take-All Society*. New York: Free Press, 1995.

Fraser, Nancy. "Heterosexism, Misrecognition, and Capitalism: A Response to Judith Butler," in Nancy Fraser (ed.), *Fortunes of Feminism: From State-Managed Capitalism to Neoliberal Crisis*. New York: Verso, 2013, 175–186.

Galbraith, John Kenneth. *The Affluent Society*. Boston: Houghton Mifflin, 1958.

Galbraith, John Kenneth. *The New Industrial State*. Boston: Houghton Mifflin, 1978.

Gauthier, David. "No Need for Morality: The Case of the Competitive Market," *Philosophic Exchange*, Vol. 13, No. 1, Summer 1982, article 2, 41–54.

Gilman, Charlotte Perkins [Stetson]. *Women and Economics: A Study of the Economic Relation Between Men and Women as a Factor in Social Evolution*. Boston: Small, Maynard & Company, 1899.

Greenstein, Share. *How the Internet Became Commercial: Innovation, Privatization, and the Birth of a New Network*. Princeton, NJ: Princeton University Press, 2015.

Guizzo, Danielle and Iara Vigo de Lima. "Polanyi and Foucault on the Issue of Market in Classical Political Economy: Complementary Approaches to the Radical Theory of Social Control," *Review of Radical Political Economics*, Vol. 49, No. 1, 2017, 100–113.

Habermas, Jurgen. *The Structural Transformation of the Public Sphere: An Inquiry into a Category of Bourgeois Society*. Cambridge, MA: MIT Press, 1989.

Hall, Stuart. "Popular-Democratic vs. Authoritarian Populism: Two Ways of 'Taking Democracy Seriously'," in Alan Hunt (ed.), *Marxism and Democracy*. London: Lawrence and Wishart, 1980, 157–185.

Hall, Stuart, Chas Critcher, Tony Jefferson, John Clarke, and Brian Roberts. *Policing the Crisis: Mugging, the State, and Law and Order*. London: MacMillan, 1978.

Haraway, Donna Jeanne. *Crystals, Fabrics, and Fields: Metaphors That Shape Embryos*. Berkeley: North Atlantic Books, 2004.

Hartog, Hendrik. *Man and Wife in America: A History*. Cambridge, MA: Harvard University Press, 2000.

Harvey, David. *The Condition of Postmodernity: An Enquiry into the Origins of Cultural Change*. Oxford, UK: Blackwell, 1990.

Honig, Bonnie. *Public Things: Democracy in Disrepair*. New York: Fordham University Press, 2017.

Honneth, Axel. *The Struggle for Recognition: The Moral Grammar of Social Conflicts*. Cambridge, MA: MIT Press, 1996.

Honneth, Axel. "From Desire to Recognition: Hegel's Grounding of Self-Consciousness," in *The I in We: Studies in the Theory of Recognition*. Cambridge, UK: Polity Press, 2012a, 3–18.

Honneth, Axel. "The I in We: Recognition as a Driving Force," in *The I in We: Studies in the Theory of Recognition*. Cambridge, UK: Polity Press, 2012b, 201–216.

Horkheimer, Max and Theodor W. Adorno. *Dialectic of Enlightenment*. New York: Seabury Press, 1972.

Howard, Vicki. *From Main Street to the Mall: The Rise and Fall of the American Department Store*. Philadelphia: University of Pennsylvania Press, 2015.

Howell, Martha C. *Commerce Before Capitalism in Europe 1300–1600*. New York: Cambridge University Press, 2010.

Jackson, Kenneth T. *Crabgrass Frontier: The Suburbanization of the United States*. New York: Oxford University Press, 1985.

Jameson, Fredric. *Allegory and Ideology*. London: Verso, 2019.

Jamieson, Patrick E. and Daniel Romer. "Cultivation Theory and the Construction of Political Reality," in Kate Kenski and Kathleen Hall Jamieson (eds.), *The Oxford Handbook of Political Communication*. New York: Oxford University Press, 2017, 595–604.

Klein, Melanie. *Envy and Gratitude and Other Works*. New York: Free Press, 1984.

Kruse, Kevin M. and Thomas J. Sugrue. *The New Suburban History*. Chicago: University of Chicago Press, 2006.

Kuiper, Edith. "The Construction of Masculine Identity in Adam Smith's *Theory of Moral Sentiments*," in Drucilla K. Barker and Edith Kuiper (eds.), *Toward a Feminist Philosophy of Economics*. New York: Routledge, 2003, 145–160.

Lamoreaux, Naomi R. "The Mystery of Property Rights: A U.S. Perspective," *Journal of Economic History*, Vol. 71, No. 2, June 2011, 275–306.

Langlois, Ganaele and Greg Elmer. "Impersonal Subjectivation from Platforms to Infrastructures," *Media, Culture & Society*, Vol. 41, No. 2, 2019, 236–251.

Lasch, Christopher. *Haven in a Heartless World: The Family Besieged*. New York: Basic, 1977.

Latour, Bruno. *An Inquiry into Modes of Existence: An Anthropology of the Moderns*. Cambridge, MA: Harvard University Press, 2013.

Maifreda, Germano. *From Oikonomia to Political Economy: Constructing Economic Knowledge from the Renaissance to the Scientific Revolution*. Burlington, VT: Ashgate, 2012.

Marx, Karl. *Capital*. Vols. I–III. New York: International Publishers, 1967.

Marx, Karl. *A Contribution to the Critique of Political Economy*. Edited with an introduction by Maurice Dobb. New York: International Publishers, 1970.

Massey, Douglas S. *Categorically Unequal: The American System of Stratification*. New York: Russell Sage, 2007.

Massey, Douglas S. and Nancy A. Denton. *American Apartheid: Segregation and the Making of the Underclass*. Cambridge, MA: Harvard University Press, 1993.

Mayer, Jane. *Dark Money: The Hidden History of the Billionaires Behind the Rise of the Radical Right*. New York: Doubleday, 2016.

McChesney, Robert W. *Digital Disconnect: How Capitalism is Turning the Internet Against Democracy*. New York: New Press, 2013.

McGirr, Lisa. *Suburban Warriors: The Origins of the New American Right*. Princeton, NJ: Princeton University Press, 2001.

McKendrick, Neil, John Brewer, and J. H. Plumb. *The Birth of the Consumer Society: The Commercialization of Eighteenth Century England*. Bloomington: Indiana University Press, 1982.

McKeon, Michael. "The Emergence of Gender Difference in England, 1660–1760," *Eighteenth-Century Studies*, Vol. 28, No. 3, Spring 1995, 295–322.

McKeon, Michael. *The Secret History of Domesticity: Public, Private and the Division of Knowledge*. Baltimore: Johns Hopkins University Press, 2005.

McKnight, David. *Murdoch's Politics: How One Man's Thirst for Wealth and Power Shapes Our World*. London: Pluto Press, 2013.

McLuhan, Marshall. *The Medium Is the Message*. New York: Bantam, 1967.

Mehrling, Perry. *The New Lombard Street: How the Fed became the Market Maker of Last Resort*. Princeton, NJ: Princeton University Press, 2011.

Meister, Robert. *Political Identity: Thinking Through Marx*. Cambridge, MA: Basil Blackwell, 1991.

Meister, Robert. *After Evil: A Politics of Human Rights*. New York: Columbia University Press, 2011.

Muirhead, Russell and Nancy L. Rosenblum. *A Lot of People are Saying: The New Conspiracism and the Assault on Democracy*. Princeton, NJ: Princeton University Press, 2019.

Nagel, Thomas. *The View from Nowhere*. New York: Oxford University Press, 1986.

Nelson, Julie. "Male is a Gender, Too: A Review of *Why Gender Matters in Economics* by Mukesh Eswaran," *Journal of Economic Literature*, Vol. 54, No. 4, 2016, 1362–1376.

Pateman, Carole. *Sexual Contract*. Stanford, CA: Stanford University Press, 1988.

Peck, Reece. *Fox Populism: Branding Conservatism as Working Class*. New York: Cambridge University Press, 2019.

Phillips-Fein, Kimberly. *Invisible Hands: The Making of the Conservative Movement from the New Deal to Reagan*. New York: W.W. Norton & Company, 2009.

Polanyi, Karl. *The Great Transformation*. Boston: Beacon Press, 1944.

Poovey, Mary. *Making a Social Body: British Cultural Formation 1830–1864*. Chicago: University of Chicago Press, 1995.

Poovey, Mary. *A History of the Modern Fact: Problems of Knowledge in the Sciences of Wealth and Society*. Chicago: University of Chicago Press, 1998.

Poovey, Mary. "The Liberal Civil Subject and the Social in Eighteenth-Century British Moral Philosophy," *Public Culture*, Vol. 14, No. 1, 2002, 125–145.

Poovey, Mary. *Genres of the Credit Economy: Mediating Value in Eighteenth-and Nineteenth-Century Britain*. Chicago: University of Chicago Press, 2008.

Postone, Moishe. "Anti-Semitism and National Socialism," in Anson Rabinbach and Jack Zipes (eds.), *Germans and Jews Since the Holocaust: The Changing Situation in West Germany*. New York: Holmes and Meier, 1986, 302–314.

Postone, Moishe. *Time, Labor, and Social Domination: A Reinterpretation of Marx's Critical Theory*. New York: Cambridge University Press, 1993.

Postone, Moishe. "Rethinking *Capital* in Light of the *Grundrisse*," in Marcello Musto (ed.), *Karl Marx's Grundrisse: Foundations of the Critique of Political Economy 150 Years Later*. New York: Routledge, 2008, 120–137.

Postone, Moishe and Eric Santner (eds.). *Catastrophe and Meaning: The Holocaust and the Twentieth Century*. Chicago: University of Chicago Press, 2003.

Riesman, David. *The Lonely Crowd: A Study of Changing American Character*. New Haven: Yale University Press, 1950.

Santner, Eric L. *The Weight of All Flesh: On the Subject-Matter of Political Economy*. New York: Oxford University Press, 2016.

Scott, Joan W. *Only Paradoxes to Offer: French Feminists and the Rights of Man*. Cambridge, MA: Harvard University Press, 1996.

Searle, John R. *Making the Social World: The Structure of Human Civilization.* New York: Oxford University Press, 2010.

Sewell, William H. Jr. "Crooked Lines," *American Historical Review,* Vol. 113, No. 2, April 2008, 393–405.

Shiller, Robert J. *The Subprime Solution: How Today's Global Financial Crisis Happened, and What to Do About It.* Princeton, NJ: Princeton University Press, 2008.

Smith, Adam. *An Inquiry into the Nature and Causes of the Wealth of Nations.* New York: Modern Library, 1994.

Staves, Susan. *Married Women's Separate Property in England 1660–1833.* Cambridge, MA: Harvard University Press, 1990.

Stern, Nicholas H. *Why Are We Waiting? The Logic, Urgency, and the Promise of Tackling Climate Change.* Cambridge, MA: MIT Press, 2015.

Stewart, Alexander J., Mohsen Mosleh, Marina Diakonova, Antonio A. Arechar, David G. Rand, and Joshua B. Plotkin. "Information Gerrymandering and Undemocratic Decisions," *Nature,* Vol. 573, September 5, 2019, 117–121.

Strathern, Marilyn. *Before and After Gender: Sexual Mythologies of Everyday Life.* Chicago: HAU Books, 2016.

Sugrue, Thomas J. *The Origins of the Urban Crisis: Race and Inequality in Postwar Detroit.* Princeton, NJ: Princeton University Press, 1996.

Swyngedouw, Erik. "The Perverse Lure of Autocratic Postdemocracy," *South Atlantic Quarterly,* Vol. 118, No. 2, 2019, 267–286.

Taylor, Charles. "Modern Social Imaginaries," *Public Culture,* Vol. 14, No. 1, 2002, 91–124.

Taylor, Charles. *A Secular Age.* Cambridge, MA: Harvard University Press, 2007.

Taylor, Charles. *The Language Animal: The Full Shape of the Human Linguistic Capacity.* Cambridge, MA: Harvard University Press, 2016.

Tooze, J. Adam. *Crashed: How a Decade of Financial Crisis Changed the World.* New York: Viking, 2018.

Trivellato, Francesca. *The Promise and the Peril of Credit: What a Forgotten Legend About Jews and Finance Tells Us About the Making of European Commercial Society.* Princeton, NJ: Princeton University Press, 2019.

Tucker, Robert C. *The Marx-Engels Reader.* 2nd ed. New York: W.W. Norton & Company, 1978.

Veblen, Thorstein. *The Theory of the Leisure Class: An Economic Study of Institutions.* New York: Modern Library, 1934.

Vilar, Pierre. *A History of Gold and Money 1450–1920.* London: NLB, 1976.

Warner, Michael. "The Mass Public and the Mass Subject," in Craig Calhoun (ed.), *Habermas and the Public Sphere.* Cambridge, MA: MIT Press, 1992, 377–401.

Weber, Max. *The Protestant Ethic and the Spirit of Capitalism.* New York: Scribner & Sons. 1958.

Weber, Max. *The Economy and Society: An Outline of Interpretive Sociology.* Vol. I. Berkeley: University of California Press, 1978.

Wilson, William Julius. *The Truly Disadvantaged: The Inner City, the Underclass, and Public Policy.* Chicago: University of Chicago Press, 1987.

Winkler, Adam. *We the Corporations: How American Businesses Won Their Civil Rights.* New York: W.W. Norton & Company, 2018.

Winneg, Kenneth M., Daniel M. Butler, Saar Golde, Darwin W. Miller III, and Norman H. Nie. "OnlineNews Consumption in the United States and Ideological Extremism," in Kate Kenski and Kathleen Hall Jamieson (eds.), *The Oxford Handbook of Political Communication.* New York: Oxford University Press, 2017, 809–822.

Winnicott, Donald Woods. *Babies and Their Mothers.* Reading, MA: Addison-Wesley, 1987.

Wolff, Robert Paul. *The Poverty of Liberalism*. Boston: Beacon Press, 1968.

Wu, Tim. *The Master Switch: The Rise and Fall of Information Empires*. New York: Alfred A. Knopf, 2010.

Wu, Tim. *The Attention Merchants: The Epic Scramble to Get Inside Our Heads*. New York: Alfred A. Knopf, 2016.

Zuboff, Shoshana. *In the Age of the Smart Machine: The Future of Work and Power*. New York: Basic, 1984.

Zuboff, Shoshana. *Surveillance Capitalism: The Fight for a Human Future at the New Frontier of Power*. New York: Public Affairs, 2019.

9 Contradictions

Introduction

This chapter will review the centrality of the "property in the person" in the dualities and contradictions of capitalism. We will also review the institutional provisions which manage these contradictions, along with their limits.

The individual

To summarize the key points thus far, "the individual" is a concept which emerges with the development and consolidation of capitalism. The "free" individual as property owner helps to rationalize capitalism, with the assignment of property rights to the titular owner. On the other hand, "the individual" is an isolated monad, without social connections, vulnerable to institutional sanctions administered through the state bureaucracy or the labor market. That is, this "individual" has two sides, both free and constrained.

The notion of "the individual" reflects and expresses the culture of capitalism. That is, rather than a self-evident biological fact, "the individual" is a cultural construction of modernity, unrecognizable in other periods of history.

The legacy of liberalism is to see a "long march" towards the extension of individual rights to more persons in a given society and to more societies throughout the globe (Taylor 2004, 2007; Bowles and Gintis 1986). That is, individualism is a social good and a moral value. On the other hand, in the legacy of Marx and Polanyi, "the individual" is the product of discipline who must strive for social and economic connections in order to survive.

The concept of "the individual" is endogenous, rather than universal or self-evident, according to the methodology of historical institutionalism. The individual is the presumed actor who develops the value of his "own property" in competition with other individuals. The property in question can include the person's own self, including mind and body, or other objects of value, such as land, means of production, real and financial assets.

The dualism of the role of labor in the market (Polanyi 1944) and in capitalism (Marx 1967) is central to both theorists. The fact that the worker as a "commodity" is a "fiction," for Polanyi, implies that it is both true and untrue.

For Marx, the worker is "free" in a double sense. Both theorists find that the role of labor is contradictory, which leads to "class struggle" for Marx and to "counter movements" for Polanyi. The role of labor as a commodity is time-limited, bound by the working day, yet having a profound influence for the person's life experience and prospects. While this dichotomous role of labor is "structural," with the outcomes predictable in general, there are nonetheless many "countervailing tendencies" for Marx and potential defenders of "society" for Polanyi. Both Marx and Polanyi employ holistic methodologies informed by history, yet both also analyze divisions (Cangiani 2011, 2017). For Marx it is forces and relations of production, and for Polanyi it is the economy vs. society.

In my view, these *double entendres* and contradictions lead to institutional, temporal, and spatial divisions in capitalism, such as the public/private divide and the separate locations for "work" and "home." In capitalism, the population is productive, the source of value, and so worthy of public representation. On the other hand, the worker requires discipline, and subordination, which takes place in the private sphere of the factory. The person takes on different roles, norms, and privileges in each institution and location. One behaves differently in a private commercial establishment than in a public park. The owner has a different degree of autonomy than the worker, as well as higher pay. The worker has more autonomy than the child or the retiree, and the citizen more than the immigrant. These differences among persons, who may otherwise be "equal," are routinized and naturalized. For both Marx and Polanyi, humans are "naturally" social, but the forms of relationships are significantly shaped by capitalist/market institutions. For Marx, the social nature of labor is represented by the "value" of commodities, in an unrecognizable form for the individual workers. For Polanyi, the social nature of the economy is masked in the "utopian" ideal of the self-regulating market and the double movements for protection.

In this work, the definition of the "market" is what people do with money, with which they become legally empowered to command the labor and to acquire the products of others. The profit motive, that is, making more money with an initial sum of money, is ethically legitimate, based on the incentives for increasing productivity of the economy as a whole. The presumed "autonomy" of the market is based on the set of social relationships empowered by money which allow special powers and privileges. The relationships mediated by money are presumed to be a different type or category for which the same standards of empathy and consideration do not apply. These monetary relationships are governed by promises to (re)pay, not to ethics or politics. The economy is a "separate sphere," not because of walls or boundaries but because of different norms for the money-holder in the process of expenditure. There has been a general acceptance of the market (Lisa Herzog 2013; Gauthier 1976) in contemporary theory, rather than continual critique on moral or performance grounds. There are "morality plays," nonetheless, in the politics of debt and distribution (Blyth 2013).

Politics of property in the person

In earlier work, we have discussed the "paradigm of property," such that property is considered a discrete object owned by an individual, with its social dimensions invisible (Davis 2015, 32–40). This view of property is a form of reification which enables the economy to be considered autonomous, a separate sphere, apart from "society." In this context, I contend that there is a related "politics of property in the person," extending Pateman's term.

According to Marx and Polanyi, there is a dualism embedded in the structure of the capitalist economy. That is, the worker both is and is not a commodity. This is Polanyi's "fiction" regarding labor as a commodity and Marx's view of "freedom" in a "double sense." Pateman identifies clearly that this type of property, property in the person, is a type of coercion (Pateman 1988). That is, the worker as a commodity cannot be consumed without relinquishing control over his body, at least during the working day.

This institutional structure sets up a tension within the socioeconomic system. The person may wish to retain control over his own body during the working day, or there may be degrees of autonomy granted to certain types of employment relationship. The history of the labor relationship has been studied with this potential "conflict" in mind. The employer wishes to extract labor and may reward performance above and beyond the explicit contract. The worker may resist and wish for higher pay for his compliance (Marglin 2008; Akerlof and Yellen 1986, 1990; Gordon, Edwards, and Reich 1982). Human relations professionals and psychologists, as well as management specialists like Frederick W. Taylor, have contributed to resolving this ongoing issue.

The dialectical nature of this "contested" relationship can lead to cycles of reward and discipline, with fluctuating wage levels and degrees of labor conflict. This "class" conflict can be seen in Marxian business cycles, as well as Polanyian countermovements of social reformers. In fact, these cycles can be related. In Marx's analysis, rising wages which threaten profit would lead to automation and unemployment, squeezing workers. This increased stress could be the type of factor which would lead to Polanyi's "double movement," to save society. That is, even though Polanyi stresses "society" and Marx emphases surplus and profit, the dynamics could be mutually reinforcing: double movements to resist the market would be more likely in a business cycle downturn or depression.

This economic and political double movement can be illustrated in the history of labor laws, public relief, the public franchise and associated suffrage rules, health, housing, marital law and household composition, as well as income distribution. That is, in modern industrial capitalism, the role of the state is expanded to provide for "public goods," but structured to support the private economy. In each of these areas, there is a political oscillation, reflecting a structural dilemma which can only be resolved by a type of cycle. That is, the population must be cared for, but only conditional on supporting the core of labor market discipline. There is public provision through taxes, but contingent on contribution to the performance of the economy. Costs are distributed across the population, rather than assigned to the for-profit firm, and structured to maintain that profitability. The household is "dependent" on the "family wage," or dual-earners, while also socializing children and providing elder care. These sets of related institutions can form a type of regime with respect to the degree and form of public provision, such as "varieties of capitalism" (Hall and Soskice 2001; Piore 2016; Lazonick 2009, 2010; Thelen 2014).

This core relationship of the dual role of labor is evident in the structure of other institutions, including the public/private divide, as discussed in Chapter 3. That is, the worker as a person is a citizen with rights of participation in the "public sphere." The worker as a subordinate offers his labor to be directed by the authority in the workplace, in the "private sphere." With the evolution of the market economy, the role of the population as producing and realizing value must be recognized and "represented" in the structure of the capitalist state. Alternatively, that production of value is the result of discipline and control in the workplace, which requires subordination in the private sphere. There are two private spheres, one for production and one for consumption. The former, the sphere of production, is subject to control by the owner with exclusionary property rights. The latter, the sphere of consumption, is the sphere of "freedom" (Berlin 1969), protected from state intrusion. This is the sphere of freedom and security, where the educated bourgeois becomes capable of participation in rational public debate (Habermas 1989).

There is an associated reversal of the relative value of the public and private sphere, in "ancient" vs. "modern" economies (Berlin 1969; Pocock 1975). The traditional importance of public political engagement as a requirement for self-realization has become less relevant than private "individual" choices. Writing in the 1970s, Daniel Bell also articulated the contradiction between the individual personality required for the reliable consumer, hedonism, which would conflict with the behavior expected at the workplace, and discipline (Bell 1978). Rather than blame the deficient moral character of the person, however, he did attribute these behavioral patterns to the economic system of capitalism and its divisions.

Individuation as discipline

While the market is considered as the guarantee of freedom (Friedman 1962), there is another duality to this notion. There are two principles of freedom, one in the market for the property owner and one in the state as citizen. But there are two potentially conflicting principles of market and the state.

For the property owner, the market requires contingency of means of subsistence as a type of discipline. The citizen requires autonomy or security for full deliberation regarding the public interest. To assure such independence, early suffrage laws required property ownership.

A resolution of this potential conflict between property owner and citizen is with inequality and class hierarchy in which those with greater wealth can deliberate with more security regarding the overall operation of the market

Table 9.1 Public/Private Divide

Alternate Roles	Types of Freedom	
	Public	Private
Property owner	Fair representation	Free use of property
Citizen	Secure Income and free speech	Protection of privacy

and the state. Another potential resolution is oscillation, with periods of public investment alternating with periods of austerity. A third potential resolution is expansion of public property (Davis 2018; Blyth 2002) and equalization of income, such as the policies of social democracy. A fourth resolution is the "ownership society," where the wide distribution of private property increases political support for its protection (Lamoreaux 2011; Wray 2006; Ott 2011).

Such different views can lead to checks and balances and more complete consideration of alternative positions. An alternative possibility is gridlock, where both sides are equally represented, and cannot resolve the opposing principles. Such gridlock, along with falling incomes and increasing instability, is one factor that can lead to populism in periods of economic crisis (Eichengreen 2018). That is, in spite of the conceptual distinction between public and private, the treatment of a person in the private sphere as a form of property can create backlash in the public sphere in terms of alternative political formations.

There can also be oscillation between various doctrinal approaches to the discipline of bodies, such as women and workers. For example, the doctrine of freedom of contract prevented collective bargaining for labor in the nineteenth century, to be overturned by the Supreme Court in the 1930s. Further, labor standards are subject to fluctuating definition and enforcement (Piore and Schrank 2018), and immigrants are subject to differential treatment based on skill level, state of the economy, and country of origin (Borjas 2016; Davis and Chacon 2006).

That is, the "individual" can be an aspiration for many but attainable only for the few who have enough resources and security to invest and develop "human capital" and capacities.

Inequality

Juridical protection of property as a market principle can lead to inequality, and juridical resistance to income redistribution, even over policy recommendations for economic stability. Then income inequality itself can further contribute to political instability. Such protections of property can diminish the efficacy of "democracy."

Definition of democracy

The definition of democracy in this book would include the separation and protection of property in the liberal democratic state by means of the separation of markets from government in the public/private divide (see Chapter 3). That is, property has been protected from democratic influence with the adoption of the Constitution of 1787, by checks and balances (Searle 2010, 170–171; Pistor 2019).

The usual definition of "democracy" includes only the public and the "political," such as "universal male suffrage, civil liberties, and constrained executives" (Ziblatt 2017, 5). For Berman, the "liberal conception of democracy" specifies "a government [which] must be willing and able to guarantee the rule of law; and must protect minorities and individual liberties; and leaders and citizens must respect the democratic 'rules of the game,' and treat all members of society as political equals" (Berman 2019, 6). She does not mention the specific types of property which are recognized by that rule of law, or any requirement of a minimum standard of living for all citizens (Bell 1978).

According to Polanyi, the constitutional protection of property protects the economy from the population, in spite of universal suffrage.

> The separation of powers, which Montesquieu (1748) had meanwhile invented, was now used to separate the people from power over their own economic life. The American Constitution, shaped in a farmer-craftsman's environmental by a leadership forewarned by the English industrial scene, isolated the economic sphere entirely from the jurisdiction of the Constitution, put private property thereby under the highest conceivable protection, and created the only legally grounded market society in the world. In spite of universal suffrage, American voters were powerless against owners.
>
> (Polanyi 1944, 225–226)

As a result, conservative political parties are able to support democracy as part of a class compromise to increase political stability (Ziblatt 2017, 16–21).

Property protections

The public/private divide was designed to balance citizenship in the public sphere with property "rights" in the private sphere, a form of personification as discussed in Chapter 7. See Figure 9.1.

But the constitutional provisions for protection of property can have long-term consequences towards removing this balance, representing property rights in the public sphere, as well as people. There have been long-term changes that reflect this dynamic.

First, slavery was considered property with the full protection of the Constitution. Second, property was considered an appropriate criterion for suffrage. As Chancellor Kent of New York explained at the 1821 New York State Constitutional Convention,

> Society is an association for the protection of property as well as of life, and the individual who contributes only one cent to the common stock,

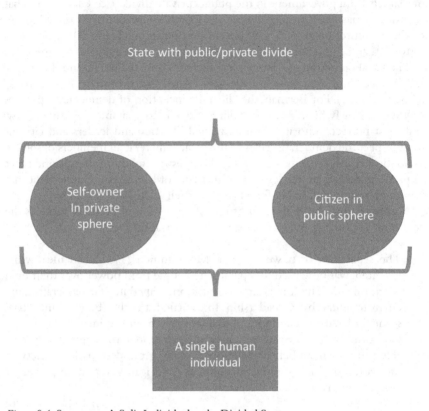

Figure 9.1 Symmetry: A Split Individual and a Divided State

ought not to have the same power and influence in directing the property concerns of the partnership, as he who contributes his thousands.

(Lepore 2018, 183)

Third, the Fourteenth Amendment, which was designed to protect former slaves, was subsequently interpreted to protect private business corporations as persons as well (Lepore 2018, 760; Mayer 2016, 226–239). Further, the doctrine of freedom of contract prevented regulation of working conditions, in the Supreme Court case Lochner 1905 (Lepore 2018, 377–378). Only nation-wide mobilization associated with the Progressive movement enabled the ratification of the income tax, the Sixteenth Amendment, in 1913 (Lepore 2018, 375–377). The Great Depression led to the protection of labor in the New Deal, with legal innovations which were developed in the early twentieth century in the New York labor movement.

Further theoretical development continued the trend towards protection of property as a foundational principle. For example, mainstream economics doesn't concern itself with the issue of inequality (Stiglitz 2015), and the Neo-liberal Thought Collective finds inequality a major driver of the economy (Mirowski 2013, 63). Doctrines like law and economics, principle–agent, and maximizing shareholder value extended principles of profit maximization to the courts and to corporate management and CEO pay practices (Lazonick 2009; Stout 2012; Fox 2009). The share of the top 1% of the population in the US has now exceeded the share in the 1920s, after a long period of relative equality in the 1950s and 1960s (Piketty 2014). The reduction of the regula-tion of campaign finance with Citizens United in 2010 has further enabled the very wealthy to dominate politics, including issues like climate change and health care (Mayer 2016; Skocpol and Hertel-Fernandez 2016). Meanwhile there is great spatial inequality in the US in health, education, and income, and declining life expectancy. Great disparities of income change the nature of the democracy (Stiglitz 2015) and have contributed to the outpouring of recent books warning of democracy's demise (Levitsky and Ziblatt 2018; MacLean 2017; Runciman 2018).

As a result of these long-term priorities, there is a decline in labor share at the global level. That is, rather than the roughly balanced distribution of income shares to each major factor of production, capital and labor, trends since the 1980s show a persistent decline in labor share (Autor 2018; Dao et al. 2017).

Contradictions

I contend that the contradictions of liberalism are related to the concept of "property in the person" (Pateman 1988; MacPherson 1962). That is, for many people, most of their lives consists in labor force participation, offering their own bodies and persons for sale as a commodity. In this case, the "consump-tion" of that commodity allows access to that person's capacities for the discrete time period of the working day. That person must respond to directions and complete tasks as assigned by the workplace authority. This can be considered a form of coercion. This notion of persons as objects for sale conflicts with the notion that this same person is a citizen with equal rights of participation in the state. This contradiction is embedded in capitalism, which is based on the use of labor power as a commodity for the production of value and surplus value, according to Marx (1967). This idea that the person is a commodity is consid-ered a "fiction," according to Polanyi, which the state must enforce (Polanyi 1944). As discussed in Chapter 2, the person as self-owner is internally divided, and can be related to the history and forms of society. That is, the modern indi-vidual is internally split, leading to forms of irrationality which are diagnosed in the helping professions, with their own histories (Moyn 2009, 328–330).

Labor market competition can lead to degradation of labor, which "society" will resist with a "countermovement" for protection. The changing structure of labor market institutions reflects this dynamic (Block and Somers 2014). In fact, much of the role of the modern liberal state is involved with the management of this dual role of labor, as both person and as commodity, such as provision for welfare, education, health, and social security. For example, welfare provision was established as early as the late thirteenth century in England (Block and Somers 2014, 124) and was used to manage the "social question" in imperial Germany in the late nineteenth century (Beck 1995). The administration of public welfare, like the Fordist production systems, is managed by bureaucratic techniques, where specific characteristics are used to "process" individuals in large impersonal systems, known as the "iron cage" (Weber 1978). Such categories then become aspects of personal identities and are used to claim greater access to resources, such as "identity politics," an ironic form of collective countermovement. An initial uneven distribution of resources can then become amplified in uneven development, with pockets of privilege, spatially, and institutionally.

There are persistent contradictions of liberalism, such as universal suffrage and the right to political participation vs. the exclusionary rhetoric of "capacity" based on property or education (Kahan 2003).

There is a contradiction between the notion of equal individuals vs. the equality of property owners, which includes property in the person, the opposite of equality (MacPherson 1962).

Case study: structure of post-war stimulus for housing

The structure of material infrastructure plays a role in individuation (Bennett and Joyce 2010; Cronon 1991; Norton 2008). That is, the material infrastructure reflects the key terms which organize the institutions in a given period. For example, there is a distinct change in urban architecture and urban design in the transition from the early modern to the modern period (Harvey 1990, 24–26, 69, 2010, 166–172). The formation of land markets (Bavel 2010) required different forms of human settlement, at once less secure and providing real estate collateral for financial assets. Domestic architecture also shifted from combined shop and home to the separation of public and private, first within the home, and then with the more complete spatial separation by residential and commercial districts. This material manifestation of domesticity helped to naturalize the separation of home and work (McKeon 2005). Home mortgages were also a feature in stabilizing the labor market, as noted by Engels (Davis 2018, 90–95). As housing became increasingly privatized after World War II, with the single-family suburban home as the norm, market competition for residential access was structured by race, income, and gender through access to finance (Dymski, Hernandez, and Mohanty 2013).

Production of space

The use of land shifted from shared usufruct on the commons to privately owned commercial agriculture, to urbanization, and subsequently suburbanization and industrial agriculture. The rent is based on agricultural productivity as well as the population density of urban building sites (Marx 1967, Vol. III, Chapters 46, 47, 808–813), subject to speculation based on capitalized value.

The importance of the role of land owners and rent as a category of income has been underestimated, according to Harvey, and the "state-finance nexus" has been instrumental in reorganizing the use of space on the requisite scale (Harvey 2010, 47–51, 54–57, 171–172, 180–183). Tax preferences for capital gains and the deductibility of interest have been important in the use of leverage to bid up land values, which then encourages further speculation (Hudson 2010). The stream of expected future wages can be used to capitalize land values as well, by means of long-term residential mortgages (Lapavitsas 2013, 167–168).

In industrial countries, housing can be provided by both the public and the private sectors, and its treatment in GDP statistics is somewhat arbitrary. For example, housing is treated as a "residential investment," with an imputed cost of housing services as part of the wage bundle in the Consumer Price Index. Home ownership is the most significant asset held by most households, other than the very rich.

The post-World War II generation faced the challenge of an economic stimulus large enough to replace the war effort (Shiller 2008; Harvey 2010, 168–172). The financing and production of private housing in the suburbs was the answer, in terms of quantity as well as form, providing a "spatial fix" as well as creation of the "homeowner" mentality. The democratization of financial assets (Ott 2011) and home ownership (Wray 2006) apparently produced the requisite respect for property to make enforcement of property rights a popular issue (Lamoreaux 2011). The rise in homeownership to roughly 60% of the households also made true the conventional wisdom that "home prices never fall," as the World War II generation certainly achieved a sizable gain in asset value and the "wealth effect." After World War II, home ownership has become a method of asset accumulation for households. The "wealth effect" enabled Greenspan to monetize home values in 2001 to avoid a Japan-style liquidity trap with home equity withdrawal (Hudson 2010, 20).

The design of housing also revealed the goal of supporting consumption rather than efficiency, with single-family homes as the standard for post-war finance, rather than apartments or coops. Rather than efficient apartment hotels which minimized housework (Hayden 1981), the design of the single-family home increased "work for mothers" (Cowan 1983), along with possibilities for consumption. At the same time, the housewife and her work were trivialized in a popular culture in which "Father Knows Best."

The single-family home became the norm for qualifying for self-amortizing home loans from the government financial institutions, Fannie Mae and Freddie Mac, with 30-year fixed rates (Shiller 2008; Kruse and Sugrue 2006). The specific location in class-and-race-differentiated suburbs affected socialization, work, and life chances for the next generation (Wilson 1987; Massey 2007; Massey and Denton 1993). Given the differentiation by income, there is an infinite demand for "moving up," as there is always a "better" neighborhood with more luxurious homes to be obtained (Chetty et al. 2014). Amenities like a clean environment, good schools, and transportation access require investment in public goods, which are unevenly provided given the reliance on local property taxes.

The interstate highway system paved the way for the automobile and mass consumption, along with dependence on fossil fuels. The design of cities changed yet again, taking the public space of city streets for the private automobile as a mass consumer durable good (Norton 2008). The individual house and car were protected private spaces, yet reliant on large-scale public goods funded by the state. Ironically, the proliferation of such consumer durables as the house and car transformed the landscape of the US, as well as its environment.

The suburbs were at once the middle-class ideal, at the same time that women (Friedan 1963) and youth culture burst out of the confines of materialist conformity (Harvey 1990, 37–38). Defense of property from taxes and from racial integration also helped fuel the conservative movement in the 1960s (McGirr 2001; Phillips-Fein 2009). Women, newly mobile between home and workforce, developed divided loyalties in electoral politics and social movements. In spite of the enormous investment of the federal government in infrastructure for water and transportation in California, it became the center of the movement to cut taxes and protect private property.

Housing and mortgage debt as disciplinary device

Home ownership enabled by mortgage debt also served as a disciplinary device (Edel, Sclar, and Luria 1984; Hudson 2010; Cooper 2017). The life cycle became increasingly driven by a series of financial obligations for home, education, and retirement (Lapavitsas 2013).

As investment was directed towards "greenfield" areas, the disinvestment in the wasteland was left for public responsibility. As those with means are mobile, the poor and disadvantaged concentrate in older urban areas and suburbs. The provision of public goods is beyond the capacity of the local public governance structure, leading to uneven development and fiscal crises. The outcome is uneven development within the US and recurrent fiscal crises (O'Connor 1973; Alcaly and Mermelstein 1977; Phillips-Fein 2017). For example, the bankruptcy of Detroit is the product of flight from unions and outsourcing, as well as the migration of blacks to the cities after Reconstruction (Florida 2017; Sugrue 1996), even while the potential of the urban form is still celebrated (Glaeser 2011).

Explaining the "neoliberal turn"

Writing in 1986, Bowles and Gintis expected that norms of democracy in the public sphere may begin to influence the private sphere towards workplace democracy (Bowles and Gintis 1986). On the contrary, with "neoliberalism" since the 1980s, market principles may have explicitly entered the public sphere instead, with privatization, market valuation, and competition (Davies 2015, 21–23).

There was a return of the rhetoric of "blaming the victim," with Poor Law Reform in 1834 and reform of welfare in the US in 1994. President Clinton may have adopted some features of neoliberalism, which had by then become a hegemonic narrative (Gerstle 2018; Block and Somers 2014). From the 1980s, neoliberalism and the "Washington Consensus" has intensified market discipline, with the end of Bretton Woods and the discipline of the metallic currency imposed with new institutional forms and rationales (Tooze 2018, 10–11).

Businesses shifted their alliance with labor with a type of "capital/labor accord," to a renewed focus on market discipline (Kotz 2015; Blyth 2002), faced with student resistance to the Vietnam War, labor unrest, and the formation of OPEC in the 1960s and 1970s.

With the forecast of climate refugees and an aging population, the demand of welfare on public finance may only increase in coming decades.

The capitalist growth model continually produces political strains, as there are persistent trends for capital labor/substitution to increase control and productivity, which displaces labor. To offset declining rates of profit, there is an increase in scale by international foreign direct investment and outsourcing to low-wage countries (Milberg and Winkler 2013).

Contemporary period

The Great Financial Crisis had many causes (Blyth 2013). The role of home ownership was one aspect. The democratization of property by means of home ownership did provide more than 60% of the households with an asset capable of accumulation of value. The family, that "unique individual" which was responsible for raising the next generation, was an integral part of the economy (Cooper 2017). In 2001, when Greenspan was seeking a stimulus for the economy, after the financial crisis of 2001, the tapping of the accumulated value of home ownership seemed like a viable strategy. Low interest rates and securitization provided a method for extracting this value by means of expanding financial markets. The infinite demand for housing, as a means for achieving higher social status, upward mobility by means of neighborhood, schools, amenities, and social connections, also proved attractive.

The growth of the financial markets was facilitated by the development of more financial "products," based on mathematical models which could ascertain the value of a certain asset, to facilitate trade (Brine and Poovey 2017). The end of Bretton Woods and the globalization of financial markets also provided more outlets for investment, along with the supreme confidence in markets from the Mont Pelerin Society framework, associated with Hayek. With increasing trends towards automation and inequality, financial investment was an appealing alternative to commodity production (Davis 2017, 130–143). The reification of money reinforced the belief that financial markets were just as promising a direction of investment as "real" investment. The possibility of "systemic risk," associated with many trades based on the same assumptions, with a single counter party such as AIG, was not recognized until after the fact.

In spite of the Great Financial Crisis of 2008, there is an acceptance and accommodation to the market among contemporary theorists (Herzog 2013;

Gauthier 1976), while ignoring the increasing inequality (Piketty 2014; Bavel 2016) and instability.

Some of the collective countermovements are regressive (Evans 2008), such as right-wing populists, fundamentalist terrorists, and white racists with potential global reach. These movements are post-liberal, collectivist rather than individualist, opposed to market forces rather than consistent with the market, and sometimes violent rather than law-abiding.

This may also prove to be a serious crisis of capitalism (Streeck 2016, 2017). The seriousness of the current global economic context may be indicated by the statement of the Business Roundtable in August, 2019, which declared a new purpose of the corporation. This new mission was to provide for stakeholders, not just maximize value for shareholders, a doctrine which had been in effect since the statement of Milton Friedman in the 1950s (Lazonick and O'Sullivan 2000; Sorkin 2019). Michael Porter, a professor at Harvard Business School, had also been recommending "creating shared value" (Porter and Kramer 2011).

It is possible that the protection of property as a first principle of government has led to increasing inequality (Pistor 2019), which is complicating macro management of the global economy. For example, there is a risk of deflation, rather than inflation, due to the "total domination of capital over labor" (McCulley 2019). Major industrial economies have very low interest rates, even negative in some cases, making addressing the next recession more difficult (Goldfarb and Kruger 2019). In addition, increasing inequality undermines the capacity for democracy. That is, the existence of vastly unequal living conditions reduces empathy and solidarity at a time when collective action to restore public goods like infrastructure, health, education, and climate resilience is more important than ever for economic performance and for well-being.

Bibliography

Akerlof, George A. and Janet L. Yellen. *Efficiency Wage Models of the Labor Market*. New York: Cambridge University Press, 1986.

Akerlof, George A. and Janet L. Yellen. "The Fair Wage-Effort Hypothesis and Unemployment," *Quarterly Journal of Economics*, Vol. 105, No. 2, May 1990, 255–283.

Alcaly, Roger E. and David Mermelstein (eds.). *The Fiscal Crisis of American Cities*. New York: Vintage Books, 1977.

Autor, David and Anna Salomons. *Is Automation Labor-Displacing? Productivity Growth, Employment, and the Labor Share*. Cambridge, MA: National Bureau of Economic Research, #24871, July 2018.

Bavel, Bas J.P. van. *Manors and Markets: Economy and Society in the Low Countries, 500–1600*. New York: Oxford University Press, 2010.

Bavel, Bas J. P. van. *The Invisible Hand? How Market Economies Have Emerged and Declined Since AD 500*. New York: Oxford University Press, 2016.

Beck, Hermann. *The Origins of the Authoritarian Welfare State in Prussia: Conservatives, Bureaucracy, and the Social Question, 1815–70*. Ann Arbor: University of Michigan Press, 1995.

Beck, Ulrich. *Individualization: Institutionalized Individualism and its Social and Political Consequences*. London: Sage, 2002.

Bell, Daniel. *The Cultural Contradictions of Capitalism*. New York: Basic Books, 1978.

Bennett, Tony and Patrick Joyce (eds.). *Material Powers: Cultural Studies, History and the Material Turn*. New York: Routledge, 2010.

Berlin, Isaiah. "Two Concepts of Liberty," in *Four Essays on Liberty*. New York: Oxford University Press, 1969, 118–172.

Berman, Sheri. *Democracy and Dictatorship in Europe: From Ancient Regime to the Present Day*. New York: Oxford University Press, 2019.

Bhattacharya, Tithi (ed.). *Social Reproduction Theory: Remapping Class, Recentering Oppression*. London: Pluto Press, 2017.

Block, Fred L. "Understanding the Diverging Trajectories of the United States and Western Europe: A Neo-Polanyian Analysis," *Politics and Society*, Vol. 35, No. 1, March 2007, 3–33.

Block, Fred L. "The Contradictory Logics of Financialization: Bringing Together Hyman Minsky and Karl Polanyi," *Politics and Society*, Vol. 44, No. 1, 2016, 3–13.

Block, Fred L. and Margaret R. Somers. *The Power of Market Fundamentalism: Karl Polanyi's Critique*. Cambridge, MA: Harvard University Press, 2014.

Blyth, Mark. *Great Transformations: Economic Ideas and Institutional Change in the Twentieth Century*. New York: Cambridge University Press, 2002.

Blyth, Mark. *Austerity: The History of a Dangerous Idea*. New York: Oxford University Press, 2013.

Borjas, George J. *We Wanted Workers: Unraveling the Immigration Narrative*. New York: W.W. Norton & Company, 2016.

Bowles, Samuel and Herbert Gintis. *Democracy and Capitalism: Property, Community, and the Contradictions of Modern Social Thought*. New York: Basic, 1986.

Brine, Kevin R. and Mary Poovey. *Finance in America: An Unfinished Story*. Chicago: University of Chicago Press, 2017.

Burawoy, Michael. "For a Sociological Marxism: The Complementary Convergence of Antonio Gramsci and Karl Polanyi," *Politics and Society*, Vol. 31, No. 2, June 2003, 193–261.

Cangiani, Michele. "Karl Polanyi's Institutional Theory: Market Society and Its 'Disembedded' Economy," *Journal of Economic Issues*, Vol. 45, No. 1, March 2011, 177–197.

Cangiani, Michele. "'Social Freedom' in the Twenty-First Century: Rereading Polanyi," *Journal of Economic Issues*, Vol. 51, No. 4, 2017, 915–938.

Chetty, Raj, Nathaniel Hendren, Patrick Kline, and Emmanuel Saez. "Where is the Land of Opportunity? The Geography of Intergeneration Mobility in the U.S.," *Quarterly Journal of Economics*, Vol. 129, No. 4, November 2014, 1553–1623.

Cooper, Melinda. *Family Values: Between Neoliberalism and the New Social Conservatism*. New York: Zone Books, 2017.

Cowan, Ruth Schwartz. *More Work for Mother: The Ironies of Household Technology from Open Hearth to Microwave*. New York: Basic, 1983.

Cronon, William. *Nature's Metropolis: Chicago and the Great West*. New York: W.W. Norton & Company, 1991.

Dao, Mai Chi, Mitali Das, Zsoka Koczan, and Weicheng Lian. "Why is Labor Receiving a Smaller Share of the Global Income? Theory and Evidence," IMF Working Paper 17/169, July 2017.

Davies, William. *The Limits of Neoliberalism: Authority, Sovereignty and the Logic of Competition*. London: Sage, 2015.

Davis, Ann E. "The Process of Provisioning: The Halter for the Workhorse," *Journal of Economic Issues*, Vol. XLIX, No. 2, June 2015, 449–457.

Davis, Ann E. *Money as a Social Institution: The Institutional Development of Capitalism*. New York: Routledge, 2017.

Davis, Mike. *Old Gods, New Enigmas: Marx's Lost Theory*. New York: Verso, 2018.

Davis, Mike and Justin Akers Chacon. *No One is Illegal: Fighting Violence and State Repression on the U.S.-Mexican Border*. Chicago: Haymarket Books, 2006.

Dymski, Gary, Jesus Hernanedez, and Lisa Mohanty. "Race, Gender, Power and the US Subprime Mortgage and Foreclosure Crisis: A Meso Analysis," *Feminist Economics*, Vol. 19, No. 3, 2013, 124–151.

Edel, Matthew, Elliott D. Sclar, and Dan Luria. *Shaky Palaces: Home Ownership and Social Mobility in Boston's Suburbanization*. New York: Columbia University Press, 1984.

Eichengreen, Barry. *The Populist Temptation: Economic Grievance and the Political Reaction in the Modern Era*. New York: Oxford University Press, 2018.

Evans, Peter. "Is an Alternative Globalization Possible?" *Politics and Society*, Vol. 36, No. 2, June 2008, 271–305.

Florida, Richard. *The New Urban Crisis: How our Cities are Increasing Inequality, Deepening Segregation, and Failing the Middle Class, and What We Can Do About It*. New York: Basic Books, 2017.

Fox, Justin. *The Myth of the Rational Market: A History of Risk, Reward, and Delusion on Wall Street*. New York: Harper Business, 2009.

Friedan, Betty. *The Feminine Mystique*. New York: Norton, 1963.

Friedman, Milton. *Capitalism and Freedom*. Chicago: University of Chicago Press, 1962.

Gauthier, David. *Morals by Agreement*. Oxford: Clarendon Press, 1976.

Gerstle, Gary. "The Rise and Fall (?) of America's Neoliberal Order," *Transactions of the Royal Historical Society*, Vol. 28, 2018, 241–264.

Giroux, Henry A. *The Terror of Neoliberalism: Authoritarianism and the Eclipse of Democracy*. Boulder: Paradigm Publishers, 2004.

Glaeser, Edward L. *Triumph of the City: How Our Greatest Invention Makes Us Richer, Smarter, Greener, Healthier, and Happier*. New York: Penguin, 2011.

Goldfarb, Sam and Daniel Kruger. "Investors Ponder Negative Bond Yields in the U.S.," *Wall Street Journal*, August 11, 2019.

Gordon, David M., Richard Edwards, and Michael Reich. *Segmented Work, Divided Workers: The Historical Transformation of Labor in the United States*. New York: Cambridge University Press, 1982.

Habermas, Jurgin. *The Structural Transformation of the Public Sphere: An Inquiry into a Category of Bourgeois Society*. Cambridge, MA: MIT Press, 1989.

Hall, Peter A. and David Soskice (eds.). *Varieties of Capitalism: The Institutional Foundations of Comparative Advantage*. New York: Oxford University Press, 2001.

Harvey, David. *The Condition of Postmodernity: An Enquiry into the Origins of Cultural Change*. Oxford, UK: Blackwell, 1990.

Harvey, David. *A Brief History of Neoliberalism*. New York: Oxford University Press, 2005.

Harvey, David. *The Enigma of Capital and the Crises of Capitalism*. New York: Oxford University Press, 2010.

Harvey, David. *Seventeen Contradictions and the End of Capitalism*. New York: Oxford University Press, 2014.

Hayden, Dolores. *The Grand Domestic Revolution: A History of Feminist Designs for American Homes, Neighborhoods, and Cities*. Cambridge, MA: MIT Press, 1981.

Herzog, Lisa. *Inventing the Market: Smith, Hegel, and Political Theory*. New York: Oxford University Press, 2013.

Hudson, Michael. "The Transition from Industrial Capitalism to a Financialized Bubble Economy," Levy Economics Institute Working Paper No. 627, October 2010.

Kahan, Alan S. *Liberalism in Nineteenth-Century Europe: The Political Culture of Limited Suffrage*. New York: Palgrave MacMillan, 2003.

Kotz, David. *The Rise and Fall of Neoliberal Capitalism*. Cambridge, MA: Harvard University Press, 2015.

Kruse, Kevin M. and Thomas J. Sugrue (eds.). *The New Suburban History*. Chicago: University of Chicago Press, 2006.

Lamoreaux, Naomi R. "The Mystery of Property Rights: A U.S. Perspective," *Journal of Economic History*, Vol. 71, No. 2, June 2011, 275–306.

Lapavitsas, Costas. *Profiting without Producing: How Finance Exploits Us All*. London: Verso, 2013.

Lazonick, William. *Sustainable Prosperity in the New Economy? Business Organization and High-Tech Employment in the United States*. Kalamazoo, MI: W.E Upjohn Institute for Employment Research, 2009.

Lazonick, William. "Innovative Business Models and Varieties of Capitalism: Financialization of the U.S. Corporation," *Business History Review*, Winter 2010, 675–702.

Lazonick, William and Mary O'Sullivan. "Maximizing Shareholder Value: A New Ideology for Corporate Governance," *Economy and Society*, Vol. 29, No. 1, February 2000, 13–35.

Lepore, Jill. *These Truths: A History of the United States*. New York: W.W. Norton and Company, 2018.

Levitsky, Steven and Daniel Ziblatt. *How Democracies Die*. New York: Crown, 2018.

MacLean, Nancy. *Democracy in Chains: The Deep History of the Radical Right's Stealth Plan for America*. New York: Penguin, 2017.

MacPherson, C. B. *The Political Theory of Possessive Individualism: Hobbes to Locke*. Oxford: Clarendon Press, 1962.

Marglin, Stephen A. *The Dismal Science: How Thinking Like an Economist Undermines Community*. Cambridge, MA: Harvard University Press, 2008.

Marx, Karl. *Capital*. New York: International Publishers, 1967.

Massey, Douglas S. *Categorically Unequal: The American System of Stratification*. New York: Russell Sage, 2007.

Massey, Douglas S. and Nancy A. Denton. *American Apartheid: Segregation and the Making of the Underclass*. Cambridge, MA: Harvard University Press, 1993.

Mayer, Jane. *Dark Money: The Hidden History of the Billionaires Behind the Rise of the Radical Right*. New York: Doubleday, 2016.

McCulley, Paul. Dinner speaker. Twenty-Eighth Annual Hyman P. Minsky Conference. Levy Institute, Bard College, Annandale-on-Hudson, April 17, 2019.

McGirr, Lisa. *Suburban Warriors: The Origins of the New American Right*. Princeton, NJ: Princeton University Press, 2001.

McKeon, Michael. "The Emergence of Gender Difference in England, 1660–1760," *Eighteenth-Century Studies*, Vol. 28, No. 3, Spring 1995, 295–322.

McKeon, Michael. *The Secret History of Domesticity: Public, Private and the Division of Knowledge*. Baltimore: Johns Hopkins University Press, 2005.

Milberg, William and Deborah Winkler. *Outsourcing Economics: Global Value Chains in Capitalist Development*. New York: Cambridge University Press, 2013.

Mirowski, Philip. *Never Let a Serious Crisis Go to Waste: How Neoliberalism Survived the Financial Meltdown*. New York: Verso, 2013.

Moyn, Samuel. "The Assumption by Man of His Original Fracturing: Marcel Gauchet, Gladys Swain, and the History of the Self," *Modern Intellectual History*, Vol. 6, No. 2, 2009, 315–341.

Norton, Peter D. *Fighting Traffic: The Dawn of the Motor Age in the American City*. Cambridge, MA: MIT Press, 2008.

O'Connor, James R. *The Fiscal Crisis of the State*. New York: St. Martin's, 1973.

Ott, Julia C. *When Wall Street Met Main Street: The Quest for an Investors' Democracy*. Cambridge, MA: Harvard University Press, 2011.

Pateman, Carole. *The Sexual Contract*. Stanford, CA: Stanford University Press, 1988.

Phillips-Fein, Kimberly. *Invisible Hands: The Making of the Conservative Movement from the New Deal to Reagan*. New York: W.W. Norton & Company, 2009.

Phillips-Fein, Kimberly. *Fear City: New York's Fiscal Crisis and the Rise of Austerity Politics*. New York: Metropolitan Books, 2017.

Piketty, Thomas. *Capital in the Twenty-First Century*. Cambridge, MA: Harvard University Press, 2014.

Piore, Michael J. "Varieties of Capitalism Theory: Its Considerable Limits," *Politics and Society*, Vol. 44, No. 2, 2016, 237–241.

Piore, Michael J. and Andrew Schrank. *Root-Cause Regulation: Protecting Work and Workers in the Twenty-First Century*. Cambridge, MA: Harvard University Press, 2018.

Pistor, Katharina. *The Code of Capital: How the Law Creates Wealth and Inequality*. Princeton, NJ: Princeton University Press, 2019.

Pocock, J.G.A. *The Machiavellian Moment: Florentine Political Thought and the Atlantic Republican Tradition*. Princeton, NJ: Princeton University Press, 1975.

Polanyi, Karl. *The Great Transformation*. Boston: Beacon Pres, 1944.

Porter, Michael E. and Mark R. Kramer. "Creating Shared Value: How to Reinvent Capitalism – and Unleash a Wave of Innovation and Growth," *Harvard Business Review*, January–February 2011, 1–17.

Runcimann, David. *How Democracy Ends*. New York: Basic, 2018.

Searle, John R. *Making the Social World: The Structure of Human Civilization*. New York: Oxford University Press, 2010.

Shiller, Robert J. *The Subprime Solution: How Today's Global Financial Crisis Happened, and What to Do About It*. Princeton, NJ: Princeton University Press, 2008.

Silver, Beverly J. and Giovanni Arrighi. "Polanyi's 'Double Movement': The *Belle Epoques* of British and U.S. Hegemony Compared," *Politics and Society*, Vol. 31, No. 2, June 2003, 325–355.

Skocpol, Theda and Alexander Hertel-Fernandez. "The Koch Network and Republican Party Extremism," *Perspectives on Politics*, Vol. 14, No. 3, September 2016, 681–699.

Sorkin, Andrew Ross. "How Shareholder Democracy Failed the People," *The New York Times*, August 20, 2019.

Stiglitz, Joseph E. *The Great Divide: Unequal Societies and What We Can Do About Them*. New York: W.W. Norton & Company, 2015.

Stout, Lynn A. *The Shareholder Value Myth: How Putting Shareholders First Harms Investors, Corporations, and the Public*. San Francisco: Berrett-Koehler, 2012.

Streeck, Wolfgang. *How Will Capitalism End? Essays on a Failing System*. New York: Verso, 2016.

Streeck, Wolfgang. *Buying Time: The Delayed Crisis of Democratic Capitalism*. 2nd ed. New York: Verso, 2017.

Sugrue, Thomas J. *The Origins of the Urban Crisis: Race and Inequality in Postwar Detroit*. Princeton, NJ: Princeton University Press, 1996.

Taylor, Charles. *Sources of the Self: The Making of Modern Identity*. New York: Cambridge University Press, 1989.

Taylor, Charles. *Modern Social Imaginaries*. Durham, NC: Duke University Press, 2004.

Taylor, Charles. *A Secular Age*. Cambridge, MA: Harvard University Press, 2007.

Taylor, Charles. *The Language Animal: The Full Shape of the Human Linguistic Capacity*. Cambridge, MA: Harvard University Press, 2016.

Thelen, Kathleen. *Varieties of Liberalization and the New Politics of Social Solidarity*. New York: Cambridge University Press, 2014.

Tooze. J. Adam. *Crashed: How a Decade of Financial Crises Changed the World*. New York: Viking, 2018.

Veblen, Thorstein. *The Theory of the Leisure Class: An Economic Study of Institutions*. New York: Modern Library, 1934.

Wacquant, Loic. *Punishing the Poor: The Neoliberal Government of Social Insecurity*. Durham, NC: Duke University Press, 2009.

Weber, Max. *Economy and Society: An Outline of Interpretive Sociology*. Berkeley: University of California Press, 1978.

Wilson, William Julius. *The Truly Disadvantaged: The Inner City, the Underclass, and Public Policy*. Chicago: University of Chicago Press, 1987.

Wray, L. Randall. "Neocons and the Ownership Society," *Challenge*, Vol. 49, No. 1, January–February 2006, 44–73.

Ziblatt, Daniel. *Conservative Parties and the Birth of Democracy*. New York: Cambridge University Press, 2017.

10 Backlash

Backlash

The term "backlash" suggests repetition and irrationality. This is not the typical sequence for economics, which is rational, linear, and progressive. A recent discussion of the "madness of crowds" mentioned Gustave Le Bon, who witnessed the Paris Commune in 1871, feeling both fascinated and appalled at the capacity for group contagion (Davies 2019, 8–12). Other examples include crowd reactions to financial markets, and the "mania" that can spread among investors, even if not present at the same time and place (Kindleberger 1989; MacKay 1932). Pocock mentioned the whimsical nature of "Fortuna" and the impact on personalities from the uncertainty in newly emergent financial markets (Pocock 1975).

In spite of these examples, economics assumes the rational "individual" whose actions are based on objective information, not influenced by social phenomena. Values and beliefs serve to discipline individual behavior but result from the spontaneous emergence of markets and morals, according to the Mont Pelerin Society (Brown 2019, 28–39, 42–44), not "society." The argument in this book is that "individuation" is the outcome of institutional design, which channels behavior into manageable and predictable forms, such as the public/private divide. Any inadequacies of this form of institutional representation can generate "mobs" and open resistance to existing values.

As discussed earlier in Chapters 2 and 5, there is a type of "doubling" in capitalist institutions, which are "fictional" but have real effects. The acceptance of unreality in everyday life is indicated by the now-conventional phenomena such as "reality TV" and "virtual reality." While behavioral economics studies the types of irrationality in individual decision-making, it can be argued that it is the structure of the economy itself that is "irrational."

The concept of protection of property, however reified, can justify tax cuts, deregulation, and privatization as part of its "protection," a founding principle of John Locke and the US Constitution of 1787. Neoliberalism, principle–agent alignment, and maximizing shareholder value (Stout 2012) are other ideas that can be used to justify inequality. As inequality in the twenty-first century surpasses the levels last reached in the 1920s (Stiglitz 2015; Piketty 2014), there is a justifiable rage, but channeled differently depending on dominant ideas. The individualism promoted by Thatcher was supplemented by the influential novels of Ayn Rand in the US, who celebrated the creative individual, consistent with Nietzsche (McKibben 2019, 85–101).

The return of the term "socialism" to recent electoral campaigns in 2016 and 2018 may be a reaction to the dominance of neoliberalism, perhaps consistent with Polanyi's "double movement."

Double movement

In foundational capitalist institutions like double-entry bookkeeping, there is a dichotomy between the "real" and the "financial," the identification of the specific commodity and its monetary value (Brine and Poovey 2017). That is, there is an institutional basis for Polanyi's "double movement" in accounting, as well as the "fictional" commodities.

The analysis of Karl Polanyi regarding the self-regulating market as a "utopian fiction" can be used as an aid to understanding political movements in the twentieth and the twenty-first centuries, in my view. The operation of the market requires the action of the state, which then violates the principle of the self-regulating market and the separation of the market from society, what we call the "public/private divide." The state acts both to support the market and then also to protect both firms and labor from its effects. These contradictory tendencies then impair the operation of the market. According to Polanyi, both fascism and the New Deal were a reaction to market gridlock (Polanyi 1944, 242–244), which is an inevitable result of the strains of the "utopian self-regulating market."

Polanyi reviews each market for the "fictional commodities," labor, land, and money. For example, to "separate labor from other activities of life and to subject it to the laws of the market was to annihilate all organic forms of existence and to replace them by a different type of organization, an atomistic and individualist one" (Polanyi 1944, 163). Only Owen understood that "individualization" was not feasible, given the effect of society on the worker (Polanyi 1944, 127–129, 258A–258B).

> The smashing up of social structures [was necessary] in order to extract the element of labor from them. . . . Only the penalty of starvation . . . was deemed capable of creating a functioning labor market. . . . It was necessary to liquidate organic society, which refused to permit the individual to starve.
>
> (Polanyi 1944, 164–165)

Legislation like the Anti-Combination Laws of 1799–1800 and the Poor Law Amendment of 1834 were important to "repeal the right to live" (Polanyi 1944, 80–83). That is, "*laissez-faire* itself was enforced by the state" (Polanyi 1944, 139). The "collectivist" backlash of the 1870s and 1880s was "spontaneous" and was observed across a politically diverse range of industrializing countries, with workman's compensation, health, education, and factory legislation (Polanyi 1944, 146–150). Protectionism in the late nineteenth century in turn led to imperialist rivalry and depression, and the failure of the separation of the state and the market (Polanyi 1944, 200–219). According to Polanyi, the same dynamic was repeated in the 1930s, with the destruction of the "free trade" regime and the return to war.

That is, the market has been the governing mechanism of the global economy since the early nineteenth century, but this "free market" is a utopian myth (Mazower 2012). The periodic breakdowns and reactions are evidence for this repeated pattern.

There are various methods for periodizing the US economy to make these patterns of double movement more visible. As one of the fictional commodities, which is also a human person with the potential of political agency, labor is an important focus.

There were notable changes in labor relations, from the doctrine of freedom of contract, which restricted the formation of unions, to the Wagner Act of 1935, which legalized unions and the right to organize. After World War II, the Taft Hartley Act of 1947 undercut coordination across unions and allowed states to permit "right to work" laws. After the end of Bretton Woods in the early 1970s, fewer restrictions on foreign direct investment and outsourcing reduced manufacturing employment in the US and contributed to the decline of unionization. The neoliberal consensus of Thatcher and Reagan was explicitly anti-union.

Each durable regime would have a moral foundation. For example, the New Deal would stress safe working conditions, social security, and rights

Table 10.1 Periodization of US Political Regimes

Period	Turning Points	Types of Labor
1812–1860	War of 1812 to beginning of Civil War	Indentured, slave, and wage labor
1865–1890	Populism; emergence of national market and large-scale enterprises	Wage labor and emergence of unions; Reconstruction and Jim Crow Laws
1890–1930	Corporate capitalism	Methods of mass production; professionalization of management, social science, journalism, finance
1930–1970	New Deal regime	Rights to organize; consumer society; social benefits; increasing equality
1980–2008	Neoliberalism	Declining unionization, globalization of investment and production; increasing inequality; contingent social benefits
2013–present	Populist backlash	Restrictions on immigration and affirmative action; global labor surplus

Sources: Gerstle 2018; Livingston 2001; Kotz 2015

to organize. Neoliberalism would emphasize individual responsibility, work effort, family, and religion. Further, the promise of individual opportunity would enable entrepreneurship and innovation. The development of an affluent consumer society based on "identity" and conspicuous consumption may undercut these values, nonetheless, leading to contradictions within each regime (Gerstle 2018).

Ideas have been important in the development of political alliances (Blyth 2002). For example, the threat of communism had an impact on the New Deal and its class compromise between capital and labor (Gerstle 2018, 253–255). There may have been structural contradictions in the "Postwar Liberal Consensus" (Mason and Morgan 2017; Jessop et al. 1988). Slow job growth in the 1960s may have led to "white backlash" (Carter 1995, 349). The fall of communism emboldened neoliberalism after 1989. Some observers see the rise of populism as a collective backlash against neoliberal individualism, which had undercut the power of unions, increased inequality, and had deregulated finance, making the Great Financial Crisis of 2008 more likely (McKean 2019; Tooze 2018). Like the "Southern Strategy" of Goldwater and Nixon, the Trump campaign rhetoric stokes a white nationalist, cross-class identity in contrast to American black and "brown" immigrants from Arab, Central and South American countries. This strategy may be especially appealing to lower-middle and working-class Americans, who are threatened by "free trade" and the global labor surplus, who have been bypassed by the urban knowledge economy. Like nationalism in the nineteenth century, this rhetoric may counter the appeal of class-based alliances, which are a greater threat to the protection of property.

The power of ideas: Hayek vs. Polanyi

Two near-contemporaries, Friedrich Hayek (1899–1992) and Karl Polanyi (1886–1964), viewed the wreckage of World War I and II from different vantage points. To Hayek, the greatest threat was socialism, and for Polanyi the greatest threat was liberalism (Yergin and Stanislaw 1998), which each viewed as utopian. For Hayek the preferred policy was the spontaneous emergence of markets and values, undisturbed insofar as possible by the government (Brown 2019, 29–39), even while Mirowski documents the internal inconsistencies of this position (Mirowski 2013, 68–88). For Polanyi, the market was a "utopian" dream, requiring the active role of the government to construct and maintain the three "fictional" commodities, land, labor, and money (Polanyi 1944).

The observation that the economy is an incentive system presents a contradiction for Hayek and neoliberalism, who view the market as natural. That is, if the market is the outcome of human nature, the role of incentives is presumably unnecessary. This contradiction between the presumed spontaneous emergence of the market and the requirement of market design was also noted by Mirowski (2013, 303–313).

Structure of the welfare system

The structure of the welfare system reveals the importance of market incentives. In exploring and explaining the "power" of the ideas of "market fundamentalism," Block and Somers (2014) compare two welfare regimes separated by hundreds of years, the Elizabethan Poor Laws of the seventeenth through the nineteenth centuries in the United Kingdom to the twentieth-century United States. The effect of the structure of the Poor Laws was to blame the victim, rather than economic structure or business cycles. According to this narrative based on Malthus, aid to the poor removes the discipline of scarcity on both work and procreation and has the "perverse" effect of worsening the problem of poverty (Block and Somers 2014, 145–149). The Welfare Reform of the twentieth century in the US had the same narrative structure (Block and Somers 2014, 177–192).

This narrative reveals the contradiction of "the individual" as the foundation for economics, in my view. On the one hand, the individual is autonomous and fully formed, with a distinctive, unique character, which has no reference to socialization, education, or cultural values. On the other hand, this individual is susceptible to "incentives," which reward work and punish laziness, and apply stigmas to deviant behavior. In fact, the justification of the entire market system is its incentives, which motivate work and effort. Yet this market system is also founded on the notion of the "individual," which is immune to such external influences. Similarly, the notion of "austerity" is used periodically to reinforce the discipline of the market system in spite of the public capacity to support poor relief and provide public goods (Blyth 2013).

Framework of micro and macroeconomics

This inconsistency is particularly evident in microeconomics, with the market merely responding to the preferences of the exogenous "individual," on the one hand, and actively shaping those preferences, on the other. This inconsistency is present in macroeconomics as well. For example, financial markets presumably operate with rational investors with diverse expectations and risk preferences who make investments based on individual self-interest to maximize the financial rate of return. Yet financial markets are subject to contagion and imperfect information, which opens a role for reliance on convention and self-fulfilling "bubbles." Further, to be effective at the macro level, investment projects must be aggregated, ideally coordinated by the interest rate and the marginal efficiency of capital. The inadequacies of these financial market mechanisms Keynes pointed out and ultimately recommended the "euthanasia of the rentier" and a greater role for government (Keynes 1964, 315–326). The greater knowledge available to the government, and the greater capacity for coordination for the economy as a whole, led him to conclude that "the duty of ordering the current volume of investment cannot safely be left in private hands" (Keynes 1964, 320).

Yet Keynes did not take the next step and develop a "social" economy (Davis 2017). Rather, his key economic categories are monetary aggregates, and the behavioral drivers are psychological tendencies, such as liquidity preference, the marginal propensities to consume and invest, "animal spirits," and "expectations" (Keynes 1964, 246–247). Keynes makes note of "capitalistic individualism" but recommends income distribution policies and an enlarged role for the state for the stabilization of the economy (Keynes 1964, 374–381). Money is treated as a durable commodity like any other, with its "own rate of return" (Keynes 1964, 222–223). Keynes' recommended policy for unemployment is a notable contrast with the neoclassical preference for deflation, nonetheless, while also challenging their assumption that unemployment is voluntary and requires discipline. Alternatively, Keynes' position is that unemployment can be involuntary, and the experience of deflation can adversely affect expectations and so lead to a self-enforcing downward spiral. Keynes does understand the macro economy as a simultaneous, self-reinforcing performance which is interdependent and potentially volatile, rather than the neoclassical conceptualization of regular patterns of predictable behavior (Keynes 1964, 250–254). This very division within economics of micro from macro is also a result of these different treatments of the concept of "the individual."

Institutional economics

Modern contributions such as "behavioral economics" incorporate irrational preferences, without fully theorizing the social, the influence of one person on another. Rather the goal is to make more accurate predictions and to develop policies which "nudge" towards improved performance, a new application of "paternalism" (Thaler and Sunstein 2008). Exceptions are institutional economists like Veblen, who discuss "conspicuous consumption" as the attempt to influence one's status with respect to peers. Reviewing the long-term history of the market, Bavel finds that factor markets are always embedded in social and political institutions. He finds a type of Polanyian "double movement" in the acquisition of political power along with wealth for the elites formed by the market, which then constrains the market operation. He finds a cycle, with a rise and fall of markets in a range of geographies and periods of history, different from the teleology which assumes that markets rise throughout history and around the globe (Bavel 2016).

Economics avoids "the social" by assuming an exogenous, anti-social **homo economicus**, who is self-interested, rational, for whom more is better, with an income constraint, and therefore responsive to relative prices. In this sense, modern economics is true to Thatcher's statement: "there is no such thing as society."

Social factors cannot be easily isolated from economics, nonetheless, with phenomena such as financial "contagion" (Shiller 2015) as well as "efficiency wages," where the level of wages is designed to influences performance (Akerlof and Yellen 1986, 1990). The experience of long-term unemployment tends to degrade skills, as well as self-respect and motivation (Sennett and Cobb 1972), as in the concept of "discouraged workers." The absence of positive role models and social connections can breed unemployment in a particular location (Chetty et al. 2014; Rajan 2019). Absence of educational and employment opportunities can breed attitudes which are in fact unemployable, as in the era of exclusion of women from higher education. The pricing of risk in an economic model without a full account of the social tends to underprice that risk, leading to economic instability (Brine and Poovey 2017). The economy is social and has social effects, a consideration which is explicitly excluded from the formal economics discipline.

The "power of ideas" to which Block and Somers refer may be explained by the dualities of the labor market, where a person both is and is not a commodity. The market embodies "freedom," according to mainstream economics, while the "property in the person" is a form of domination, according to Pateman. These institutional regularities transmit similar contradictions, which are evident across countries and centuries (Blyth 2002). The narratives of shifting the "blame" to certain categories of individuals, such as the "undeserving poor" or the immigrant, shields the attribution of the problem to the system, helping to stabilize and legitimate the market. That is, the abstract market system may depend on personification of certain categories of persons who shoulder the blame for the market dysfunction when it is not "utopian" in effect. In this sense, the "self-regulating market" is "fiction," according to Polanyi (1944).

Time and space

Although money is presumably useful in managing time (Goetzmann 2016), there are several flaws in this argument. Economists assume "overlapping generations" (or OLG) models (Bullard 2019) and continuous homogenous abstract time (Ogle 2015). Yet there is demographic variability, contingency in current economic performance, and uncertainty regarding future prospects. Such uncertainty can be managed by derivative contracts, which are valued in the present, at the "strike price." The availability of financial trades to offset uncertainty has led to decreases in long-term real investment and greater financial instability (Rajan 2005). That is, the search for safe assets in the present has jeopardized long-term investment for the future (Brine and Poovey 2017).

When savings and pension funds are vulnerable to financial instability, the newly bankrupt savers and pensioners are enraged, driven to desperation, and even suicide (as was observed during the Great Depression in the 1930s). The bailouts of the financial firms after the Great Financial Crisis of 2008 also led to widespread protest movements as well. The promises behind the issue of financial contracts were broken, undermining trust and compliance.

Further, faced with global issues like climate change, the financial markets are ill-suited to address this issue, due to collective action problems (Olson 1965), externalities, public goods, as well as uncertainty, and the short-term bias of the calculation of present discounted value (PDV). More active industrial policy such as the "Green New Deal" would violate the presumed "freedom" of individual private property owners. That is, the constitutional guarantees of the protection of individual private property would be threatened by taxation and new regulations imposed on the use of property.

Appeals to the doctrine of public trust (Blumm and Wood 2013) have sought to regain the conceptual whole of a nation, or the earth, and the implicit promise of property protection for future generations. A new form of politics arises when the next generation mobilizes to protect their own futures.

When faced with warnings from central bankers like Mark Carney regarding the potential of climate change to impact financial markets, the response in the US has been to attack climate science rather than consider the associated risks. The paradigm of property is at stake, with its commitment to property rights and individualism, which is apparently a greater threat to existing governance and value systems than the potential impacts of climate change on the costs of food, transportation, displacement of climate refugees, loss of infrastructure and capital stock, and stranded assets (McKibben 2019).

Crisis of representation

There is a long legacy of "representation" in liberal states, from electoral methods to select public officials, to reinforce the notion of the "sovereignty" of the nation consisting of the entire population. The state would seek to understand "public opinion" in order to govern in the interests of its constituency. Yet the "values" in the liberal state are somehow "fluid," depending on the state of the economy and business expectations. Several basic concepts seem to be self-fulfilling, even tautological:

> Investors seek to understand the expectations of other investors, to be able to make the best wager on the financial markets in the present, like a "casino," as Keynes understood;
> Politicians seek to appeal to the largest number of people and to mobilize public opinion, which is then vulnerable to influence by public media and political campaigns;
> Consumers seek status according to the latest fashion, which is subject to influence by the consumer response to the latest fashion;
> Money is backed by public debt, the safety and stability of which depends on the sentiments of consumers and businesses, or "animal spirits," another concept from Keynes;
> Prices influence decisions in the market, and reflect consumer preferences, but in turn are influenced by fashion and income distribution, as well as oligopoly and technology;
> Global supply chains lead to increasing profit for multinational corporations, while hollowing out the productive capacity and skills of the US labor force.

The economy itself is performative, with no actual anchor, but more like a flotilla of vessels subject to waves of sentiment. Money is real, and a matter of life and death for wage laborers, yet money is subject to influence by the system as a whole. The growth of the system as a whole can provide rising standards of living but is contingent on performance in each moment.

That is, money represents the person, the community, and its property, but nonetheless money does not provide an absolute standard. Rather than its objectivity, the fact that money and markets reflect subjectivity is part of its utility and its ongoing fluctuations.

The economy claims to facilitate expression of human nature, not to shape it, but its operation does affect incentives, at the very least, and also its values. When life decisions are made based on present and future financial values, any instability in those financial values can disturb real lives.

In the nineteenth century, Nietzsche could observe that the human person resembled a "dividual," due to industrialization and fragmentation of the self (see Chapter 1). In the twenty-first century, such dissociation is even more notable. As expressed by Donna Haraway in "A Cyborg Manifesto," the unity of the "self" was even more elusive in the late twentieth century.

> The self is the One who is not dominated, who knows that by the service of the other, the other is the one who holds the future, who knows that by the experience of domination, which gives the lie to the autonomy of the self. To be One is to be autonomous, to be powerful, to be God; but to be One is to be an illusion, and so to be involved in a dialectic of apocalypse with the other. Yet to be other is to be multiple, without clear boundary, frayed, insubstantial. One is too few, but two are too many.
>
> (Haraway 1991)

The logic of automation has extended so far as to eliminate prospects of employment for vast numbers of the global labor surplus (Davis 2018, 2–7). Addiction to online social media is widespread, by design (Zuboff 2019, 449–451). Identity politics has become more contentious and contested, with "white" a new category of persons who claim special consideration. The "post-modern self" online is a series of presentations, with a distributed identity on social media platforms and no clear future (Simanowski 2018, 34–36, 68–69). Families and communities are disrupted by outsourcing and globalization (Cooper 2017). In such a context, the search for recognition and stable new affiliations may become more desperate.

Populism

Populism can be defined as a mobilization of political expression outside the conventional channels of political process. The term "populism" resonates with the Latin definition of "the people" (Urbinati 2014, 160–169) and makes claims to legitimacy by a more true representation of the wishes of the entire people.

The justification of representative democracy was based on the "sovereignty" of the people, after hereditary monarchy, and so the existence of more direct communication of the people's interest could be used to rationalize changes in political parties or institutions. The rise of populism can also be attributed to gridlock in existing political channels (Eichengreen 2018) or economic instability.

The claim to "true" expression of "the people" can be grounded on mobilization of the less powerful, or the disadvantaged, as a challenge to existing hierarchies. Instead of counting ballots and weighing checks and balances, populism can include total identification with a charismatic leader (Urbinati 2019) who crosses the usual boundaries of the public/private divide. There is a unity of interests, rather than pluralism and compromise. In the US, nineteenth-century populism was an expression of unrest among farmers and laborers in reaction to economic inequality and the rising political power of large corporations, such as railroads and banks. Women were active in the movement, which supported restrictions on immigrants and blacks, while also critical of capitalism (Lepore 2018, 330–353; Postel 2007). The Progressive movement addressed some of the same issues, while also appealing to professionalization in business management, municipal governance, journalism, and finance (Livingston 1986), with claims to "objective" expertise as a new source of legitimacy.

In the wake of the Great Financial Crisis of 2008, the government bailed out the financial system, protecting confidence in money and credit instead of the debtor (Tooze 2018, 166–201), repeating the trauma of the 1930s, diagnosed by Polanyi (1944). With increasing inequality, the risks of oligarchy increase (Balkin 2018).

Because the economy is not considered "social," political mobilization is "outside" the market and apparently unrelated. Living in the "utopian" self-regulating" market economy for which "there is no alternative," according to Thatcher, there is little discourse available for expressing discontent. Yet political unrest since the Great Financial Crisis (GFC) of 2008 may be related to this breakdown of the market economy. In fact, the twenty-first century turn to "populism" in industrial countries in the West is another version of Polanyi's "counter movement," in my view.

Other commentators agree that individualism and competitive emulation are unstable sources of motivation. The global economy after 1989 no longer provides access to secure positions for the now-competing, upwardly aspiring "individuals" from the newly modernizing countries of Asia and Central Europe. The model of the "bourgeois individual" emphasizes effort and responsibility, with the tendency towards blaming oneself for any failures. "Young men of promise" who cannot find secure positions commensurate with their talents can be prone to rage, especially in countries where modernization has undermined traditional privileges (Mishra 2017; Davies 2015). Rather than motivating, competition can be destabilizing.

Competition for work tends to generate a struggle of all against all, which destroys all the values of solidarity and humanity, and sometimes produces direct violence. Those who deplore the cynicism of the men and women of our time should not omit to relate it to the economic and social conditions which favour or demand it and which reward it.

(Bourdieu 1998, 84)

Nietzsche's concept of "ressentiment" has been used to understand this rage turned inward into dissatisfaction with oneself (Brown 2018, 25–26, 2019, 174–182). An "authoritarian personality" and strong identification with the leader can also result from the "*introjection* of an irrational society" (Gordon 2018, 64–67; italics in original; Stenner and Haidt 2018).

Populism can offer a new identity and a new group of like-minded individuals. The mobilization of such new groups challenges existing elites and seeks to elevate and to redefine the "common people" in more positive terms. The "public good" is articulated by a charismatic leader, rather than the result of quantitative electoral protocols. Rather than tolerance for multiple points of view, there is a respect for common knowledge expressed by the true members of the nation, rather than immigrants or outsiders (Mudde and Kaltwasser 2017). There have been populist parties historically in the US, with political leanings both to the right and to the left (Judis 2016). In the turn of twenty-first-century Italy, early exposure to entertainment TV is associated with electoral support for populist parties (Durante, Pinotti, and Tesei 2019).

The methods by which coalitions and alliances can form are diverse and subject to study as the dominant neoliberal paradigm comes increasingly under question. Such factors can include the following:

Ideas to mobilize alliances and to express and articulate "interests" (Blyth 2002)
Contradictions and class fractions (Davis 2018, 155–178)
Poor economic performance
Inequality, stoking polarization (Stiglitz 2015)
Resources for think tanks and marketing strategies in politics (Mayer 2016; Skocpol and Hertel-Fernandez 2016; Sheingate 2016)
Discourse
Charisma

Twenty-first century populist leaders boldly defy market imperatives, such as balanced budgets, and free trade, appearing to have the interests of the people at heart as a first priority. Yet when such policies disrupt economic performance, the instability and unemployment can cause further unrest, as Polanyi predicted.

Backlash

We have noted the ambivalence of the economics profession on the relationship between the economy and humans. On the one hand, the economy is a natural expression of human nature and the tendency to "truck and barter," and, on the other, the economy influences behavior by means of "incentives," which should not be disturbed by government intervention. If it can be understood that the economy, the market, has an effect on humans, then it is also possible that there can be a "backlash" against that effect, even if not expressed in those terms.

There was an intensification of market discipline and a turn to neoliberalism after the end of the Bretton Woods monetary accord in the 1970s, which had removed the metallic monetary standard. This turn created a "deep crisis of modern politics" (Tooze 2018, 10–13). Waves of movements, from left (feminist, black, sexual preference) and from the right (right to life, free market) have been mobilized across the decades (Kruse and Zelizer 2019). Identity groups may have become more relevant in this context, a turn to protective affiliation, but also providing more opportunities for political entrepreneurs (Sides, Tesler, and Vavreck 2018), perhaps also shifting attention away from increasing economic inequality.

The struggle for "position" in the economy may have become more intense with the following trends:

Labor is no longer necessary for commodity production (Livingston 2001)

Major industries, such as petroleum, shipping, and agriculture, are having a cumulative impact on the ecology

Subjectivity is less "grounded," with changing gender roles in employment and the household (Bauman and Leoncini 2019)

Sex is technologically separate from reproduction, enabling more flexible social relations

Biology is increasingly subject to conscious design

Social relations are increasingly mediated by technology

Under these conditions, the historical variation of the "self" is observable in a person's own lifetime (Livingston 2001).

The appeal of populism can be understood as follows:

A Shift from individual to groups

The categories used by various identity groups show a resemblance to the categories of routine bureaucratic processing, which allocate privilege and rights to exclusion (Koselleck 2018). In reaction to affirmative action programs, the identity of "white" has increased in salience as well (Kruse and Zelizer 2019, 354–355).

A Shift from equal to hierarchical

Instead of claims to equality among competing categories, there is now a declaration of hierarchy and merit, and the nation belonging to its white Christian founders (Lind 1996).

Response to invidious comparisons

The pervasive competition can undermine self-confidence and self-esteem (Davies 2015; Stanfield 1986, 60–61) and "repressive desublimation" can lead to "nihilism" and lack of commitment (Brown 2019, 165–169).

Change in political strategy

Political polarization has become a more acceptable strategy, from Nixon's "southern strategy" and "silent majority," (Lepore 2018, 631–639) to Trump's even more divisive rhetoric and policies (Kruse and Zelizer 2019, 351–358).

The ambiguous welfare state

The welfare state is nearly ubiquitous in advanced industrial countries but is often a political football.

For example, the welfare state provides income supports to those unable to work but is resented by those who are forced to work for low wages. The politicization has become even more controversial when illegal immigrants are able to access the same benefits as citizens and taxpayers. When so-called populist political parties shifted their positions to support these social programs with public benefits for citizens, they have been able to make substantial gains in electoral politics. The center-left parties were already compromised by earlier support for neoliberalism and had less flexibility (Berman and Snegovaya 2019).

Populism in the US and Europe

The financial crisis originated from Wall Street, and the bailout preserved Wall Street's biggest banks, making the lack of fairness evident. There were reactions from the Right (Tea Party) and Left (Occupy), with discontent articulated and mobilized by Bernie Sanders and Donald Trump (Tooze 2018, 14–21, 394–395, 468–470, 568–575). The neoliberal policies of the EU exacerbated the ripple effect and contributed to the populist response (Tooze 2018, 396–403).

The Great Financial Crisis revealed the involvement of government in the financial market and the politics of money (Tooze 2018, 9–13, 398), and relevance of the state in the protection of large corporations. As a result, the legitimacy of the state was newly undermined.

Although the liberal state promises fairness, public representation, and equality, it is also acknowledged that elections are acceptable as long as nothing important is decided and the public/private divide is maintained (Searle 2010, 170–173).

As president, Donald Trump continues to ignore the discipline of the public private divide, maintaining his businesses while in office and appointing and terminating public officials based on personal loyalty.

Conclusion

The dilemma for the liberal state is to uphold equality and fairness while also maintaining hierarchy and authority of money and property. Increasing inequality since the 1980s has undercut the appeal of that rhetoric. Further, the "individual" was never a stable, bounded, or given category, and institutions which make that presumption are inconsistent and uneven.

The explosion of rage and frustration intensified as the economy slowed after the GFC, and the inherent contradictions are more clearly exposed: government priorities are for protection for money and property, in spite of claims of equality and opportunity for "individuals."

Bibliography

Akerlof, George A. and Janet L. Yellen. *Efficiency Wage Models of the Labor Market*. New York: Cambridge University Press, 1986.

Akerlof, George A. and Janet L. Yellen. "The Fair Wage-Effort Hypothesis and Unemployment," *Quarterly Journal of Economics*, Vol. 105, No. 2, May 1990, 255–283.

Balkin, Mack M. "Constitutional Rot," in Cass R. Sunstein (ed.), *Can it Happen Here? Authoritarianism in America*. New York: HarperCollins, 2018, 19–36.

Bauman, Zygmunt and Thomas Leoncini. *Born Liquid: Transformations in the Third Millennium*. Cambridge, UK: Polity Press, 2019.

Bavel, Bas J. P. van. *The Invisible Hand? How Market Economies Have Emerged and Declined Since AD 500*. New York: Oxford University Press, 2016.

Berman, Sheri and Maria Snegovaya. "Populism and the Decline of Social Democracy," *Journal of Democracy*, Vol. 30, No. 3, July 2019, 5–19.

Block, Fred L and Margaret R. Somers. *The Power of Market Fundamentalism: Karl Polanyi's Critique*. Cambridge, MA: Harvard University Press, 2014.

Blumm, Michael C. and Mary Christina Wood. *The Public Trust Doctrine in Environmental and Natural Resources Law*. Durham, NC: Carolina Academic Press, 2013.

Blyth, Mark. *Great Transformations: Economic Ideas and Institutional Change in the Twentieth Century*. New York: Cambridge University Press, 2002.

Blyth, Mark. *Austerity: The History of a Dangerous Idea*. New York: Oxford University Press, 2013.

Bourdieu, Pierre. *Acts of Resistance: Against the Tyranny of the Market*. New York: New Press, 1998.

Brine, Kevin R. and Mary Poovey. *Finance in America: An Unfinished Story*. Chicago: University of Chicago Press, 2017.

Brown, Wendy. "Neoliberalism's Frankenstein: Authoritarian Freedom in Twenty-First Century 'Democracies'," in Wendy Brown, Peter E. Gordon and Max Pensky (eds.), *Authoritarianism: Three Inquiries in Critical Theory*. Chicago: University of Chicago Press, 2018, 7–43.

Brown, Wendy. *In the Ruins of Neoliberalism: The Rise of Antidemocratic Politics in the West*. New York: Columbia University Press, 2019.

Bullard, William. Dinner speaker. Levy Institute Minsky Conference. Bard College, Annandale-on-Hudson, New York, April 2019.

Carter, Dan T. *The Politics of Rage: George Wallace, the Origins of the new Conservatism, and the Transformation of American Politics*. New York: Simon & Schuster, 1995.

Chetty, Raj, Nathaniel Hendren, Patrick Kline, and Emmanuel Saez. "Where Is the Land of Opportunity? The Geography of Intergeneration Mobility in the U.S.," *Quarterly Journal of Economics*, Vol. 129, No. 4, November 2014, 1553–1623.

Cooper, Melinda. *Family Values: Between Neoliberalism and the New Social Conservatism.* New York: Zone Books, 2017.

Davies, William. *The Limits of Neoliberalism: Authority, Sovereignty and the Logic of Competition.* London: Sage, 2015.

Davies, William. *Nervous States: Democracy and the Decline of Reason.* New York: W.W. Norton & Company, 2019.

Davis, Ann E. *Money as a Social Institution: The Institutional Development of Capitalism.* New York: Routledge, 2017.

Davis, Mike. *Old Gods New Enigmas: Marx's Lost Theory.* New York: Verso, 2018.

Durante, Ruben, Paolo Pinotti, and Andrea Tesei. "The Political Legacy of Entertainment TV," *American Economic Review,* Vol. 109, No. 7, 2019, 2497–2530.

Eichengreen, Barry. *The Populist Temptation: Economic Grievance and the Political Reaction in the Modern Era.* New York: Oxford University Press, 2018.

Faludi, Susan. *Backlash: The Undeclared War Against American Women.* New York: Crown, 1991.

Faludi, Susan. *Stiffed: The Betrayal of the American Man.* New York: Perennial, 2000.

Fraser, Nancy. "A Triple Movement? Parsing the Politics of Crisis After Polanyi," *New Left Review,* Vol. 81, May–June 2013, 119–132.

Gerstle, Gary. "The Rise and Fall (?) of America's Neoliberal Order," *Transactions of the Royal Historical Society,* Vol. 28, 2018, 241–264.

Goetzmann, William N. *Money Changes Everything: How Finance Made Civilization Possible.* Princeton, NJ: Princeton University Press, 2016.

Gordon, Peter E. "The Authoritarian Personality Revisited," in Wendy Brown, Peter E. Gordon and Max Pensky (eds.), *Authoritarianism: Three Inquiries in Critical Theory.* Chicago: University of Chicago Press, 2018, 45–84.

Haraway, Donna J. *Simians, Cyborgs, and Women: The Reinvention of Nature.* New York: Routledge, 1991.

Hochschild, Arlie. *Strangers in their Own Land: Anger and Mourning on the American Right.* New York: New Press, 2016.

Horkheimer, Max and Theodor W. Adorno. *Dialectic of Enlightenment.* New York: Seabury Press, 1972.

Jessop, Bob, Kevin Bonnett, Simon Bromley, and Tom Ling. *Thatcherism: A Tale of Two Nations.* Cambridge, UK: Polity Press, 1988.

Judis, John B. *The Populist Explosion: How the Great Recession Transformed American and European Politics.* New York: Columbia Global Reports, 2016.

Kazin, Michael. *The Populist Persuasion.* Basic, 1995.

Keynes, John Maynard. *The General Theory of Employment, Interest, and Money.* New York: Harcourt, Brace & World, 1964.

Kindleberger, Charles. *Manias, Panics, and Crashes: A History of Financial Crises.* New York: Basic, 1989.

Koselleck, Reinhart. *Sediments of Time: On Possible Histories.* Stanford, CA: Stanford University Press, 2018.

Kotz, David M. *The Rise and Fall of Neoliberalism Capitalism.* Cambridge, MA: Harvard University Press, 2015.

Kruse, Kevin M. and Julian E. Zelizer. *Fault Lines: A History of the United States Since 1974.* New York: W.W. Norton & Company, 2019.

Lepore, Jill. *These Truths: A History of the United States.* W.W. Norton & Company, 2018.

Levitsky, Steven and Daniel Ziblatt. *How Democracies Die.* New York: Crown, 2018.

Lind, Michael. *The Next American Nation: The New Nationalism and the Fourth American Revolution.* New York: Simon & Schuster, 1996.

Livingston, James. *Origins of the Federal Reserve System: Money, Class, and Corporate Capitalism, 1890–1913*. Ithaca, NY: Cornell University Press, 1986.

Livingston, James. *Pragmatism, Feminism, and Democracy: Rethinking the Politics of American History*. New York: Routledge, 2001.

Lynskey, Dorian. *The Ministry of Truth: The Biography of George Orwell's 1984*. New York: Doubleday, 2019.

MacKay, Charles. *Extraordinary Popular Delusions and the Madness of Crowds*. Boston: L.C. Page, 1932.

Mason, Robert and Iwan Morgan (eds.). *The Liberal Consensus Reconsidered: American Politics and Society in the Postwar Era*. Gainesville: University Press of Florida, 2017.

Mayer, Jane. *Dark Money: The Hidden History of the Billionaires Behind the Rise of the Radical Right*. New York: Doubleday, 2016.

Mazower, Mark. *Governing the World: The History of an Idea*. New York: Penguin, 2012.

McKean, Benjamin. "Populism and Global Justice: Separated at Birth?" Global Justice and Populism Workshop. European University Institute, Florence, June 3–4, 2019.

McKibben, Bill. *Falter: Has the Human Game Begun to Play Itself Out?* New York: Henry Holt and Company, 2019.

Mirowski, Philip. *Never Let a Serious Crisis Go to Waste: How Neoliberalism Survived the Financial Meltdown*. London: Verso, 2013.

Mishra, Pankaj. *Age of Anger: A History of the Present*. New York: Farrar, Straus and Giroux, 2017.

Mudde, Cas and Cristobal Rovira Kaltwasser. *Populism: A Very Short Introduction*. New York: Oxford University Press, 2017.

Muller, Jan-Werner. *What is Populism?* Philadelphia: University of Pennsylvania Press, 2016.

Ogle, Vanessa. *The Global Transformation of Time: 1870–1950*. Cambridge, MA: Harvard University Press, 2015.

Olson, Mancur. *The Logic of Collective Action: Public Goods and the Theory of Groups*. Cambridge, MA: Harvard University Press, 1965.

Packer, George. *The Unwinding: An Inner History of the New America*. New York: Farrar, Strauss, and Giroux, 2013.

Piketty, Thomas. *Capital in the Twenty-First Century*. Cambridge, MA: Harvard University Press, 2014.

Pocock, J.G.A. *The Machiavellian Moment: Florentine Political Thought and the Atlantic Republican Tradition*. Princeton, NJ: Princeton University Press, 1975.

Polanyi, Karl. *The Great Transformation*. Boston: Beacon Press, 1944.

Postel, Charles. *The Populist Vision*. New York: Oxford University Press, 2007.

Rajan, Raghuram G. "Has Financial Development Made the World Riskier?" Cambridge, MA: National Bureau of Economic Research Working Paper 11728, November 2005.

Rajan, Raghuram G. *The Third Pillar: How Markets and the State Leave the Community Behind*. New York: Penguin Press, 2019.

Runciman, David. *How Democracy Ends*. New York: Basic, 2018.

Searle, John R. *Making the Social World: The Structure of Human Civilization*. New York: Oxford University Press, 2010.

Sennett, Richard and Jonathan Cobb. *The Hidden Injuries of Class*. New York: Vintage, 1972.

Sheingate, Adam. *Building a Business of Politics: The Rise of Political Consulting and the Transformation of American Democracy*. New York: Oxford University Press, 2016.

Shiller, Robert J. *Irrational Exuberance*. 3rd ed. Princeton, NJ: Princeton University Press, 2015.

Sides, John, Michael Tesler, and Lynn Vavreck. *Identity Crisis: The 2016 Presidential Campaign and the Battle for Meaning in America*. Princeton, NJ: Princeton University Press, 2018.

Simanowski, Roberto. *Facebook Society: Losing Ourselves in Sharing Ourselves*. New York: Columbia University Press, 2018.

Skocpol, Theda and Alexander Hertel-Fernandez. "The Koch Network and Republican Party Extremism," *Perspectives on Politics*, Vol. 14, No. 3, September 2016, 681–699.

Snyder, Timothy. *The Road to Unfreedom: Russia, Europe, America*. New York: Tim Duggan Books, 2018.

Stanfield, J. Ron. *The Economic Thought of Karl Polanyi: Lives and Livelihoods*. New York: St. Martin's Press, 1986.

Stenner, Karen and Jonathan Haidt. "Authoritarianism is Not a Momentary Madness, but an Eternal Dynamic Within Liberal Democracies," in Cass R. Sunstein (ed.), *Can it Happen Here? Authoritarianism in America*. New York: HarperCollins, 2018, 175–220.

Stiglitz, Joseph E. *The Great Divide: Unequal Societies and What We Can Do About Them*. New York: W.W. Norton & Company, 2015.

Stout, Lynn A. *The Shareholder Value Myth: How Putting Shareholders First Harms Investors, Corporations, and the Public*. San Francisco: Berrett-Koehler, 2012.

Thaler, Richard H. and Cass R. Sunstein. *Nudge: Improving Decisions Regarding Health, Wealth, and Happiness*. New Haven: Yale University Press, 2008.

Tooze, J. Adam. *Crashed: How a Decade of Financial Crisis Changed the World*. New York: Viking, 2018.

Urbinati, Nadia. *Democracy Disfigured: Opinion, Truth, and the People*. Cambridge, MA: Harvard University Press, 2014.

Urbinati, Nadia. "Between Democracy and Something Else: The Hard Case of Populism in Power," Global Justice and Populism Workshop. European University Institute, Florence, June 3–4, 2019.

Vance, J. D. *Hillbilly Elegy: A Memoir of a Family and a Culture in Crisis*. New York: Harper Collins, 2018.

Wilentz, Sean. *The Politicians and the Egalitarians: The Hidden History of American Politics*. New York: W.W. Norton & Company, 2016.

Williams, Joan C. *The White Working Class: Overcoming Class Cluelessness in America*. Cambridge, MA: Harvard Business Review Press, 2017.

Yergin, Daniel and Joseph Stanislaw. *Commanding Heights: The Battle Between the Government and the Market Place that Is Remaking the Modern World*. New York: Simon & Schuster, 1998.

Zuboff, Shoshana. *Surveillance Capitalism: The Fight for a Human Future at the New Frontier of Power*. New York: Public Affairs, 2019.

11 Alternatives

If "the individual" is an invention as a component part of an epistemological system of individual private property, what is the alternative? This chapter will review the existing paradigms related to the individual and property and then consider alternative paradigms and institutional arrangements.

Paradigms

From the work of science studies, there is greater understanding of the influence of scientific paradigms on the world views of natural scientists and social scientists. There are similar concepts like "Background" (Searle 2010) and "social imaginary" (Taylor 2004; Anderson 2006), as well as culture, which provide meaning systems and norms in a given period of history or geographical location. It is not clear whether the "Anthropocene" is the mark of a new conceptual orientation, similar in scope to the shift from Ptolemy to Copernicus, with a greater understanding of the role of humans as a major influence on the evolution of the earth's systems (Subramanian 2019).

Modernity

There is a standpoint of the moderns (Latour 1993, 2017, 14–24; Descola 2013, 57–88) which separates humans from all of nature. According to this perspective, humans are capable of self-awareness, reflection, and conscious moral choices, while the rest of nature is perceived as "objects," accessible to exploration with impersonal scientific methods and tools. Such a doctrine of human exceptionalism and "bounded individualism" is a not helpful starting point for rethinking human interrelations with other species (Haraway 2016, 30–35).

Standpoints

Because of the contemporary importance of reification and commodification, as discussed in Chapter 2, there is an emphasis on "objects" instead of living beings. Science has been instrumental in aid of capitalism (Marx 1967, Vol. I, Chapter 15), with claimed "objectivity" of scientists (Shapin and Shaffer

1985; Daston and Galison 2007; Latour 1993, 2013). In searching for alternative standpoints, feminists have developed a particular perspective on science and methodology, with a large literature (Merchant 1979, 2003; Harding 1986, 2015; Keller 1983, 2010; Hrdy 1981, 2009; Haraway 1989, 1991).

An alternative to divisions among categories of people with competing claims is to develop "Self-realization," with an expanded concept of the Self (Naess 1989). That is, instead of focusing on the "individual" inside an envelope of skin, the notion of the "Self" expands into relationships with other humans, other species, and global processes upon which any given human person depends. If the human person is integrally connected to nature, the realization of that person will include nature as well.

Technology

Some visions of the future build on advanced technology, which renders human individuals "useless" and consequently reduces the relevance of individualism. Given advances in biology, organisms can be seen as simply functions of information systems, like DNA. Following this trajectory into the future results in visions such as "techno-humanism" or even "dataism," where the goal is to expand data and algorithms per se (Harari 2017). Haraway designates this perspective as C^3I, or "command-control-communication-intelligence, the military's symbol for its operations theory (Haraway 2016, 6, 34, 56). This view is part of the "abstraction" related to money and capitalism, to render persons and objects as commensurable in the context of financial circuits (Davis 2017, 149–156). The reach of information technology and the internet can even replace the market, according to recent theorists, and collapse the difference between capitalism and communism (Posner and Weyl 2018, 277–289; Harari 2017, 430–440). Harari even refers to the "dividual," but this time immersed in data and algorithms instead of indigenous communities (Harari 2017, 383), as discussed in Chapter 1.

The predominance of information technology in shaping visions of the future is manifest in Harari's discussion of code in the realm of biology, as well as computers.

> The new technologies of the twenty-first century may thus reverse the humanist revolution, stripping humans of their authority, and empowering non-human algorithms instead. . . . It is crucial to realize that this entire trend is fueled more by biological insights than by computer science. It is the life sciences that concluded that organisms are algorithms.
>
> (Harari 2017, 401–402)

Haraway (2000, 91) calls this "genetic fetishism," mistaking the genetic code as a concrete object instead of the process of creation of living species.

> The DNA molecules are never working in isolation. They are always working in interaction with other cell structures. The most common way of

saying it is that the smallest unit of life is the cell, not the gene, but the gene is always in interaction with these cellular histories. It is always in process, yet – and this is the issue – we talk about it as if it were merely a simple, concrete thing.

(Haraway 2000, 95)

Cultures

If one can be critical regarding the inherited narratives that are recounted by each religion and people, does the narrative then become discretionary? What status is attributed to myths (Castro 2014) and the origin stories (Okin 1979; Pocock 1957; Shiller 2019)?

Recent work by anthropologists has developed an extended framework for understanding the epistemology of the modern West in contrast with a variety of indigenous societies (Descola 2013, 115–125). For example, modern "naturalism," which views humans as distinct and the rest of nature as subject to impersonal laws, can be differentiated from "animism," which views humans and animals as having a common subjectivity, while their bodies are distinct. These differences in bodies affect the ecological niche and distinctive patterns of predator and prey, all of whom are aware of each other and who seek mutual accommodation. In this context a shaman's ritual intervention can help make compensation for such necessities. One's "prey" can consist of other tribes as well as other species, all of whom share a common subjectivity and mutual awareness. In this context, humans as omnivores are not so different from "cannibals" in their awareness of common life among all species, including ones that form one's own sustenance (Viveiros de Castro 2009). Further, in modern industrial economies, human labor is "consumed" in the process of production, as discussed in Chapter 5, what may be considered a form of autophagy.

Integrating anthropological research on varieties of relationships, Descola (2013, 309–335) distinguishes symmetrical from non-symmetrical forms of "attachment." He catalogues "gift," "exchange," and "predation" as relationships among equals, which are potentially reversible. In contrast he suggests that "production," "protection," and intergenerational "transmission" are hierarchical. The role of "production" is particularly important in Western economic thought, which prioritizes the role of the agent or creator, as ontologically distinct from the materials which form the resources for the work. This agent, or "subject," is accorded respect and status for this role of initiator and designer, often in imitation of a deity. This emphasis on agency and production is not universal to other collective entities. By contrast, in the "animistic" societies, there is often a relationship of mutual respect, even among predators and prey. Other alternative world views are found in China and Africa, which emphasize holistic transformations.

While Marx considers production as hierarchical (Descola 2013, 321–322), and often exploitive, for example, it is also possible to consider work as cooperative and collaborative, even as the labor process transforms the persons and the material. For example, there is a "socialist" tradition which precedes Marx. So rather than Descola's catalogue of production as inherently hierarchical and unequal, perhaps this is particularly true of Western economic systems, such as capitalism, since the fifteenth century.

Environmental ethics

There have been powerful leaders of the Conservation and Preservation movements who have sought to protect unique ecologies and landscapes from development (Leopold 2013; Muir 1997). Yet these efforts have remained divided between market and non-market public goods, and hence have been limited in terms of achieving a comprehensive ecological synthesis. That is, those protected spaces are still vulnerable from global ecological processes, and the scale is not sufficient to sustain those ecological processes. Recently writers from a variety of perspectives have addressed environmental ethics directly (Jedediah Purdy 2015; Clowney and Mosto 2009).

The consumer economy has sought novel products and experiences to stimulate production and sales. Rather than more intense personal pleasures from bodily sensations (sugar, caffeine, immersion in virtual reality, alcohol, hallucinogens, nicotine), it is possible to seek deeper interpersonal understanding and more diverse relationships with other beings (Haraway 2016).

Pricing the environment

There has been a long-standing critique of Gross Domestic Product as a measure of economic performance and human welfare (Stiglitz, Sen, and Fitoussi 2010). There is literature which stresses accounting for different types of capital, like social, human, and natural (Bourdieu 1986). Various techniques exist for valuing natural capital (Costanza 2015; Daily 1997, 2002; Fourcade 2011). Yet often these techniques depend on importing market prices into ecological contexts to estimate replacement costs of ecosystems services, or present discounted value of future resource flows. By importing market prices, however, one repeats the distortion of markets, such as monopoly, externalities, income inequality, and imperfect information.

It is conceptually possible to measure directly social, human, and environmental resources which contribute to sustainability and human development. That is, rather than measure inputs and outputs in money terms, one could develop direct physical measures of both environmental resources and human development. This approach recalls the mid-twentieth-century "socialist calculation debate" between Hayek and Lange (Cockshott and Cottrell 1993; Cockshott et al. 2009). For example, the technology exists to measure carbon sinks and emissions globally by specific location, providing a basis for direct management of these flows. Human development, such as life expectancy and literacy, can also be measured directly, in relation to investments in education and family support. Profit and the value of production in market prices need not be the only or best measure of ecological sustainability and human flourishing, or the only incentive system.

A further difficulty of using market techniques is illustrated by the concept of "present discounted value." That is, there is an assumption of an infinite, global market with interest-earning assets available for trade. The value in the present of long-term assets redeemed in the future is the sum of the interest returns over its lifetime, discounted. This assumes that there are interest returns and that there is a global financial market with which these assessments can be made. Moreover, the further in the future any given payoff remains, the lower its discounted value, providing less incentive for making long-term investments. As a result, there is debate with respect to choice of discount rate, which makes decisions for the long-term difficult to calculate (Nordhaus 2013, 2015; Stern 2015).

Further, techniques of cost/benefit analysis make assumptions about how humans assess benefits on an individual basis, with no consideration of externalities or changing ethical values.

Declaration of interdependence

Rather than independence of "the individual," and the assumption of infinite markets, there could be a celebration of relation to the "other," with mutuality, reciprocity, recognition. There could be an attitude of love and fascination with, not domination and separation from, nature.

Architects and engineers who maintain an understanding and a priority on natural systems can improve both productivity and sustainability by designing with nature (McDonough and Braungart 2002).

There are awe-inspiring examples of the interconnections of life which are increasingly being discovered by scientists:

a) One example is "how microbes made the earth inhabitable" (Falkowski 2015). That is, without microbes and the "Great Oxidation Event," the atmosphere of the earth would not have abundance of oxygen for energy transport in most living cells.
b) There is an increasing understanding of the division of labor within cells and the interaction among cell components (Dolgin 2019).
c) Microbes living in the human gut have a significant impact on human health (Zeevi et al. 2019).
d) Another example of interdependence is the structure of subatomic particles in the nucleus, nucleons, which is affected by whether or not they are located inside an atomic nucleus at a given moment (Feldman 2019).
e) Electron transfer chains provide the energetic basis of life of all forms (Raana et al. 2018).

That is, there are common elements in all life forms which provide a basis for greater understanding of interconnections.

New subjectivity

Instead of the "view from nowhere" (Nagel 1986), one can develop an aware-ness of both subjective and objective points of view (Searle 2010; Gazzaniga 2018). With advances in cognitive neuroscience, one can imagine an emotional state, which is reflected in the biophysical state of the neurons in one's brain. In fact, the subject in the MRI tube can report his own feelings while simultane-ously the machine produces the image of the specific neurons which are firing. The state of knowledge is such that currently this is an observation, a descrip-tion, while in the foreseeable future the possibility exists of intentionally creat-ing a specific state of mind by biophysical means. While each brain is unique, certain consistent features allow for diagnosis and control. Certain compounds have hallucinogenic properties which have induced, "altered," states of mind across cultures and millennia.

The presence and identification of one's unique self in an expansive, chang-ing universe is the product of modern science, which also provides the capacity for reaching beyond one's own body. Such scientific advance can be for the purpose of better health, quality of life, and longevity, or control (Davies 2015). The political, economic, and ethical uses of science are now at question.

Unified vision of a single earth

Rather than "individual" self-interest and anthropocentrism, and pleasure from domination from the top of the food chain, a more enlightened, even "rational," view would reconsider the place of humankind for the future generations of all species. Drawing from modern science and ethics, rather than a return to an idealization of the pre-modern enchantment of nature, there would be a new understanding, appreciation, and pleasure from interdependence and intercon-nection. With reasonable institutional reforms (Speth 2012) and transition to renewable energy (Yergin 2011; Prentiss 2015), a new sustainable economy is feasible within the existing property paradigm, except for the political will to make the necessary changes.

Terrestrials

A shift in mindset is also timely to mobilize the initiative, innovation, and com-prehensive vision for a sustainable future. Rather than universals based on a "view from nowhere" (Nagel 1986; Latour 2018), there is needed a study of unique earth systems from the point of view of resilience and sustainability. Methods based on "Galileon objects" have the same universal laws (Latour 2018, 67–77) anywhere in the galaxy but may be less useful in understanding evolution of species on earth.

Humans are "grounded" on living earth ecosystems, brought "down to earth," in common with humus, another term for soil (Latour 2018, 4–5, 92; Haraway 2016, 32). Humans are integrated with, resulting from, and constitut-ing part of, earth processes.

Latour (2018) uses the term "Terrestrials" to indicate the presence of humans among other species on earth, considered in all of its diversity and interdependent ecosystems. Instead of the "modern constitution" (Latour 1993) which separates humans from nature, he proposes a new awareness of humans in nature and nature in humans (Moore 2015). A "Terrestrial" would be located in a specific landscape, with knowledge of its unique niche and its relationship with other living beings.

Grounded in modern science, human habitation on the earth would benefit from a deeper understanding of earth processes, such as biogeochemical cycles and the niches occupied by varieties of species. The common elements of metabolism, reproduction, and evolution would be explored across species, as well as the common mechanisms found in multiple organisms as the result of evolution, such as mitochondria within cells. Rather than the human/nature distinction, humans would be co-residents of the planet earth, with a broader perspective on mutual interactions.

With such a perspective, there would be a new voice, a first-person plural, a "we" which encompasses all living beings in the critical zone, the atmosphere of the earth. In the context of an infinite universe, the atmosphere is limited and fragile, affected by industrial and consumption processes, requiring care and close monitoring.

Instead of "the individual" in the universal, infinite market, there are relationships and responsibilities within climate limits. Instead of the human for whom the earth was created, there is a variety of species with whom we interact. As Latour points out, at present, there is much scientific knowledge on which to draw, but no institutional mechanism. That is, there is no "representation" of Terrestrials, which makes organization of an earth-based politics more difficult.

Unified electron chain for consilience?

In Falkowski's view, all life on earth shares the same nano-machines for processing electrons for energy. Mitochondria, DNA, and proteins are evolutionarily conserved from the first microbes to complex living beings, interacting with the atmosphere, ocean, land, and living bodies of plants and animals. These nutrient cycles are known and shared, and cross the disciplinary boundaries of physics, chemistry, biology, sociology, and psychology. The energy for movement, reproduction, and information storage is based on the same processes. Plants and animals live in communities which share waste-nutrient symbiosis and communicate with chemical signals, if not articulate speech.

Life on earth influenced the earth itself, which in turn shaped the evolution of life. These long-term dynamic interactions are studied on the millennial, global scale. If the future of evolution is now in human hands (Harari 2017; McKibben 2019), with the capacity for DNA modification (CRSPR) and artificial intelligence (AI), then at least a conceptual understanding of earth systems is also necessary, with such tools as climate modeling. If humankind inhabits one earth, then the tools of advanced science may facilitate a greater understanding of that interrelationship, which cannot be divided into a separate "nature" as object.

> Now if property, in the sense of the capacity to appropriate, is part of how Euro-Americans reproduce themselves, so too is knowledge. For what has to be returned to the self comes both as things for bodily consumption and as abstract qualities that enhance the equally abstract self, which is exactly where knowledge belongs. Knowledge of the world is a powerful means of connection to it (distinction from it). Yet, as we have already seen, for Euro-Americans it is much more than a means: knowledge about the world is returned to the person who already knows enough to seek it. Its end in fashioning subjectivity makes it something as an end in itself.
>
> (Strathern 2005, 153)

Alternative institutions

In earlier chapters we have proposed that "society" which seems unnecessary to Thatcher is instead represented abstractly by the money or specific currency of the nation-state. Rather than a divided society, with a public/private divide based on the market, it is possible to have a single unified society based on humans living on the earth. Rather than fictional commodities and double vision, one could eliminate the market in land and labor and have communities settled based on ecological principles, with an integration of natural and social science. Scientific advances in understanding biogeochemical flows and balances provide the basis for new social forms, such as a global federation of regional ecological commonwealths (Davis 2017, 2019).

Sustainable communities could be founded in unique ecosystems, aware of their contingency in terms of social cohesion and ecological resilience. Forms of human community, as well as value systems, are important for global ecology, and that integration is central to sustainability in the long term.

The belief that money is valuable in itself, and that it accumulates in value, helps to blind us to the degradation of the earth. The alternative model is a world without money, guided by interpersonal regional ecological communities, according to priorities based on human needs and ecological implications. Such a world is no longer divided into public and private by financial circuits, and economics is no longer separated from the rest of social science by the reification of money. The dichotomy between individual and social is reduced by interpersonal regional communities rooted in the land, bound by common residence on the earth, and living with full awareness of its global ecological processes.

There are models available for local self-government. It is conceivable to return to the geographically centered corporation of early modern city-states (Wickham 2015), or self-governing municipal corporations in the colonial period (Hartog 1983). Cities like the Republic of Florence from 1200–1500 provide a model for local self-government (Najemy 1982). The re-purposing and re-use of the corporate form has been long-standing, with the possibility of returning from global to local forms (Padgett 2001, 2012a, 2012b).

Other models are available from the study of the commons, or "common pool resources" (CPR), studied by Elinor Ostrom and her colleagues (https://iasc-commons.org). There are long-standing institutions which have successfully managed CPRs without relying on states or markets and individual private property. Communities which conform to certain design principles are durable, according to her research, and can solve the problems of free riders and collective commitment (Ostrom 1990, 2010). Norms and monitoring are important, as well as accurate information, graduated sanctions, and recognition from higher levels of government.

Concepts of urban redesign are available from architects with a sustainability priority, based on public goods instead of individual consumerism (Duany, Plater-Zyberk, and Speck 2000), such as the Congress on the New Urbanism (www.cnu.org). Other new vision comes from the concept of "smart cities," integrated with advanced information technology (www.sidewalklabs.com). The irony of the housing market is that the prime determinants of home prices are based on local public goods, such as location, transportation access, quality of schools, and environmental amenities. It is not clear whether or not local property taxes are sufficient to support those assets. Even if funds were available, the local governments are often dominated by real estate interests, since they are no longer independent self-governing units but administrative divisions of the state with variable rights to "home rule."

Other models are available from history. For example, American farmers' associations in the late-nineteenth-century US developed cooperatives to maintain community autonomy in the face of the increasing scale and monopoly power of railroads and corporations in the late-nineteenth-century US (Postel 2007). There were friendly societies, where immigrants from a specific country would form communities in the new location to pool resources and provide solidarity.

Other innovations are formed at local and state levels, as well as national. For example, there are new relationships with food which are formed by Community Supported Agriculture (CSA), where cooperatives create a direct tie between consumers and specific farmers for the crop of a given season. Such relationships reduce food transportation costs, provide fresh produce, and acquaint members with new food preferences and possibilities, like local heirloom varieties, which are better suited to the local ecology. Worker-owned enterprises provide another model (Kruse 2013; Blasi, Freeman, and Kruse 2013). Public benefit corporations are modified to blend the for-profit mission to take into account the public interest, such as the Empire State Development Corporation of New York State. Sovereign wealth funds provide pooled collective investments for the national interest, another model (Clark, Dixon, and Monk 2013). In summary, there are various options for which type of collective is founded, on what basis, and for what mission, rather than merely a series of "unique individuals," as discussed in Chapter 7.

As indicated by Wilson (2016), there is need to preserve "half" of the earth to maintain existing biodiversity (Kolbert 2006, 2014). The land assembly of such an order of magnitude is not feasible with eminent domain a parcel at a time (Heller 2008; Heller and Ricks 2008), or by the existing public domain. A new paradigm is needed for landed property, not real estate valued in financial terms, but ecology. For example, Goldstein has developed the concept of "greenwood in the bundle of sticks," where special ecological regulations would apply to property in land (Goldstein 2005). A single ruling in the Supreme Court could apply to all land consistently across the country, with different treatment for different ecologies. Other innovative legal approaches could include public trust, a colonial doctrine brought to the twenty-first century by lawsuits brought by the next generation to protect their future property rights, such as "Juliana" (Blumm and Wood 2013). The general capacity to form such impersonal organizations is considered an advance of civilization for North and co-authors (North, Wallis, and Weingast 2009).

Global ecological federation

To focus on ecology directly, the foundation for the state would take a new form. Individual private property with absolute rights is no longer the foundation, but rather shared use or "usufruct." The states would no longer issue currency which is used for expansion of the financial circuits, M – M'. Rather than real estate markets which can bid for the ground under one's feet, there is an ecological territory within which there is cohesive governance for each community. The fiscal military state is no longer necessary, as war is no longer legal. The discipline in each community is based on qualifications for full participation, with the prohibition from government service as a sanction, or ultimately the threat of exile, as was exercised in Florence by the local republican government of that period (Najemy 1982).

Rather than legal institutional collectives like corporations, which can be mobile and multinational, there are ecological preserves with distinctive characteristics, like a watershed. There are regional ecological communities, with territories designed to encompass a cohesive ecological region, and a global federation of such communities. Such ecological units as a watershed can encompass related geographies, managing the many uses of water as solvent, feedstock for bioenergy, amenity, waste disposal, energy transport through phase changes, and transportation. There are scientific advisory bodies who can assist each region in its ecological regeneration goals.

Rather than function as a business corporation with a financial budget constraint, there are ecological constraints, based on scientific and shared knowledge of each region. Instead of management to increase output per unit of time, like the corporation, there would be allocation of working time of the population towards shared goals, like a family or community, with new standards of efficiency. The first priority would be agricultural production for basic nutrition of all residents, within the constraints of ecological preservation, followed by health, education, and care of children and the elderly. Third, the construction of infrastructure for water, sewer, transport, communication, and power would be the focus of community investments, with technology designed for long-term sustainability. Scientific research, commodity production, entrepreneurship and innovation would also provide opportunities for employment, based on qualifications, skills, and interests. Each region would receive an allocation of basic nutrients, such as water, carbon, nitrogen, oxygen, sulfur, phosphorus, and energy, with which to manage its production, construction, and consumption. Surveys would be conducted with information technology regarding preferences of the residents, along with assessment of ecological resilience, for the deliberation and discussion of plans for the future.

Governance would be inclusive, with rotating service among all qualified residents. All humans are citizens of the earth at birth. The preparation for all residents of this governing role would be a basic priority for education, communication, and deliberation skills. There is no public/private divide because there is no separation of market and state. There would be a global federation of all such regional communities. Instead of for-profit social media, the internet would be a public utility dedicated to the determination of needs and priorities of residents, as well as coordinating production and environmental remediation, and sharing relevant research findings and models at the global level.

The goal of the community is its own development and sustainable preservation. Rather than mediation through money and the market, there are direct, interpersonal relationships based on co-habitation and ecological regeneration. Residential permits would be based on commitment and contributions to the ecology and the community, rather than the ability to pay. Environmental quality would be a community resource and a public good, not subject to market rationing.

Individual and cultural expression would be valued and shared among residents at the regional and global levels.

Each community would focus on developing its own capacity for self-government by focusing on education, deliberation, and regeneration. Within the governing institutions, there would be special assignments for education, health, food production, and ecological sustainability. Cultural values and political institutions are the topic of deliberation and reflexivity, in order to focus on long-term development of the population and its environment.

The priority of each region would be to secure provision for the population (Power 2004; Davis 2015), without contingency based on market performance.

Specific methods of population reproduction and control would be the subject of community deliberation, along with sexual norms and practices, within the constraints of biogeochemical budgets.

At the global and local level, biogeochemical budgets are the basic governance mechanism. For example, carbon, representing the importance to humans of energy, beginning with fire and the resulting deforestation (Williams 2003), is the basic budget which must be balanced. For example, emissions from each region must be balanced with carbon sinks, with the possibility of trading among regions (like Kyoto Clean Development Mechanism). Other nutrients, such as nitrogen, phosphorus, water, and sulfur, would also be monitored on a global basis.

Each region would be a distinct entity, with relationships among the regions based on global ecological concerns, as well as deliberation, innovation, and shared models of successful ecological management.

"We, the people, hereby define a new relationship among ourselves and with the globe." In self-governing ecological communities, there is a new first-person plural, empowered and aware of our own goals and impacts on ourselves and our ecological futures.

Self-conscious, inclusive, deliberative social construction of institutions is the essence of democracy, and "collective intentionality" (Searle 2010), rather than reification of abstract concepts like "property," "money," and the self-regulating market.

Rather than an economy based on abstract inputs and outputs, there would be concrete flows of resources, habitats, and human generations, managed collectively for the purpose of sustainability and personal development.

Conclusion

One can prioritize the discreet bounded human "individual" only through hubris or ignorance. As a social science construct consistent with capitalism, the concept of "the individual" supports the myth of perpetual universals as the objective foundation for human knowledge.

Rather than reification of abstract categories like "the individual" and "property" there are direct human relationships in an ecological context at each geographic scale. One can redefine "democracy" to provide for inclusive deliberation and "collective intentionality," no longer within the confines of "property" and "money," the labor, land and real estate markets, and the public/private divide.

There would be a global federation of ecological communities united in the pursuit of sustainability and human development, sharing resources, innovations, and earth's bounty.

Bibliography

Anderson, Benedict. *Imagined Communities: Reflections on the Origin and Spread of Nationalism.* London:Verso, 2006.

Blasi, Joseph, Richard Freeman, and Douglas Kruse. *The Citizen's Share: Putting Ownership Back into Democracy.* New Haven:Yale University Press, 2013.

Blumm, Michael C. and Mary Christina Wood. *The Public Trust Doctrine in Environmental and Natural Resources Law.* Durham, NC: Carolina Academic Press, 2013.

Bourdieu, Pierre. "The Form of Capital," in J. Richardson (ed.), *Handbook for Theory and Research for the Sociology of Education.* NewYork: Greenwood Press, 1986, 241–258.

Castro, Eduardo BatalhaViveiros de. *Cannibal Metaphysics:A Post-StructuralAnthropology.* Minneapolis, MN: Univocal, 2014.

Clark, Gordon L., Adam D. Dixon, and Ashby H. B. Monk. *Sovereign Wealth Funds: Legitimacy, Governance, and Global Power*. Princeton, NJ: Princeton University Press, 2013.

CLAS Collaboration. "Modified Structure of Protons and Neutrons in Correlated Pairs," *Nature*, Vol. 566, February 21, 2019, 354–358.

Clowney, David and Patricia Mosto (eds.). *Earthcare: An Anthology in Environmental Ethics*. New York: Rowman & Littlefield Publishers, Inc., 2009.

Cockshott, W. Paul and Allin Cottrell. *Towards a New Socialism*. Nottingham, UK: Russell Press, 1993.

Cockshott, W. Paul, Allin Cottrell, G. J. Michaelson, I. P. Wright, and V. M. Yakovenko. *Classical Econophysics*. New York: Routledge, 2009.

Costanza, Robert, et al. *An Introduction to Ecological Economics*. Boca Raton: CRC Press, 2015.

Daily, Gretchen. *Nature's Services: Societal Dependence on Natural Ecosystems*. Washington, DC: Island Press, 1997.

Daily, Gretchen and Katherine Ellison. *The New Economy of Nature: The Quest to Make Conservation Profitable*. Washington, DC: Island Press, Shearwater Books, 2002.

Daston, Lorraine and Peter Galison. *Objectivity*. New York: Zone Books, 2007.

Davies, William. "The Return of Social Government: From 'Socialist Calculation' to 'Social Analytics'," *European Journal of Social Theory*, Vol. 18, No. 4, 2015, 431–450.

Davies, William (ed.). *Economic Science Fictions*. London: Goldsmiths Press, 2018.

Davis, Ann E. "The Process of Provisioning: The Halter for the Workhorse," *Journal of Economic Issues*, Vol. XLIX, No. 2, June 2015, 449–457.

Davis, Ann E. "The Practical Utopia of Ecological Community," in Richard Westra, Robert Albritton, and Seongjin Jeong (eds.), *Varieties of Alternative Economic Systems: Practical Utopias for an Age of Global Crisis and Austerity*. New York: Routledge, 2017, 52–70.

Davis, Ann E. "Salvation or Commodification? The Role of Money and Markets in Global Ecological Preservation," *Review of Radical Political Economics*, Vol. 51, No. 4, December 2019, 536–543.

Davis, Mike. *Old Gods, New Enigmas: Marx's Lost Theory*. New York: Verso, 2018.

Descola, Philippe. *Beyond Nature and Culture*. Chicago: University of Chicago Press, 2013.

Dolgin, Elie. "The Secret Conversations Inside Cells," *Nature*, Vol. 567, March 14, 2019, 162–164.

Duany, Andres, Elizabeth Plater-Zyberk, and Jeff Speck. *Suburban Nation: The Rise of Sprawl and the Decline of the American Dream*. New York: North Point Press, 2000.

Falkowski, Paul G. *Life's Engines: How Microbes Made the Earth Inhabitable*. Princeton, NJ: Princeton University Press, 2015.

Feldman, Gerald. "Origin of Neutron and Proton Changes in Nuclei," *Nature*, Vol. 566, February 21, 2019, 332–333.

Fourcade, Marion. "Cents and Sensibility: Economic Valuation and the Nature of 'Nature'," *American Journal of Sociology*, Vol. 116, No. 6, May 2011, 1721–1777.

Gazzaniga, Michael S. *The Consciousness Instinct: Unraveling the Mystery of How the Brain Makes the Mind*. New York: Farrar, Straus and Giroux, 2018.

Goldstein, Robert J. "Greenwood in the Bundle of Sticks: Fitting Environmental Ethics and Ecology into Real Property Law," *Boston College Environmental Affairs Law Review*, Vol. 25, Winter 1998, 347–428.

Goldstein, Robert J. *Ecology and Environmental Ethics*. Aldershot: Ashgate, 2004a.

Goldstein, Robert J. (ed.), *Environmental Ethics and Law*. Aldershot: Ashgate, 2004b.

Goldstein, Robert J. *Greenwood in the Bundle of Sticks*. Aldershot: Ashgate, 2005.

Harari, Yuval Noah. *Homo Deus: A Brief History of Tomorrow*. New York: Vintage, 2017.

Haraway, Donna J. *Primate Visions: Gender, Race, and Nature in the World of Modern Science.* New York: Routledge, 1989.

Haraway, Donna J. *Simians, Cyborgs and Women: The Reinvention of Nature.* New York: Routledge, 1991.

Haraway, Donna J. *How Like a Leaf: Donna J. Haraway;* an Interview with Thyrza Nichols Goodeve. New York: Routledge, 2000.

Haraway, Donna J. *Manifestly Haraway.* Minneapolis: University of Minnesota Press, 2016a.

Haraway, Donna J. *Staying with the Trouble: Making Kin in the Chthulucene.* Durham, NC: Duke University Press, 2016b.

Harding, Sandra G. *The Science Question in Feminism.* Ithaca, NY: Cornell University Press, 1986.

Harding, Sandra G. *Objectivity and Diversity: Another Logic of Scientific Research.* Chicago: University of Chicago Press, 2015.

Hartog, Hendrik. *Public Property and Private Power: The Corporation of the City of New York in American Law, 1730–1870.* Chapel Hill: University of North Carolina Press, 1983.

Heller, Michael. *Gridlock Economy: How Too Much Property Wrecks Markets, Stops Innovation, and Costs Lives.* New York: Basic Books, 2008.

Heller, Michael and Rick Hills. "Land Assembly Districts," *Harvard Law Review,* Vol. 121, No. 6, April 2008, 1465–1527.

Hornborg, Alf, J. R. McNeill, and Joan Martinez-Alier. *Rethinking Environmental History: World-System History and Global Environmental Change.* New York: Altamira Press, 2007.

Hrdy, Sarah Blaffer. *The Woman That Never Evolved.* Cambridge, MA: Harvard University Press, 1981.

Hrdy, Sarah Blaffer. *Mothers and Others: The Evolutionary Origins of Mutual Understanding.* Cambridge, MA: Harvard University Press, 2009.

Keller, Evelyn Fox. *A Feeling for the Organism: The Life and Work of Barbara McClintock.* San Francisco: W.H. Freeman, 1983.

Keller, Evelyn Fox. *The Mirage of a Space Between Nature and Nurture.* Durham, NC: Duke University Press, 2010.

Kolbert, Elizabeth. *Field Notes from a Catastrophe: Man, Nature, and Climate Change.* New York: Bloomsbury, 2006.

Kolbert, Elizabeth. *The Sixth Extinction: An Unnatural History.* New York: Henry Holt, 2014.

Kruse, Douglas. *Sharing Ownership, Profits, and Decision-Making in the Twenty-First Century.* Bingley, UK: Emerald, 2013.

Latour, Bruno. *We Have Never Been Modern.* Cambridge, MA: Harvard University Press, 1993.

Latour, Bruno. *An Inquiry into the Modes of Existence: An Anthropology of the Moderns.* Cambridge, MA: Harvard University Press, 2013.

Latour, Bruno. *Facing Gaia: Eight Lectures on the New Climatic Regime.* Cambridge, UK: Polity Press, 2017.

Latour, Bruno. *Down to Earth: Politics in the New Climatic Regime.* Cambridge, UK: Polity Press, 2018.

Leopold, Aldo. *Sand County Almanac.* New York: Library of America, 2013.

Lewontin, Richard and Richard Levins. *Biology Under the Influence: Dialectical Essays on Ecology, Agriculture, and Health.* New York: Monthly Review Press, 2007.

Marx, Karl. *Capital.* New York: International Publishers, 1967.

McDonough, William and Michael Braungart. *Cradle to Cradle: Remaking the Way We Make Things.* New York: North Point Press, 2002.

McKibben, Bill. *Falter: Has the Human Game Begun to Play Itself Out?* New York: Henry Holt and Company, 2019.

Merchant, Carolyn. *The Death of Nature: Women, Ecology, and the Scientific Revolution.* San Francisco: Harper & Row, 1979.

Merchant, Carolyn. *Reinventing Eden: The Fate of Nature in Western Culture.* New York: Routledge, 2003.

Moore, Jason W. *Capitalism in the Web of Life: Ecology and the Accumulation of Capital.* New York: Verso, 2015.

Muir, John. *Nature Writings.* New York: Library of America, 1997.

Naess, Arne. *Ecology, Community and Lifestyle; Outline of an Ecosophy.* New York: Cambridge University Press, 1989.

Nagel, Thomas. *The View from Nowhere.* New York: Oxford University Press, 1986.

Najemy, John M. *Corporatism and Consensus in Florentine Electoral Politics, 1288–1400.* Chapel Hill: University of North Carolina Press, 1982.

Nordhaus, William D. *The Climate Casino: Risk, Uncertainty, and Economics for a Warming World.* New Haven: Yale University Press, 2013.

Nordhaus, William D. "Climate Clubs: Overcoming Free-Riding in International Climate Policy," *American Economic Review,* Vol. 105, No. 4, 2015, 1339–1370.

North, Douglass Cecil, John Joseph Wallis, and Barry R. Weingast. *Violence and Social Orders: A Conceptual Framework for Interpreting Recorded Human History.* New York: Cambridge University Press, 2009.

Okin, Susan Moller. *Women in Western Political Thought.* Princeton, NJ: Princeton University Press, 1979.

Ostrom, Elinor. *Governing the Commons: The Evolution of Institutions for Collective Action.* New York: Cambridge University Press, 1990.

Ostrom, Elinor. "Beyond Markets and States: Polycentric Governance of Complex Economic Systems," *American Economic Review,* Vol. 100, June 2010, 641–672.

Padgett, John F. "Organizational Genesis, Identity, and Control: The Transformation of Banking in Renaissance Florence," in James E. Rauch and Alessandra Casella (eds.), *Networks and Markets.* New York: Sage Foundation, 2001, 211–257.

Padgett, John F. "The Emergence of Corporate Merchant-Banks in Dugento Tuscany," in John F. Padgett and Walter W. Powell (eds.), *The Emergence of Organizations and Markets.* Princeton, NJ: Princeton University Press, 2012a, 121–167.

Padgett, John F. "Transposition and Refunctionality: The Birth of the Partnership System in Renaissance Florence," in John F. Padgett and Walter W. Powell (eds.), *The Emergence of Organizations and Markets.* Princeton, NJ: Princeton University Press, 2012b, 168–207.

Pocock, J. G. A. *The Ancient Constitution and Feudal Law: A Study of English Historical Thought in the Seventeenth Century.* New York: Cambridge University Press, 1957.

Posner, Eric A. and E. Glen Weyl. *Radical Markets: Uprooting Capitalism and Democracy for a Just Society.* Princeton, NJ: Princeton University Press, 2018.

Postel, Charles. *The Populist Vision.* New York: Oxford University Press, 2007.

Power, Marilyn. "Social Provisioning as a Starting Point for Feminist Economics," *Feminist Economics,* Vol. 10, No. 3, 2004, 3–19.

Prentiss, Mara. *Energy Revolution: The Physics and the Promise of Efficient Technology.* Cambridge, MA: Harvard University Press, 2015.

Purdy, Jedediah. *After Nature: A Politics for the Anthropocene.* Cambridge, MA: Harvard University Press, 2015.

Raana, Hagal, et al. "Modular Origins of Biological Electron Transfer Chains," *PNAS,* Vol. 115, No. 6, February 6, 2018, 1280–1285.

Searle, John R. *Making the Social World: The Structure of Human Civilization.* New York: Oxford University Press, 2010.

Shapin, Steven and Simon Schaffer. *Leviathan and the Air-Pump: Hobbes, Boyle, and the Experimental Life*. Princeton, NJ: Princeton University Press, 1985.

Shiller, Robert J. *Narrative Economics: How Stories Go Viral and Drive Major Economic Events*. Princeton, NJ: Princeton University Press, 2019.

Snow, C. P. *The Two Cultures and the Scientific Revolution*. New York: Cambridge University Press, 1959.

Speth, James Gustave. *America the Possible: Manifesto for a New Economy*. New Haven: Yale University Press, 2012.

Stern, Nicholas H. *Why Are We Waiting? The Logic, Urgency, and the Promise of Tackling Climate Change*. Cambridge, MA: MIT Press, 2015.

Stiglitz, Joseph E., Amartya Sen, and Jean-Paul Fitoussi. "Mismeasuring Our Lives: Why GDP Doesn't Add Up: The Report," in *Commission on the Measurement of Economic Performance and Social Progress*. New York: New Press, 2010.

Strathern, Marilyn. *Kinship, Law and the Unexpected: Relatives are Always a Surprise*. New York: Cambridge University Press, 2005.

Subramanian, Meera. "Humans versus Earth," *Nature*, Vol. 572, August 8, 2019, 168–170.

Swyngedouw, Erik and Henrik Ernstson. "Interrupting the Anthropo-obScene: Immuno-biopolitics and Depoliticizing Ontologies in the Anthropocene," *Theory, Culture, and Society*, Vol. 35, No. 6, November 2018, 3–30.

Taylor, Charles. *Sources of the Self: The Making of Modern Identity*. New York: Cambridge University Press, 1989.

Taylor, Charles. "Modern Social Imaginaries," *Public Culture*, Vol. 14, No. 1, 2002, 91–124.

Taylor, Charles. *Modern Social Imaginaries*. Durham, NC: Duke University Press, 2004.

Taylor, Charles. *A Secular Age*. Cambridge, MA: Harvard University Press, 2007.

Taylor, Charles. *The Language Animal: The Full Shape of the Human Linguistic Capacity*. Cambridge, MA: Harvard University Press, 2016.

Viveiros de Castro, Eduardo. *Cannibal Metaphysics: For a Post-Structural Anthropology*. Minneapolis: Univocal Press, 2009.

Wickham, Chris. *Sleepwalking into a New World: The Emergence of Italian City Communes in the Twelfth Century*. Princeton, NJ: Princeton University Press, 2015.

Williams, Michael. *Deforesting the Earth: From Prehistory to Global Crisis*. Chicago: University of Chicago Press, 2003.

Wilson, Edward. O. *Consilience: The Unity of Knowledge*. New York: Random House, 1998.

Wilson, Edward O. *Half-Earth: Our Planet's Fight for Life*. New York: W.W. Norton & Company, 2016.

Yergin, Daniel. *The Quest: Energy, Security, and the Remaking of the Modern World*. New York: Penguin, 2011.

Zeevi, David, et al. "Structural Variation in the Gut Microbiome Associates with Host Health," *Nature*, Vol. 568, April 4, 2019, 43–48.

12 Conclusions

Methodology

One goal of this book is to further develop the methodology of historical institutionalism, as discussed in Chapter 3. There are three aspects of this methodology: the key term, the related institutions, and the associated expertise. In the case of "the individual," this concept has a plausible real, material dimension, by the discreet body of a single person. Yet the interdependencies of that person loom so large, in terms of provision of necessities, socialization, environmental interdependence, as well as technology and culture, that the interconnections may be of greater salience than the singular body. No human person can survive alone, and solitary confinement is the most severe form of punishment and can lead to mental instability.

The strategy in this work is to identify the historical and cultural evolution of this term, the individual, along with the specific institutions, such as property and the market, and the expertise, such as law and economics, along with psychology and sociology.

Some leading institutionalists, such as Mark Blyth and Fred Block, emphasize the importance of "ideas." Yet the approach in this work, by contrast, is to see "ideas" as part of the paradigm of terms, institutions, and expertise. The "ideas" do not exist alone but are part of language statements that specify functions and coordinate actions, as discussed in Chapter 7. These language statements must provide legitimacy to the institutional arrangements, so that the persons within the institution understand and support the role and function of their enactments and performances, as well as the overall purpose.

Humans are cognitive beings, and communication is a significant source of order and purpose, as well as identity, recognition, and satisfaction. For this insight, the work of John Searle on language is extremely important, along with the dual emphasis of Karl Marx and Karl Polanyi on roles as well as actions, ideas along with behavior.

Another aspect of this methodology is the historical approach to understand how the entire complex of the key term, the institutions, and expertise changes over time. For this, study of the long duree of capitalism and the market is a key resource, and such a study can provide in turn a better understanding of the pressures and contradictions which can lead to change. Following Polanyi and Blyth, this first quarter of the twenty-first century seems like a time of "great transformations."

Centrality of "the individual"

The central position of this book is that "the individual" is embedded in a complex system of meaning and relationships, contrary to the conventional understanding of the term. The Lockean origin story contains a narrative of property, an object which mediates the relationship to the deity and to the earth. Humankind has rights to the earth, as "property," for its own sustenance. As property producers, workers form a state for mutual protection. By means of reification, this property becomes the central "object," a "double entendre" in the sense of purpose and in the sense of its composition in a material form. This property becomes the purpose of the state and of relationships of production and citizenship, which then replaces them. The purposes of human society are "objectified," no longer human. The "individual," once empowered as a property owner, becomes subjected to other imperatives to increase the value of his property. That "value," which is social and systemic, is expressed in money terms, which is considered a characteristic of individual private property. Thus "the individual" is part of the world view of property, whose history can be traced and subject to critical analysis.

Legacy of property

Western civilization is grounded on key concepts from Ancient Greece and Rome, with a view of politics as the highest expression of humankind. The polis, with debate and deliberation, is the model for Western notions of freedom. Yet the model citizen of these societies was a free male who owned land and slaves. In this context, property was a criterion of political enfranchisement and a marker of status.

In seventeenth-century England, the notion of modern forms of governance was based on this tradition. For Locke, property was a key term providing the rationale for the state. The source of property was more democratic. Property was formed by a person mixing his labor with the soil. He could then claim a portion of the commons which God had given to mankind as his own, justified by the needs for his own sustenance and his own labor. With money, the provisos are modified, such that accumulation beyond one's own needs is allowed, servants can be employed who do not have a claim to their own property, and inequality is justified by the increased productivity of the enclosure of the commons. The individual owner is the citizen of the state, which is formed by agreement among such owners to protect their property from others and from the state.

The state, as a contract among founders for the protection of property, becomes symbolized by that property and its expanding value, rather than the human relationship among equals and deliberation among citizens. Freedom is protection of property, not the rights and relationships of citizenship, as "property" became reified.

The individual and property

The political enfranchisement of the individual property owner is important for modern governance. The individual further expresses his personality by means of property and assures his own conditions of life, his own independence. Such independence and rationality of ownership assures the legitimacy of the government formed on that basis.

The individual is so empowered to take from nature and to view nature as an object. His work on nature expresses his intention, his creativity, and his unique mark.

Every individual is a self-owner, at least of his own labor power. But some individuals own more than their own labor power, including land and financial assets. So all individuals are equal owners, but some are more equal than others. Each person will seek to increase his own value, in competition with others, generating inequality as an outcome.

There are several paradoxes with such a state formed on that basis. One noted among theorists is that a state strong enough to protect property is also strong enough to extract it (Lamoreaux 2011). Another is that inequality of property ownership threatens the legitimacy of its exclusive privileges and the consensus among owners once non-owners are allowed the franchise (MacPherson 1962).

Equality and domination

Originally the formation of a state of property owners by means of a social contract is based on equality. But the individual owner is empowered to command nature and non-owners. The trust in the legitimacy of such a state is undermined by these contradictions between equality and domination.

Property and governance

Property is the foundation of both the public and private spheres.

In the public sphere, franchise and influence are based on property, which may shape the type of rules which are written and the enforcement of property.

In the private sphere, the ownership of property is protected for profit from production and investment, and for private enjoyment.

The goal of the expansion of the value of property, M – M', is present in both spheres, as the "wealth of nations" is the goal of the state. This common goal may jeopardize the checks and balances and countervailing power of property. Originally the US Constitution of 1787 was written to protect the minority property owners from the poor majority from "below." It is perhaps ill-suited to guard against dominance from an oligarchy of wealth and monopoly power from "above."

Money is protected by the state, based on public assets and wealth capacity. But money is also considered a private good, owned by any holder of cash. Financial circuits undergird property and its protection and enforce the adherence of any holder to behavioral norms of the expansion of wealth.

Property is both "freedom" and "coercion." Owners are free to choose based on investment incentives, and owners only of their own labor power must choose an employer in order to live. That is, incentives for owners are positive and for non-owners are negative. The market, which allocates such opportunities to individuals, is viewed as a realm of freedom, in spite of imperfections of the market which are widely known. Especially since the rise of "neoliberalism" in the 1980s, only the market is considered "freedom," and the government is considered "coercion."

Property requires parceling the earth and restricting non-owners. This paradigm views the earth and other people as instrumental for human needs and satisfaction. As a result, society is divided into spheres, and persons have multiple selves.

The market is perfect enough to substitute for morals, according to Gauthier (1982). But that depends on several assumptions, including fair initial endowment, no externalities, perfect competition, and wages sufficient to cover the cost of reproduction. Without these assumptions, there is no guarantee of reward for merit, or absence of desperation to meet basic needs, or distorted prices due to monopoly and inequality, or depletion of public goods. In spite of the significance of these provisos, the market remains the dominant mechanism of global governance (Mazower 2012; Polanyi 1944), with a set of ideas that Block and Somers call "Market Fundamentalism" (Block and Somers 2014). Yet the market is based on "fictions" (Block 2018), such as infinite financial markets, which are existentially threatened by terrorism, nuclear war, and climate change. The daily financial markets, based on trades in the instant, are poorly adapted to deal with long-term eventualities, no matter how inevitable or inescapable.

Reification

A state based on property conceives the object of property as the goal of the state. The object itself is the source of status, independence, and security. Yet this focus upon the object tends to reify the social relationships which are necessary to produce it, trade it, consume it, and to protect it. The object itself seems sufficient. The rhetorical focus becomes the protection of the object rather than the sustenance of the relationships.

One example of such an outcome is the treatment of women as exclusive "owners" of reproductive capacity, and the treatment of women as "sex objects," as if the only goal of society were genital coitus and the only relations between men and women were erotic (Strathern 1988, 311–318, 2016, 207, 232–244). The assignment of sex to women enables the elision of the relationships that are necessary for childbirth, child care, and socialization. This process simply becomes "women's work," and social responsibility for the next generation becomes privatized in the household, enforced by the "marriage contract" (Pateman 1988). Women become the symbol of sex and reproduction. Control of women's sexuality and the assignment of chastity outside of marriage becomes the primary method of managing the population. The assignment of guilt to women and the enforcement of laws against abortion become a political mantra for re-imposition of responsibility upon women (Cooper 2017). Evangelicals battle the #MeToo movement in heightened political contests at present.

The treatment of women owning their fertility, as in Roe v. Wade, is an example of the dilemmas of individual self-ownership. That is, sexuality, childbirth, and socialization are eminently social and relational, yet the paradigm of individual private property renders this process as owned by women. This assignment of responsibility brings with it the combination of empowerment and subordination that is associated with this distinct role.

Another example is the invisibility of public power behind private property and finance (Grandin 2019, 45; Davies 2017).

Ownership becomes the central relationship, expressed in the ostensible value of the object. As a result, relationships become invisible. This reification of relationships, along with the differential treatment of women, by marital status, race, and class, is an example of the systematic reversal of life and death in the capitalist system.

Mobility

One advantage of the individual and individual private property is its mobility. The individual owner can trade property, the individual worker can relocate to secure employment, and property itself can change, in composition, location, and in value. With the individual status and personality reliant on property, nonetheless, these changes can be disruptive, with ramifications in political expressions. The loss of access to property can lead to alienation and to insecurity, even while the role of government is to protect exclusive access by owners against non-owners.

One resolution was continual growth of territory (Grandin 2019) and of economic output (Harvey 2014). For example, expansion of GDP is assumed, and the focus is the comparative size and "rate" of growth among nations in the competition for political and economic power.

Relationships

The production of property requires the commodification of parcels of the earth and the lives of the peoples. This formation of "fictional" commodities shapes the substances of the earth and those lives into distinct molds. The "real" commodities produced for profit for sale become the focus of the sphere of circulation, the "market," while the sphere of production is in a shroud of secrecy. The "equality" of property owners applies only to the sphere of circulation, where commodities are obtained for consumption by means of effective demand. The "value" thus realized returns to the property owners for reinvestment into further production of commodities.

The process of commodification of "fictional" commodities, like the land and the labor, is managed by the state by means of "unique individuals," like corporations and families, and the associated laws and regulations. This process is relatively invisible, and unquestioned, like a physical, financial, and legal infrastructure. The source of meaning for human lives, love, and work is managed by the "property" in labor and in gender, protected and reproduced by the state.

The relationship between property rights and human rights is complex. On the one hand, the purpose of property is to reproduce human life. On the other hand, the purpose of property, both finance and real, is to produce a stream of earnings for the reproduction of capital. At times these relationships are complimentary and at times contradictory.

Ethics

There is a moral case to be made for the value of every human person. Due to reification, however, "individualism" does not effectuate that moral value. Instead, "individualism" is often taken to mean the right to use one's property strictly according to one's own interests. There is an elision of property rights and human rights. A self-owning person is equivalent to a wage laborer who is for sale, under conditions and with rewards beyond his control.

Human lives are put at risk for the benefit of the expansion of property "values" which are proxies for human pleasures. But human lives and human pleasures are separated due to the distinct financial circuits of the reified symbol of human pleasure, money.

The necessity of finding a job and spouse drives one's life plans. Competition with others influences one's self-concept and human relationships, and the goal to raise the next generation of workers.

In contrast to these norms of the property paradigm, the notion of a life secure in a "grounded" community, clearly focused on human needs, is nearly unimaginable.

Issues

The property system itself is revealing stress based on these contradictions.

a) Threats to "democracy" (or majority rule by enfranchised but unequal citizens) (Levitsky and Ziblatt 2018; Runciman 2018; Maclean 2018; Mounk 2019; Diamond 2019); political gridlock.
b) Environmental impact of the treatment of nature as an object.

c) Limits to growth of the capitalist model based on exploitation of nature and workers.
d) Reproduction of an impoverished population, in terms of social cohesion, provision of minimal needs, and development of capacities.

Yet what we call "democracy" is more like a republic, and perhaps even an oligarchy with the increasing concentration of wealth in the US. Elections can be like plebiscites without widespread participation in recruitment of candidates and without fair electoral procedures. Further, the constitutional protection of property can leave the people without significant control over the economy, as Polanyi points out (Polanyi 1944), and worsening inequality (Piketty 2014; Stiglitz 2015). If "the individual" has never been free, the periodic elections within context of Madisonian checks and balances (to reduce factions as in the Federalist Paper #10) do not reduce the discipline of the economy but maintain and enforce it for the production of the "wealth of nations."

As the public sphere becomes absorbed into the private sphere with neoliberalism, the protagonists of the Left are the only remaining defenders of bourgeois liberties, such as rule of law, separation of powers, free press, and free speech. The oligarchy in the US finesses such fine distinctions as the public/private divide in the interests of its own aggrandizement.

Alternative world view

The individual and individual private property are key concepts for a particular world view. Alternatives include the celebration and exploration of interdependencies among peoples and the environment.

Rather than see the earth and other humans as instruments for one's individual, personal satisfaction, the role of humans can be viewed as part of nature, integrally indivisible, the source of enlightenment.

Alternative institutions

Rather than separate households from the land by means of the labor and real estate markets, it is possible to design human settlement in discreet ecosystems, such as a watershed, and management of that ecosystem with sustainable principles, along with human flourishing. Human communities can grow along with the ecology, as interdependent living systems, in cohesive coordinated efforts with the simple goal of sustainability rather than the expansion of the value of money and property.

Resistance

While some may prefer such alternative systems for aesthetic or ethical reasons, there is a system of privilege embedded in "the individual" and regime of individual private property. Those with power in the existing system may prefer that system and actively resist change, equipped with the authority and resources of that existing system.

Such simultaneous "Great Transformations" of political economy and paradigms are fraught with risk, as are "great revolutions."

Trends

Given the conceptual foundation of the state, based on individualism and individual private property, and the expansion imperatives of capitalism, there are certain long-term trends:

• Automation of employment
• Increasing inequality
• Energy from fossil fuels rather than animal, human, or renewable; resulting in climate change

That is, rather than simply a trend towards advancing technology, there is a "direction" of technology towards substitution for labor, a trend noted by Smith and Marx. This direction has led to the increasing control of production, advances in information technology and communication, and advances in artificial intelligence. As opportunities for employment diminish, those with financial wealth are able to invest in increasing biological and intellectual capacity, further increasing inequality. Even if methods to improve living standards for the large majority of the population are available as "low tech," the direction of innovation is towards "high tech" solutions such as genetic engineering of food and human biology, and space travel, as envisioned by Elon Musk, Ray Kurzweil, and Jeff Bezos.

As substitution for fossil fuel would require active industrial policies to manage such a transition, resistance to such an expanded role of the government may prevent this change, even with the consequences for habitat on earth. Ideas based on individualism, as well as the expanded options for money in campaign finance and investments in the associated think tanks and electoral methods, may block the needed changes for a sustainable future (Mayer 2016; McKibben 2019; MacLean 2018).

There are tipping points, such as sufficient inequality to undermine democracy and self-reinforcing climate trends that worsen climate change, like melting arctic glaciers, ocean acidification, drought, and deforestation. In such a context,

> Instead of galvanizing heroic innovation and international cooperation, growing environmental and socioeconomic turbulence may simply drive elite publics into more frenzied attempts to wall themselves off from the rest of humanity.
>
> (Davis 2018, 211)

The denial of "society" by neoliberals like Thatcher may have been persuasive enough to change society in terms of major concepts, institutions, and expertise, an ironic yet world-altering achievement.

Bibliography

Block, Fred L. *Capitalism: The Future of an Illusion*. Oakland: University of California Press, 2018.

Block, Fred L. and Margaret R. Somers. *The Power of Market Fundamentalism: Karl Polanyi's Critique*. Cambridge, MA: Harvard University Press, 2014.

Blyth, Mark. *Great Transformations: Economic Ideas and Institutional Change in the Twentieth Century*. New York: Cambridge University Press, 2002.

Blyth, Mark. *Austerity: The History of a Dangerous Idea*. New York: Oxford University Press, 2013.

Cooper, Melinda. *Family Values: Between Neoliberalism and the New Social Conservatism*. New York: Zone Books, 2017.

Davies, William. *The Limits of Neoliberalism: Authority, Sovereignty, and the Logic of Competition*. London: Sage, 2017.

Davis, Mike. *Old Gods New Enigmas: Marx's Lost Theory*. New York: Verso, 2018.

Diamond, Larry. *Ill Winds: Saving Democracy from Russian Rage, Chinese Ambition, and American Complacency*. New York: Penguin Press, 2019.

Eichengreen, Barry. *The Populist Temptation: Economic Grievance and the Political Reaction in the Modern Era*. New York: Oxford University Press, 2018.

Gauthier, David. "No Need for Morality: The Case of the Competitive Market," *Philosophic Exchange*, Vol. 13, No. 1, Summer 1982, article 2, 41–54.

Grandin, Greg. *The End of the Myth: From the Frontier to the Border Wall in the Mind of America*. New York: Henry Holt and Company, 2019.

Harvey, David. *Seventeen Contradictions and the End of Capitalism*. New York: Oxford University Press, 2014.

Lamoreaux, Naomi R. "The Mystery of Property Rights: A U.S. Perspective," *Journal of Economic History*, Vol. 71, No. 2, June 2011, 275–306.

Levitsky, Steven and Daniel Ziblatt. *How Democracies Die*. New York: Crown, 2018.

MacLean, Nancy. *Democracy in Chains: The Deep History of the Radical Right's Stealth Plan for America*. New York: Penguin Books, 2018.

MacPherson, C. B. *The Political Theory of Possessive Individualism: Hobbes to Locke*. Oxford: Clarendon Press, 1962.

Mayer, Jane. *Dark Money: The Hidden History of the Billionaires Behind the Rise of the Radical Right*. New York: Doubleday, 2016.

Mazower, Mark. *Governing the World: The History of an Idea*. New York: Penguin, 2012.

McKibben, Bill. *Falter: Has the Human Game Begun to Play Itself Out?* New York: Henry Hold and Company, 2019.

Mirowski, Philip. *Never Let a Serious Crisis Go to Waste: How Neoliberalism Survived the Financial Meltdown*. New York: Verso, 2013.

Mounk, Yascha. *The People vs. Democracy: Why our Freedom is in Danger and How to Save It*. Cambridge, MA: Harvard University Press, 2019.

Pateman, Carole. *The Sexual Contract*. Stanford, CA: Stanford University Press, 1988.

Piketty, Thomas. *Capital in the Twenty-First Century*. Cambridge, MA: Harvard University Press, 2014.

Polanyi, Karl. *The Great Transformation*. Boston: Beacon Press, 1944.

Runciman, David. *How Democracy Ends*. New York: Basic Books, 2018.

Stiglitz, Joseph E. *The Great Divide: Unequal Societies and What We Can Do About Them*. New York: W.W. Norton & Company, 2015.

Strathern, Marilyn. *The Gender of the Gift: Problems with Women and Problems with Society in Melanesia*. Berkeley: University of California, 1988.

Strathern, Marilyn. *Kinship, Law and the Unexpected: Relatives are Always a Surprise*. New York: Cambridge University Press, 2005.

Strathern, Marilyn. *Before and After Gender: Sexual Mythologies of Everyday Life*. Chicago: HAU Books, 2016.

Index

Printed in the United States
by Baker & Taylor Publisher Services